DON AND MANDARIN

DON AND MANDARIN

MEMOIRS OF AN ECONOMIST

DONALD MACDOUGALL

JOHN MURRAY

© Donald MacDougall 1987

First published 1987
by John Murray (Publishers) Ltd
50 Albemarle Street, London W1X 4BD
All rights reserved
Unauthorised duplication
contravenes applicable laws

Typeset by Inforum Ltd, Portsmouth

Printed and bound in Great Britain
by Butler & Tanner, Frome

British Library Cataloguing in Publication Data

MacDougall, Donald
Don and Mandarin : memoirs of an economist.
1. MacDougall, Donald   2. Economist —
Great Britain — Biography
I. Title
330'.092'4   HB103.M1/

ISBN 0-7195-4424-6

CONTENTS

ILLUSTRATIONS

ACKNOWLEDGEMENTS

Many people have helped me in the preparation of this book. I am particularly indebted to Martin Holmes, of Lady Margaret Hall, Oxford; and to Doug McWilliams and Max Wilkinson, who read and commented on early drafts of most chapters; also to numerous others for help of various kinds, including Sir Campbell Adamson, Lord Barber, Lady Birkenhead, David Butler, Sir Alec Cairncross, Sir Norman Chester, Jimmy Clark, John Clarke, Peter Davies, Lord Diamond, Leslie Dicks-Mireaux, John Dunkley, Lesley Green, Dominic Harrod, Duff Hart-Davis, Sir Gordon Hobday, Jack Hyde, Ken Johnson, Michael Kaser, T. C. Keeley, Keith McDowall, Simon Miller, Sheila Murray, Lady Simon, Audrey Skeats, Debby Stevens, Linda Turner, Eleanor Vallis, Alastair Wallace. For permission to reproduce illustrations my thanks are due to Universal Pictorial Press and Agency, Ltd., 10; the *Financial Times*, 11, 14, 15; *CBI News*, 16. Finally, I am extremely grateful to Roger Hudson, of John Murray, for his wise guidance during the final stages of drafting and his skilful management of the production of the book.

TO MARGARET

1

EARLY LIFE: 1912–39

ALTHOUGH I was born on the twenty-sixth of October 1912 it was not until some time later – in fact in the winter of 1978/9 – that I began to realise how much my life may have been influenced by King Ja Ja. I was idly turning the pages of the *Magazine of the Barbados Hotel Association*, while enjoying what I like to think was a well-earned holiday in the sun, and came across an article entitled 'The Slave Who Became A King And Was Exiled in Barbados'. It was about Ja Ja, who had had a brief sojourn on the island nearly ninety years earlier; and to my surprise and excitement I discovered that he had been closely associated with my maternal grandfather, George Miller.

I had long known that he had traded in West Africa; but the article, and subsequent research, revealed that he and his brother, based on Glasgow, had only really got going in the Niger Delta in the early 1870s as the result of an arrangement they came to with the former slave of a neighbouring King. Ja Ja, as the ex-slave was called, gained such power in his own region that he was recognised by the local British Consul as King of Opobo. This greatly helped my grandfather and his brother to establish themselves in defiance of violent and persistent antagonism from rival traders, mostly based on Liverpool. The quarrel continued for many years. It culminated in the victory of the Liverpool interests and Ja Ja's arrest by the acting British Consul in 1887, and subsequent deportation to St Vincent in the West Indies – despite protests by a deputation sent by Ja Ja to London for which my grandfather acted as spokesman when they visited the Foreign Office.

Ja Ja was moved to Barbados in 1891 and just over two months later left for his homeland, having been given permission by the British Government and when he showed signs of being seriously ill. He died on the way, in the Canary Islands, but his body was carried home where he was accorded a royal funeral lasting thirty-two days.

Despite Ja Ja's fate, the Miller brothers continued to trade in West Africa and made a fair amount of money; but it seems quite possible that, without his help during their first fifteen years or so in the area, they might never have done so. My grandfather, who died in the early 1920s, left some money in trust for his grandchildren. But he had ten children, most of whom survived him and were provided for, so the total left over for grandchildren was limited. Moreover, as he had fourteen of these, the share of each was considerably diluted; but mine came in handy in the following way. A year or so before the end of my school days, I decided I would like to go to University. But there was the little problem of finance. The possibilities of a Scholarship or of getting money from the taxpayer did not really arise. Nor did I feel able to seek parental aid. My father, who died when I had just turned seventeen, had wanted to be a doctor, but considered it his duty when his father retired, being the eldest son, to help run the family china business; and this, to put it mildly, had not done at all well. My mother's income from investments, though considerable, was not sufficient to bear the strain, especially with the Great Depression gathering pace. So the only possibility was my grandfather's Trust. This was not supposed to be available till I was 21, which would be too late; but fortunately a lawyer decided it would be consistent with my grandfather's wishes if I got some earlier for educational purposes; and this enabled me to go to Balliol. Without this money, my whole future life could have been very different, and a good deal less enjoyable and interesting. So that is why I feel a debt of gratitude to King Ja Ja of Opobo.

I was born and brought up in Glasgow and went to school at Kelvinside Academy – a mile or so from my home – until I was nearly fourteen. The standard cannot have been very high because I was top of the class every year until my last, when I was delighted to come second, because I disliked being called a swot. No one I know now will believe it, but quite early on I got the first prize for handwriting in my class. It was a great pity, because it made me over-confident and my writing progressively deteriorated until it became quite illegible, which it has been for many years.

It was also a pity that, during my last two years at Kelvinside, when most of the boys in my class were doing science, my parents decided that I should instead learn Greek. They thought it would be useful when I went to Shrewsbury where they planned to send me; my elder brother was already there. So four little boys were taught Greek by someone whom the school engaged specially for the job. I studied it for a further three years at Shrewsbury, which enabled me later to take the New Testament in Greek as a subsidiary subject in the Higher Certificate – broadly the equivalent of 'A' levels – when I was specialising in maths. I passed with flying colours. This was partly because my Greek was adequate, but also because, after many years of regular attendance at religious services where lessons were read, the New Testament had so sunk into my mind that I only had to get the odd sentence or two of a passage of Greek for translation into English and most of the rest came tumbling out.

I shall always regret not learning about useful things like light, heat, sound and electricity at school in Glasgow; and my science teaching at Shrewsbury was, as I recall it, mostly historical and seldom got beyond the eighteenth century. All this, coupled with the fact that my father (in other respects a kind, tolerant person) would not let me use his tools (though I had a pedal fretsaw with which I made jigsaw puzzles), meant that in adult life I was completely useless on practical matters about the house or to do with a car. My Greek was of no use whatsoever after I left school – except in doing maths where a knowledge of the alphabet is handy, but hardly takes five years to acquire – and before long I had forgotten every word of it. This did not, however, prevent me reading, with great enjoyment, the excellent English translations available of classical Greek literature. I read Thucydides' *Peloponnesian War* at the time of the Suez crisis in 1956 and worked out that the ancient ships they used over two thousand years earlier seemed able to move at least as fast about the Mediterranean as the Royal Navy.

At Kelvinside Academy the winter game was rugby. I was no good at it, particularly after I became short-sighted following an attack of scarlet fever and could not see much without glasses. Fortunately my mother – a lovable person whom I never heard speak ill of anyone and who, I am happy to say, survived until I was well into my forties – thought I was delicate and gave me notes which got me off most days when I was supposed to be playing. But one summer I had a moment of athletic glory when competing in a sack race during the School Sports. Actually I came in last, but the people from the local cinema – which showed shots of local events between ordinary films – were not fussy. One of them put me on his shoulder in my sack and had me photographed; and a few days later I made my screen debut as the winner of the race.

At an early age I was introduced to problems of political economy. At the debating society we had 'Hat Nights' at which you drew a question out of a hat and had to open a debate on it after a couple of minutes' preparation. Churchill was then Chancellor of the Exchequer, and one question I drew was 'Should Winston tax the doughnut?' Another was a moral question, but with economic overtones: 'Should the blind lodger pay for the hall light?' It was not a bad training.

I also studied avidly the review of industry and commerce published annually by the *Glasgow Herald* on or about every New Year's Day, and was proud to read what a relatively important centre Glasgow still was. Alas how things changed. When, shortly before the Second World War, I was working for the (Barlow) Royal Commission on the Geographical Distribution of the Industrial Population, I discovered that the slow economic growth between the wars in all but one of the depressed areas of Britain could be largely explained by the heavy concentration in them, at the start of the period, of old industries destined to decline. The odd man out was mid-Scotland (of which Glasgow and the surrounding areas were a major part). After the First World War it had its fair share of expanding, declining and other industries. But its subsequent overall growth was far below the national average, because most *individual* industries grew more slowly, or declined more rapidly, than they did in the rest of the country.

I sometimes wonder whether the explanation was, in part at least, sociological. Many of the boys at Kelvinside Academy planned, as a matter of course, to go into the family business, which – I sometimes thought – they felt owed them a living, even if they did not exert themselves unduly. More important in explaining the inter-war experience of the area was that some at least of their fathers may have felt likewise; and sometimes their attitude towards 'the workers' seemed to me at worst contemptuous and at best lacking in understanding.

I quite enjoyed my time at Kelvinside. The same can scarcely be said about Shrewsbury, where I began my boarding school life when just short of fourteen. Some have described their time at public school as the happiest in their life. At the other extreme Prince Edward said, in a television interview in 1984, that the Prince of Wales 'hated' his time at Gordonstoun. While I would hardly say that of Shrewsbury, I would place myself near the Prince Charles end of the spectrum. But I made some good friends. One was Hartley Ayre. He left a year earlier than I did and that summer took me for my holidays to Newfoundland where he lived.

My academic performance at Shrewsbury was adequate but undistinguished. I never came first in anything, as I had at Kelvinside. I got some prize for maths in my last year, but only because there were several to be handed out to boys specialising in the subject in the Sixth Form, and there were just four of us. The only sports I was moderately good at were rowing and cross-country running. In my last year I actually came second in a race in which the whole school took part – except for the best runners, with the equivalent of school colours, who did not compete!

Unlike Shrewsbury, it would be no exaggeration to say that my five years at Balliol were among the happiest in my life. The contrast could hardly have been greater. I enjoyed a wonderful sense of freedom – one no longer felt cooped up – and most of the things I missed at school I found at Oxford. Creature comforts were immeasurably better; one's time was far less regimented; there were far fewer petty restrictions and rules – although some would make the modern undergraduate smile, like the prohibition on going into a pub, and the segregation of the sexes. There were, of course, no co-residential colleges; and, though I could take a girl out to dinner or the theatre, the entry of men into women's colleges was strictly regulated. I once went to one with a few other males to have tea with some girls; and they had to be chaperoned by a female don.

Movements in the opposite direction were less restricted but women had to be out of Balliol by dinner time. I was in a delegation to the Master – Sandy (later Lord) Lindsay – to request a relaxation of this rule. He said it was an interesting question which he would be glad to discuss with the undergraduates on the following Sunday after dinner in the Junior Common Room. He came as promised and talked reasonably and eloquently about the matter, but at such length that, by the time he had finished, most of his audience had melted away; and the rump that was left did not have the spirit to carry on the fight. So the whole thing fizzled out.

It was a good example of one of the techniques of that wily Scot – who had, incidentally, been one of my mother's playmates when they were children in Glasgow. How very different was the technique of Maurice (later Sir Maurice) Bowra a few years later when Warden of Wadham (where I became a Fellow after the war). A deputation of students called on him with a similar request which he dealt with in summary fashion. 'Nonsense,' he said, 'Don't you know the afternoon's the time for love-making; the evening's for work'; and there was a notice in the Lodge which read: 'Gentlemen are reminded that it is not permitted to have in the College after 7.15 pm ladies, dogs or other pets'.

My main sporting activity at Balliol was rowing. One trouble – which I wish I had now – was being so light; I sometimes had difficulty making the scales show me heavier than the cox. The apogee of my rowing career was when I was in the Balliol crew that beat Eton at Henley in 1933 in the Ladies' Challenge Plate (then mainly confined to Oxbridge Colleges and public schools). Admittedly I was selected only because several of the best Balliol oarsmen were unavailable; and we were probably the second worst crew in the competition, but were lucky enough to draw Eton, probably the worst, in the first round (we were thrashed by a Cambridge College in the second). But it was a stirring experience, especially as the launches following the race were crammed with Crown Princes and the like who had been at Eton; and it was pleasant to disappoint them.

After this triumph at Henley, I rested on my laurels and gave up rowing

– a time-consuming sport – to get on with some work. But my most instructive aquatic experience had come earlier when rowing bow in a Balliol coxless four and also steering the boat with my feet, which were attached by wires to the rudder. As one faces in the opposite direction to that in which one is trying to progress this entails looking round a good deal, and the river in Oxford twists and turns. Things were even more difficult when we were practising on the busy tideway in London before the autumn term of 1932, especially as we usually went out around dusk, our coach being at work during the day. Before our first outing some joker had told me that the rule of the river was to keep to the left when the tide was flowing one way, and to the right when it was going the other; this created a difficult problem of judgement when the tide turned slack. Fortunately we got back in one piece, and subsequent outings proved less hair-raising when I heard that the rule was simply to keep to the left. It was all invaluable experience for one who later had to advise on the steering of the economy, when one could often only see through a glass darkly how that animal was behaving; when it was hard enough looking backwards, with official statistics out of date and being continually revised, and harder still to look ahead; and when governments of different persuasions were periodically succeeding each other, and not infrequently reversing course – and sometimes changing the rules governing policy – in mid-stream.

During my first year at Balliol I read for 'Honour Mathematical Moderations'. I did not work particularly hard and, somewhat to my surprise, having expected a Third Class, got a Second. Perhaps it was because I was tutored by Hubert Linfoot, the brother of my second wife. He had won a scholarship to Balliol at 16, and had a long and brilliant career, first in pure mathematics and then in optics. I believe most people reach their 'peak' in maths at a certain level, which varies from person to person. I had been rather precocious in enjoying mathematical problems at a very early age; but by 1932 I realised that I had certainly reached my peak and must turn to something else. There were really only two possibilities: engineering or PPE (Philosphy, Politics and Economics). I opted for PPE.

Many years later I recalled this momentous decision while attending my last meeting of the National Economic Development Council in March 1984. They were discussing education and one of the members, Sir Walter (later Lord) Marshall, Chairman of the Central Electricity Generating Board, made a very forthright speech in which he said – and I noted his words – that we should 'stamp out the social sciences'; their great increase over the years had been 'disastrous'; it would have been much better if 'all the good people had become technicians'. But, leaving aside the question of whether I was one of his 'good people', I am sure I made the right choice. For whatever my contribution to society as an economist, it would surely have been disastrous had I tried to become an engineer, given my abysmal ignorance of the natural sciences and lack of the most elementary practical skills.

As PPE at that time included a compulsory paper of unseen translation from two modern languages, I decided to learn German; for I only had one – French. So I arranged to spend a month of the 1932 summer vacation with a German family in Freiburg, bought an elementary textbook on the language to study on the way, and set off on what was then quite a long journey by train and boat. The father of the family was high up in the local police force and I have often wondered what happened to him, for he had far too great a sense of humour to make a good Nazi. They were already much in evidence on the streets and holding rallies, though Hitler was not yet in power. One day I asked him how I should start a letter to a girl I wished to ask out. He said 'Meine Liebe Fraülein X'. This sounded all right to me as it seemed like 'My dear Miss X'; but it meant something much more like 'My love'. I had no reply. Once he was rung up on the telephone and I heard him saying, at intervals, Ja, Ja, Ja. He eventually put the receiver down and told us, with hilarious touches of humour, that it was one of the good citizens of Freiburg complaining that he had just seen, through his binoculars, a little girl of two or three playing in her garden several miles away without any clothes on; and what was he going to do about it.

I learned some German through studying several hours most days and a good deal of conversation; and was amazed, while in Paris on the way home, how difficult I found it to remember a single word of French, despite my innumerable years at it while at school. During my next two long vacs I went to Austria: in 1933 to stay with a family in the Salzkammergut where it rained a lot and, as there were plenty of young Austrians around, I spent much of the time jabbering away in German; then in 1934 on a walking tour with my sister in the Tyrol where we lived incredibly cheaply. Germany had imposed a prohibitive tax on their nationals wishing to holiday in Austria so that the hotels were virtually empty and cut their prices to the bone. After all this, and with the aid of a few German lessons in Oxford, I had little difficulty with my German translation in PPE. My knowledge of the language proved useful in many ways during the next ten years but after that, through desuetude, I gradually forgot most of it.

Soon after going to Oxford I got interested in the Balliol College Boys' Club, of which I later became President. The Clubhouse was in what were then the slums of St Ebbes. It was open most evenings when Balliol students and 'working class' boys met to take part in a wide range of activities: woodworking, gym, billiards, darts, table tennis, boxing, amateur dramatics; and we had a library, dances, and facilities outside for football, cricket and tennis. We also had an annual camp after the end of the summer term, and occasional, much smaller, weekend camps. At the annual camp in 1935, on the Isle of Wight, I disgraced myself by getting ill – almost certainly the result of over-indulgence during celebrations of the end of 'Schools' (the final exams) – and spent much of the time in bed in a nearby farmhouse where, according to the Club's Magazine, I 'ate jellies prepared by the farmer's pretty daughters', but remember better reading a fascinating book about bees. On other occasions I stayed the course. Once this made me late for a camp of the cavalry section of the University Officers' Training Corps, which I joined purely to learn to ride free – I had no wish to take part in cavalry charges, which everyone assured me were obsolete. When I arrived, my good friend, Lord David Douglas-Hamilton, a keen supporter of the Boys' Club who spent a lot of time teaching the boys to box but had not been at their camp that year, played a dirty trick on me. We had to groom the horses and, when I asked him how to do it, never having groomed one before, he gave me detailed instructions including the washing of their private parts. When I did this, my horse – perhaps understandably – turned his head round and bit me; and I have been frightened of the beasts ever since. David, alas, was killed in August 1944.

Another friend at Balliol was Christopher Hill, who later became a distinguished historian, and Master of the College. Many of his views differed from mine, including our views on the Boys' Club, of which he disapproved. So we had a debate on it one evening in College. I was in favour of less inequality probably as much as he was, but, unlike him, did not fancy achieving this by aggravating class conflict – on the contrary. So it did not worry me that I got to know a lot of Oxford messenger boys who greeted me cheerily while riding their bicycles when I was in a tail coat and white tie on the way to take my current girlfriend to a Commemoration Ball. It must have been the same philosophy which led me, in the summer of 1934, to go to a camp for the unemployed, near Consett in County Durham (at a time when attempts were being made to make such camps suspect). It was run by about a dozen university students, under the auspices of the 'Universities Council for Unemployed Camps' which had the support of the Prince of Wales and hoped to organise at least ten such camps that summer, following a successful one at Eastnor in 1933.

On the first evening the students allotted tasks among themselves.

When it came to that of Medical Officer, and I had not yet been given a job, I found myself saddled with this one. So for ten days, before a medical student turned up – a Balliol friend, James Mason – I was in charge of the health of a hundred unemployed men, aged from 17 to over 50; I was 21. I found I could do most things, having suffered many of the complaints myself. My chief aids, apart from bandages and sticking plaster, were 'Number Nine' pills for constipation, and TCP. The last was a wonderful cure-all, which worked surprisingly well until one evening a man complained indignantly that the stuff I had just given him to gargle with for his sore throat was the same as I had prescribed that morning for his injured ankle. When I pointed out that it had helped his ankle, so why shouldn't it help his throat, he was reasonably contented. But it made me think that I would have to get some harmless dyes, and have a row of bottles of TCP of different colours on the shelf in my medical tent; but then James Mason arrived and I naturally handed over to him. But he took some time to win the confidence of my previous patients; they kept on saying: 'But the other doc said . . .'

One thing that happened while I was in charge sticks in my memory. I took a man, in great pain with a suppurating tooth, to the local dentist, who extracted it. He then begged me not to let the others in the camp know what he had done. He was sure the majority had chronic toothache, being unable to afford private dental treatment or the fare to the nearest teaching hospital where they could get free treatment from students; and he just could not cope.

Ministry of Labour officials visited the camp each week to pay out unemployment benefit, a small part of which the men paid over towards their up-keep. A letter sent to them before they came said: 'You are requested to bring with you: 1 pair gym shoes, 1 towel and 1 spare shirt. These are bare essentials and if you can you should bring shorts, pyjamas, etc. These should be packed in a kit-bag or sack, and *not* in a paper parcel.'

I enormously enjoyed reading PPE. Having read 'Maths Mods', which took a year, the College allowed me a further three years, which gave me longer at it than colleagues who had done 'Pass Mods' in the middle of their first year. My tutor in economic theory was Maurice Allen, a perfectionist who for that reason published virtually nothing, but was in my opinion brilliant. We became firm friends and worked together in subsequent incarnations. At first he was a trifle shy. He was a bachelor, and had rooms in Holywell Manor, a rather luxurious annexe of Balliol, which had just been completed and where I spent three years after my first in College. Maurice disliked getting up early – an aversion I shared. One morning I had a tutorial with him arranged for, shall we say, 9.30. I duly went into his study, but after waiting quarter of an hour thought I might as well go. It turned out that he was in his bathroom and would have had to come through the study in his dressing gown to get into his bedroom to dress; and this he felt would be too embarrassing. His teaching methods were unorthodox. He assumed I would find out for myself what elementary textbooks to read; and the first essays he set me were on abstruse, original articles which had just appeared in the learned journals, and controversial chapters of new books. But although, after my first term, I had little idea of what economics was all about, I think being flung in at the deep end did me no harm. On the contrary, puzzling my way through these difficult pieces, trying to summarise and then criticise them on paper, and finally discussing them with someone possessing such a fine mind as Maurice did, was an excellent training. It stood me in good stead when I had had a chance to read some of the elementary stuff and could apply a critical mind to it.

While Maurice was a highly trained economist, the same can hardly be said of A B Rodger, to whom I went for tutorials in 'economic organis-ation'. This was no fault of 'Rodge', as he was affectionately called. He was a historian who had been conscripted into teaching economics at a time when those trained in the subject were scarce. He once set me an essay on how to reduce unemployment. I suggested that more public works – 'investment in the infrastructure' in modern jargon – would be a good idea. He said: 'No, that wouldn't work.' When I asked why, he could only reply that 'they' had worked out that it would do nothing on balance to help. I discovered later that 'they' were using arguments similar to those popular in some circles, but not accepted by me, in the 1980s – that more investment in the public sector would 'crowd out' an equivalent amount of private investment.

I enjoyed reading politics and philosophy (although I thought moral philosophy a somewhat phony subject), but fairly soon decided to special-ise in economics; and in the academic year 1933–34 really began to work quite hard, after in effect lying rather fallow for seven years – five at Shrewsbury and my first two at Balliol. Towards the end of the year my tutors encouraged me to try for a George Webb Medley Junior Schol-arship in Political Economy. This was a University prize open to those beginning their final year of PPE and involved taking exams early in October 1934. I worked hard during the long vac, and to my surprise and delight won one of the two Scholarships on offer. It was worth £100. It also made me think I might be quite good at economics and even make it my profession; and that I should try for a 'First' in Schools.

During Schools a funny thing happened. I had learned to use a slide-rule and took it with me for the statistics paper. The invigilator, who was a philosophy or politics don, not an economist, asked me what it was. When I told him he said: 'I don't think you should be using this' and confiscated it. I then had to resort to the log tables provided to do my calculations and, not having used them for a good many years, and having forgotten the rules of thumb, had to work it all out from first principles. This took a good half hour and I also got some sums wrong, so my performance in this paper, which I had expected to be one of my best, was not so good. In the following year – and thereafter – the statistics paper stated that slide-rules might be used. I continued to use a slide-rule for the next forty-nine years, always carrying a small one in a leather case in an inside pocket of my jacket, and was desolated when, in 1984, I lost the part that slides up and down in the middle. Nor have I been able to find another small one to buy, since they seem to be regarded as obsolete with the advent of the pocket calculator. But I learned to *think* with a slide-rule; and also – long before the days of pocket calculators – that a good way of putting off someone I was arguing with was to take out my little slide-rule and start checking his calculations on it, and preparing my counter-arguments. Lord Cherwell, with whom I later worked for many years, always carried a pocket slide-rule and it was partly from him that I learned how useful it could be.

After Schools, I had nearly five weeks to wait for my *viva voce* examination – or '*viva*' for short. It was a long one, lasting over an hour. The two economics examiners were Roy (later Sir Roy) Harrod of Oxford, and C R Fay of Cambridge. Now Roy was a first-class economist, but Fay was a Reader in Economic History. He was distinguished in that subject but I did not really regard him as an economist; and much of my *viva* took the rather strange form of Roy and myself trying to persuade Fay that what I had written in my economics papers was correct.

After the *viva*, like most candidates, I gave an official in the Examination Schools my address on the day when the results would be published, and money for a telegram telling me my Class. I then drove to Scotland in my ancient car – a 1927 Morris Cowley I had bought for £10 – to stay with my mother in Argyll. Not long after, I returned from a day's fishing to find the fatal telegram, opened it, and read the one word 'Second'. I was devastated, but somewhat consoled by quite a flood of letters that arrived soon after, including four from my tutors, saying that they thought the examiners had made a mistake. Maurice Allen's told me that Roy Harrod had argued strongly for my getting a First, and that he considered me the

best economist in the Schools. This was encouraging; and I was completely consoled a fortnight later when I heard I had been awarded the
George Webb Medley Senior Scholarship, which is in effect given to the
best economist of the year in PPE. I was also pleased at the prospect of
being able to draw £300 a year, tax free, for two years, the value of the
Scholarship – quite a lot of money in those days.

Fay was a strange fellow. He kept on sending me, and Harrod,
postcards (never a letter) for many years after this, about everything under
the sun. He never mentioned my degree, or anything remotely connected
with it, until one day – it may well have been twenty to twenty-five years
later – he sent a postcard to Roy, who sent it on to me, which said, in
effect: 'I think we ought to have given MacDougall a First.' So I got one
posthumously, as it were.

In the autumn of 1935 I returned to Oxford as a graduate. I moved from
Holywell Manor a hundred yards or so to the end of Manor Road where I
had found digs in what was then a delightfully quiet little corner of
Oxford. The house overlooked the Cherwell at one of the places where
punts were hired out, and my landlady looked after me magnificently.

To my delight, Roy Harrod was appointed my University supervisor
(although I continued to see a lot of Maurice Allen who was extremely
helpful). Until then, apart from my *viva*, I had never talked to Harrod, but
while an undergraduate had been to his lectures in Christ Church where I
was struck by his stimulating style and clarity of exposition. I was then too
lacking in knowledge of economics to recognise also his great originality,
but have long since come to regard him as one of the most original of the
many economists I have known, and I doubt whether he received the full
recognition he deserved. He was a most conscientious supervisor. I saw
him many times during my first term as a graduate and deluged him with
theoretical and mathematical stuff on the theory of the firm. Then right at
the end of the term, I got a letter from him dated 6 December – I had seen
him that morning – that I feel worth quoting almost in full.

I am a little worried about your work and not quite certain whether I am the right
person to supervise you. But the latter point can be considered later.

What I feel would be really good for you would be to take up your pen and put
down on paper what you consider to be the problems set in the screed I have and
what, if any, the solutions given without ever using a so-called mathematical
symbol of any kind. Perhaps this is an impossible task. But I am seriously worried
by your failure to express either on paper or orally what your problems are in the
language of literature or even of literary logic. It may be that you will win through
as a mathematical economist. But I do feel that in the present condition of
economics, your weakness on the literary side may be an impediment.

At first I found this hurtful, then started preparing a defence of what I was doing, but after further reflection decided that Roy was absolutely right. He was indeed understating his case because, quite apart from the merits and demerits of mathematical economics as such – and I have become increasingly sceptical of much of it – one who had only scraped a Second in Maths Mods could never have been really distinguished in the field.

Roy's advice at this stage was among the most important I have had in my life. I completely changed course and started studying the iron and steel industry. I found masses of statistics in the trade journals of blast furnaces being blown in, damped down, re-lined and so on. I visited steel works near Glasgow in the vacations and had long discussions with those running them about how they took their decisions on these and other matters. All this proved most stimulating to my theoretical work, which I continued, and gave me many insights. In the end, and after numerous further discussions with Roy, I produced a paper on 'The Definition of Prime and Supplementary Costs' – containing hardly any mathematics – which he thought was marvellous and should be submitted to Keynes, as Editor of the *Economic Journal*, for inclusion in that illustrious publication.

I was over the moon when I got a letter from Keynes on 4 July 1936 saying he would be glad to accept a version of it for the *Journal*, but asking if I could try to shorten it considerably. He went on to make some extremely helpful suggestions about how this might be done. I was flattered by the trouble he had taken and by the length of his letter; and impressed by the modest way in which the great man suggested possible changes. His last sentence read: 'If you would be so kind as to attempt another version, it would be easier for both of us to come to a conclusion whether or not it is an improvement.'

I took a room in a pub in Islip, a village a few miles north of Oxford, to have peace and quiet to get on with the revision. I also had further help from Roy Harrod, including the suggestion that I should mention Keynes' recently published *General Theory of Employment, Interest and Money* early in my article to arouse the interest of the reader; I did so in the first sentence, one of my first efforts in the noble art of Public Relations. On 28 July I sent Keynes the revised version – which I am sure was greatly improved by the shortening and other changes he had suggested – and got a reply dated 29 July accepting it for the *Journal*; it appeared in the September issue. In this letter he raised some further points about my 'definition', on which I commented in a reply to him a week later. So altogether our correspondence on the matter was quite voluminous.

About half way through the three weeks or so I spent revising my article I had to break off and go for an interview at Leeds University where I had applied for an Assistant Lectureship. My success in getting this job, after failing to get several others I had applied for – academic posts were at that time not easy to come by – was, I believe, due in no small part to the conditional acceptance of my article for the prestigious 'EJ', together with generous references from Roy Harrod, Maurice Allen and others.

During my last year at Oxford I went to a series of London/Cambridge/Oxford seminars for graduate students in economics. Oxford was very much the junior partner; we had only a handful of such students. One day four or five or us piled into my old car and drove to Cambridge for one of these seminars. I had trouble with the car on the way – not an unusual occurrence – and we arrived late, having had no lunch. We crept into the back of the room where the meeting was taking place, and found ourselves listening to what was, to us, a largely unintelligible discussion. It was a few months before the publication of Keynes' *General Theory*. We knew nothing of many of its revolutionary new ideas, terminology and concepts; but the Cambridge students (and somehow some of those from London) seemed quite at home, having heard Keynes and others lecturing on them (and even, it is said, through climbing into Keynes' rooms at night and reading his proofs). We felt so embarrassed and out of it that, as soon as the seminar was over, we slunk away, not even staying for tea, and drove straight back to Oxford. But I am proud to say that on the day the *General Theory* was published, I was able to talk about and criticise it at a meeting that very evening. One of the regular discussions that the few economic graduate students in Oxford used to hold happened to have been arranged for then; and a small part of Keynes' book was closely related to my research.

I was able to check the proof of my article in time to set sail in the middle of August for Kiel to do some reading in the splendid library of the Institut für Weltwirtschaft. I went on a Russian ship which was going on to Leningrad. I was almost the only passenger getting off at Kiel and it was an embarrassing, and even rather frightening, experience. Many of those on the ship were friends of Russia, while the quayside was lined with menacing looking Hitler Jugend. But I got ashore safely and after some useful study went to Berlin for an Anglo–German Conference, having been nominated as a participant by my future boss in Leeds, Professor J. Harry Jones. We had the services of Hitler's personal interpreter, Paul Schmidt. I cannot comment on his other qualities or activities, but certainly admired his amazing professional skill. He translated both ways and could listen to a speech lasting twenty minutes without taking a note, and then repeat it in the other language, often more cogently than the original speaker. I also remember talking, in a quiet corner, with a dissident, who kept on looking over his shoulder; and flying back to

London – it was my first flight. We came down three times on the way and during every descent I was violently sick. This symbolised my feelings after attending the Conference, where the patent insincerity of the discussion and the repeated assertions by the Germans that war between our countries was unthinkable made me highly suspicious.

My suspicions were confirmed when I got to Leeds and made friends with Henry (later Sir Henry) Hardman, then an extra-mural tutor in economics at the University. He had studied deeply the rise of Hitler (and of Mussolini), taught me much about the dangers facing the country, and greatly influenced my thinking. He joined the Ministry of Food in 1940, stayed in the Civil Service after the war, and in 1963 became Permanent Secretary at the Ministry of Defence.

During the years before the war I was thus much preoccupied with the German menace. I was not reassured by a conference of British and German economists I attended in Dresden in July 1938 on the general theme of, believe it or not, 'peaceful change'. A couple of months later I was sufficiently concerned during the Munich crisis to send a telegram to my MP. He replied in a letter dated 29 September 1938, the day after Chamberlain returned from meeting Hitler and proclaimed 'peace for our time': 'I have received your telegram of the 21st inst. This is the gravest crisis the country has faced since 1914 and I do not think you can do better than follow the example of the whole House of Commons and place your trust in Mr Chamberlain to see us through our difficulties.' During the year or so before the war broke out I spent quite a lot of time arranging for four German and Austrian students, either Jewish or threatened by the Nazis for other reasons, to come to Britain and pursue their studies at Leeds. Some had had some pretty frightening experiences, including incarceration in a concentration camp. Despite infuriating bureaucratic and other difficulties and delays – as much on the British as on the German side – the operation succeeded.

The shock of moving from the beauty and cleanliness of Oxford to the ugliness and dirt of Leeds was considerable. The city is, broadly speaking, at the north-east corner of a huge conurbation which at that time was full of buildings belching out filthy smoke and, as the prevailing wind was from the south-west, a lot of dirt fell on Leeds. If I sat reading a book near an open window I sometimes had to blow the soot off it several times between turning over one page and the next; and buildings quickly got grimy and black. During my first term I lived in digs conveniently close to the University but in a rather run down terrace and a house which was filled throughout with smoke whenever the landlady deigned to cook a meal for the occupants, which tended to be at unpredictable intervals.

But we were a friendly lot of young men doing various jobs – I think I
was the only academic. On some evenings we played vingt-et-un; but I
was often too busy preparing lectures and once, so as not to appear too
unsociable, said I would go away for a couple of hours and guarantee them
all against loss for a premium of sixpence each; I made a small profit.
Then, when a remark by Dr Blunt, Bishop of Bradford, effectively ended
the conspiracy of silence about Edward VIII and Mrs Simpson, a
journalist who was one of our company took up the public telephone in the
house, rang up the Bishop's home, said he was from the *Daily X*, and
asked to speak to the Bishop. His wife said he was not available.
Undaunted and unashamed, he rang again saying he was from the *Daily
Y*, but without success. He tried again as correspondent of the *Daily Z*,
and it was only after he had run through virtually all the press that he
admitted defeat in the face of the stout defence of the Bishop's lady – who
was not the daughter of a Lieutenant-Colonel for nothing – and decided
he had done the best he could for his paper; I was never quite sure which
one ie was.

In my second term I moved to more salubrious lodgings, further from
the University but within walking distance and therefore good for
my health. Here I met a much more scrupulous and respectable journalist, who was to become a life-long friend – and godfather to my daughter.
He was Stephen (Steve) Bonarjee, then leader writer for *The Yorkshire
Evening News*. This seemed to me a terrible job because he had to get up at
an unearthly hour to read the press and have his leaders written before
mid-morning; and he had to go back in the afternoon too. In 1938 he
joined *The Manchester Guardian* and after six years in the Army went to the
BBC. There he pioneered current affairs programmes – first on radio,
then on television – in a way that I do not think has received the
recognition it deserved. Steve seemed to know everyone concerned with
current affairs and quite often got me to do a broadcast while I was a don.

There were only five of us teaching in the Economics Department at
Leeds, and that covered everything, including economic history, industrial relations, statistics – the lot. As there were about a hundred students
taking economics in their first year, and although the numbers going on to
a second and third year were much smaller, the teaching load was heavy
and varied, and I had to mug up quite a lot of new subjects.

There was the additional problem that, from time to time, one of my
senior colleagues would phone up early in the day, apologise for being ill,
or explain that the road to Leeds was flooded, fog-bound or snow-bound
– some lived quite a long way out – and ask if I would kindly take his

lecture for him that morning. Quite a challenge, but my training at Kelvinside Academy 'Hat Nights' came in handy. I once gave a lecture, largely off the cuff, to the first year students about Tristan da Cunha, an island about which I knew absolutely nothing, but used as an example of how I imagined a tiny, isolated economy might work, to illustrate some simple economic concepts. My audience listened attentively until, when my allotted fifty minutes were up, an alarm clock – previously planted by some practical joker – went off inside the desk from which I was lecturing.

I also lectured, for extra pay, to a class of Local Government Officers one evening a week on 'the economics of public utilities and public enterprises'. A good many could do shorthand and I used to watch them taking down my lecture verbatim, even the same phrase twice when I repeated it for emphasis; and I saw some of them filling in their football pools at the same time with their left hand. I found these skills most impressive; but when, at the end of the course, I read their examination papers, full of garbled regurgitation of what I had said, I was equally depressed. I had to pass most of them, of course. But I decided that perhaps evening lectures to tired and hungry people who had already done a full day's work were not a very good form of education.

So during my first year at Leeds I was pretty fully occupied preparing lectures and classes and had little time for research or writing. But I did have time to get married, in July 1937, to Christabel (Chris) Bartrum, whom I had met during a family holiday in Austria a couple of years before. I am sorry to say that the marriage did not turn out to be a happy one, but it produced two splendid children. Our son John won a Scholarship to Winchester, which I think he enjoyed about as much as I did Shrewsbury. He followed his father to Balliol but, unlike me, got a First in PPE. He spent the next four years in India – with which he fell in love – starting with a Research Fellowship and then doing a wide variety of other things, including a spell in a Gandhian Ashram. Finally, after studying, researching and teaching in several American Universities, he settled down as Professor of Sociology at the University of Lowell in Massachusetts. He is a US citizen and married with two children. His sister Mary was less academically inclined but is wonderfully practical. She went to school at Dartington Hall and for a good many years now has been a postperson in the wilds of Argyll where her round involves driving a Landrover eighty miles a day and not only delivering the post but, as a much loved member of a widespread community, helping many in personal need.

Early in 1975 I left Chris and asked her to divorce me so that I could marry Margaret Hall, the Economics Fellow at Somerville College, whom

I had known for nearly thirty years, and who had divorced Sir Robert Hall (later Lord Roberthall) in 1968. The proceedings were completed early in 1977 and I was able to marry Margaret and, if I may steal the final words of Churchill's *My Early Life*, after mentioning his marriage in 1908, we 'lived happily ever afterwards'.

During my second and third years at Leeds I no longer had to prepare all my lectures and classes from scratch and, although they still took up a good deal of time, I had far more left over for other things. Now my Professor, J Harry Jones, was a keen sub-contractor. So I spent some of my time, while also enhancing my income, doing work which he sub-contracted to me, the usual arrangement being that I received two-thirds, while he kept one-third, of the revenue. This included marking scripts for a professional body and an overseas university which had appointed Jones as an examiner. I also wrote a good deal for *The Accountant*, with which he was closely associated, including a series on official statistics – one on employment and unemployment statistics, one on statistics of foreign trade and so on – which I found extremely useful in educating myself, and very much complementary to a more serious (unpaid) study in which I had got involved in the following way.

Section F (the economic section) of the British Association for the Advancement of Science had a year or two before set up a Research Committee to prepare a book on *Britain in Recovery* as a sequel to a previous volume on *Britain in Depression*. Jones was Chairman and got me appointed Assistant Secretary. Roy Harrod was also on the Committee as President, for 1938, of Section F. My job as 'Assistant Secretary' meant that I did much of the work (I doubt whether the Committee ever met) of collecting and editing the various contributions. There were several general chapters by different economists on recovery in the various regions, commercial policy, industrial relations and so on; and fourteen by specialists on individual industries. I wrote at the beginning a 'General Survey 1929–37' – some eighty pages long – covering the whole business cycle. I must have worked pretty hard at all this during the nine months or so after the end of the summer term of 1937, because I was able to write to Roy Harrod at the end of April 1938 saying that I had finished my own piece and had sent it, together with two-thirds of the other chapters, to Percy Ford at University College, Southampton, the Secretary of the Committee, to see it through the press. (Roy, incidentally, was shortly to surprise all of us who had regarded him as a confirmed bachelor by getting married – to 'Billa' Cresswell.)

The book was published in September 1938, soon after the annual

meeting of the British Association, which was in Cambridge that year –
and at which I gave a paper on an entirely unrelated subject; I wonder how
I ever found time to prepare it. The book received good reviews, including
favourable comments on my own piece. This also impressed Harrod and
suggested to him that I had a special aptitude for quantitative economics
(one reason why he recommended me for a fascinating war job a year
later). I thought at the time it was rather dull; and when, in the early
1970s, I was selecting pieces for inclusion in two volumes of my collected
articles, lectures, etc, I was doubtful whether to include it, partly for this
reason, partly because it was so long, but also because it might be regarded
as 'old hat' since we had learned how to prevent depressions anything like
so severe as that of the 1930s. How wrong I was, and how glad I am I
included it. In the early 1980s we had just such a depression; the subject
of how we recovered in the 1930s became topical, and when the Bank of
England held a seminar of economists to discuss it in January 1984, and I
was invited, the study I had made some forty-five years earlier turned out
to be far from irrelevant.

With *Britain in Recovery* out of the way I was able to get on with two
studies for the Barlow Commission which was appointed in June 1938
with J H Jones as a member. I have already mentioned, in the context of
mid-Scotland's relatively poor economic performance, one of these
studies. This was published as Chapter II of a memorandum by Professor
Jones appended to the Commission's Report, exactly as I submitted it to
him, except for a concluding paragraph which read: 'This chapter was
made possible by the elaborate and careful analysis of the statistical
evidence of the Ministry of Labour prepared by my colleague Mr G D A
MacDougall'. The other study was on 'Inter-war Population Changes in
Town and Country'. It was published in the *Journal of the Royal Statistical
Society* in 1940.

2

STATISTICS AT WAR

DURING the summer of 1939, as war became increasingly probable, I pored over as much as I could get hold of about the economics and statistics of the First World War and the German economy. Then, not long after the war started, I had a mysterious phone call from Roy Harrod saying he had a job for me, the nature of which he could not reveal in advance, and urging me to take the train from Leeds to Oxford without delay. This I did, and on arrival was introduced to Professor Lindemann (known to many as 'The Prof') in Christ Church Common Room.

He was a distinguished physicist who had for years worked closely with Churchill, advising him on, among other things, the growing threat of Germany. On the outbreak of war, Neville Chamberlain had immediately brought in Churchill, who had long been in the political wilderness, as First Lord of the Admiralty, and a member both of the Cabinet and of a much smaller 'War Cabinet' which he formed. Lindemann had joined Churchill as his personal adviser on scientific matters, but after a few weeks was asked to form a 'Statistical Branch' as well. He was an old friend of Roy, both having been Students (the equivalent of Fellows) of Christ Church for many years, and asked him to suggest an economist to start the branch. Roy recommended me. This was yet another of the good turns he did me which greatly influenced, and helped to advance, my career; though I found it hard to conceal my blushes on reading, in his memoir of *The Prof*, this passage: 'I regard my choice of man on that occasion as a stroke of genius, and my best contribution to the defeat of Hitler. One single act may presumably do more to frustrate the enemy than six years of honest plodding.'

Prof and I somehow clicked from the start. We had a long conversation that evening in Christ Church during which I smoked many pipefuls of tobacco. I have not smoked for many years now and find it distasteful when someone near me puffs away continuously. But Prof, though a non-smoker – as well as a vegetarian and teetotaller – showed no signs of objecting. He must have been accustomed to Winston's cigars, but this was my first experience of his complete tolerance of those not sharing his fads. Indeed, he went further: no one fought harder to keep up the war-time ration of good red meat for the British people. After the war he was often the life and soul of the party, sipping his fruit juice while the young Oxford dons and their wives clustering round him were downing martini after martini, and somehow his conversation got more and more sparkling and amusing the more they consumed.

My new job was quickly fixed up and a few days later I arrived at the Admiralty with a trunkful of books, statistical reference works and papers with which I proceeded to fill an otherwise almost empty room. My very first task – almost immediately after I arrived – was to find out whether it was really necessary to ration sugar, as the Ministry of Food were proposing. Contingency plans for food rationing had been drawn up before the war and the Ministry were naturally itching to use their new toys. But Winston feared this would boost German morale, by suggesting that their attempted blockade of Britain through U-boats was already, so soon after the outbreak of war, starting to bring us to our knees. So I picked up my phone, rang up the Ministry and said: 'This is MacDougall, First Lord of the Admiralty's Statistical Branch, and I wonder if you would be so good as to give me some information about sugar stocks, consumption, production and imports.' The response was immediate: 'What the hell has it got to do with you?' I politely explained that my Minister, as well as being in the War Cabinet, was in charge of the Royal Navy which was responsible for convoying ships carrying to this country, among other things, sugar. Eventually, after further exchanges of this sort, I got the figures I wanted, did my sums, wrote my first memorandum as a civil servant, gave it to the Prof, who used it in his minutes to, and conversations with, Churchill, who in turn used these in correspondence with the Minister of Food and in the War Cabinet.

This was my first essay, as a youngster of 26 with no civil service experience, in the gentle art of wheedling out of officials – usually of quite long standing and much older – information which as often as not was going to be used against them. After Churchill became Prime Minister in May 1940 it became easier insofar as one had more authority to ask questions; but civil servants became more cautious about giving inform-ation which might be used by such a powerful person.

To begin with, we antagonised some people. Shortly after Roy Harrod joined the Branch at the beginning of 1940 he kept on pressing an argument that we were under-loading ships bringing in imports, long after I had discovered that it was based on a misunderstanding of the statistics. This lost us some credibility, which it took us time to regain. But we did regain it, with nearly all those we had to deal with in the departments concerned. In the end these covered nearly every one in Whitehall, but most important were the Service and supply departments and those dealing with transport, food, agriculture, labour, fuel and power, economic warfare, the Board of Trade and the Treasury. We regained our position partly because we were proved right on an increasing number of occasions, but also by being tactful, making friends with the officials concerned, showing them how we were doing our sums, trying wherever possible to get their agreement in advance, and by becoming as expert as they were – or preferably more so – on their subject; for they were, after all, the recognised authorities.

At least once the relationships I developed led to a rather comic sequence of events which went something like this. I gave Prof a minute for him to send to Churchill, covering a minute which it was suggested the latter should send to some Minister asking for a report on something or other. The PM duly sent it, the Minister passed it down the line to the chap dealing with the matter, who in turn asked me what on earth it was all about. I offered to draft a reply and he gratefully accepted; his Minister sent it to Churchill, who sent it on to Prof, who sent it to me for comment. So I had the fun of commenting on my own reply to my own question. But it was not a complete waste of time and did in fact clarify matters and shake things up.

Within a few months of my joining Prof, Harrod had recruited for him some half-a-dozen economists, mostly from the universities. The number remained at around this level throughout the war. There was some turnover, which was healthy – around fifteen economists were members of the Branch at one time or another – but the fact that it was not more rapid gave individuals time to acquire the expertise so necessary to hold their own with Departmental officials. A few of the recruits were established civil servants, but all of these had distinguished economic degrees. They included Bryan Hopkin, a Cambridge graduate, much later (as Sir Bryan) to be my successor but one as Chief Economic Adviser to the Treasury; David Bensusan-Butt, one of his contemporaries, who had compiled the index to Keynes' *General Theory* while a research student at King's College; and John Clarke, an old friend from my undergraduate days who had got a First in PPE, succeeded Hopkin as Prof's Private Secretary, and was to work again with him in 1951–53, as described in Chapter 5. We were nearly all extremely young, one notable exception being Harrod who joined when approaching the great age of forty. He left, for complex reasons I never fully understand but which he expounds in his book *The Prof*, in mid-1942. At about that time my position as Prof's right-hand man was officially recognised and I was given the title of 'Chief Assistant' – and an OBE.

To help the economists we had about half a dozen 'computers'. These were not the inanimate objects we know by this name today, but girls who worked on rather primitive calculating machines. We also had a team of 'chartists'. They had nothing in common with the agitators of the 1840s, but were talented young women – led by a man, Alan Kitching – who drew charts. Alan had had an undistinguished classical career at Balliol, but had an artistic bent and was a genius at designing and producing charts (after the war he became Drama Organiser for Oxfordshire and later Director of the Unicorn Opera in Abingdon). Churchill loved charts, and so did the Prof and so did I. So we produced many hundreds during the war, all painted in beautiful colours and collected together in innumerable loose-leaf albums or, if they were to be shown to important personages like the King or President Roosevelt, bound in cloth covers. At Churchill's request while still at the Admiralty, Prof personally presented the King's first album of charts, and explained them to him, at Buckingham Palace. Figures to bring the President's album up to date were cabled regularly to Washington; he seems to have found it compulsive reading. It was also quite common to attach a chart or two to a minute to the PM to help illustrate the argument.

They covered everything under the sun, including many aspects of shipping, manpower, imports, food, agriculture, coal, oil, timber, steel, other materials, machine tools, railways, building, prices, air, sea and land warfare, arms production, state of readiness of military units. Churchill took boxes of these to Chequers at week-ends where he would pore over them and gain such detailed knowledge that when, say, he was discussing military matters with his Chiefs of Staff, he was often able to trip them up by saying that such and such a Division in the Army had X% of its establishment of a certain type of weapon and Y% of another. Getting the figures to form the basis of all these charts was in itself a mammoth task. Particularly in the early days, the statistics in many Departments were in an appalling state and we had to do a lot of work, first making contacts and then tidying up the figures to get them consistent and into shape.

Most of our charts were on cards of a standard size, some 13 inches long and 8 inches high (though we had other shapes as well). Many, particularly those recording daily events, quickly reached the end of their 13 inches; continuation cards were then attached by tape so that they folded over neatly while still showing, when unfolded, the continuous story over as long a period as desired. They got longer and longer as the war wore on and some, containing many cards, were yards long when fully opened up (even when divided, for convenience of handling, into several charts each covering, say, twelve months).

One of the many I invented myself came to be called 'The Old School Tie' (a section of which is shown on the second page of photographs). It showed whether merchant ships were being sunk by U-boats in daylight or at night – in good, poor or no moonlight. Each twenty-four hours started at noon at the bottom of the chart, finished at noon the next day at the top, and continued again at the bottom of the chart a fraction of an inch to the right. Daylight was white and night black when there was no moonlight, blue when there was good moonlight – with the moon between its first and last quarters – and grey when there was poor moonlight. (I took a lot of time working all this out.) Red spots were then inserted showing the time of each sinking.

A section of the chart starting in, say, the autumn and ending at mid-winter naturally showed the night getting longer, and so the coloured part getting wider, just as a tie does; less obviously – and this is what made it really like an old school tie – moonless and moonlit periods happened to come out as diagonal black stripes alternating with stripes, partly of blue, partly of grey. More seriously, the chart showed how far improvements in our techniques of, and capability for, anti-U-boat warfare and other factors led German submarines, which originally attacked mostly in daylight, to do so more in moonlight and then in darkness; but also how adverse developments interrupted this tendency from time to time, sometimes severely. I suppose this was 'operational research', but I had not heard the phrase at the time.

Apart from economists, 'computers' and 'chartists', Prof at no time had more than one scientific officer in the Branch – first James Tuck and then W R Merton, both from his Clarendon Lab in Oxford. This may seem surprising since, judging by an analysis I made of his minutes to Churchill during the war, nearly one-third were on 'scientific' matters concerned mainly with technical details of instruments of war; but, of course, Prof was a scientist himself, not an economist or statistician. Counting in also a few secretaries and clerks, the total establishment was in the neighbourhood of twenty.

When Churchill became Prime Minister the scope of the Branch's work was greatly enlarged. The PM suggested that Prof should increase his staff substantially but he successfully resisted this. We moved from the Admiralty to Richmond Terrace, just across Whitehall from Downing

Street, and then – around the end of 1940 – to the St James's Park end of the 'New Public Offices', our entrance being in Great George Street. (We were thus just above the rooms to which Churchill transferred his Ministerial Headquarters from the more flimsy Downing Street buildings when the blitz got really bad.) We also became known as the Prime Minister's Statistical Branch; and after 1942, when Prof (now Lord Cherwell) had been made Paymaster-General, and an attender at War Cabinet meetings, we were sometimes known as the Office of the Paymaster-General.

I was told that during an air raid after we left Richmond Terrace a bomb penetrated the building and exploded in a cellar where we had been wont to eat sardines and drink beer during the blitz, confident that it was completely safe. While working in the New Public Offices I spent many nights sleeping well underground in what I was also assured was a bomb proof dormitory. No German plane happened to drop a bomb just on that spot to prove or disprove it.

My room was on the first floor and looked on to a courtyard which was the scene of noisy activity during much of the time I was there. First, workmen spent a long time erecting steel scaffolding covering the whole courtyard. They were keen whistlers and also enjoyed taking steel pipes as high as they could and then dropping them so that they hit the scaffolding below as often as possible on the way down, each time making a hideous clang. When the scaffolding had reached the top of the building they attached to it what looked like an enormous metal mattress, several feet thick. Now when I moved in to this office, the bottom of the courtyard looked as if it had been heavily reinforced with concrete. I concluded that below it must be part of the underground offices where the PM, Chiefs of Staff and War Cabinet used to meet, and sometimes sleep; and that the steel erection was intended to reinforce the protection from bombs already provided by the concrete. But I was uncertain whether the idea was that a bomb would bounce up and down on the mattress and fail to go off, or that the whole structure would slow its descent and make it explode opposite my window rather than on the concrete below. Then, when the whole thing was in place, someone must have decided it would not do; for it was all taken down and rebuilt to a different design, involving many more months of whistling and clanging; and by the time the second structure was completed the war was virtually over.

I have given some idea of the enormous range of topics covered by the Branch. But as the PM was such a busy man, we had to be selective in those we bothered him with. Nonetheless, apart from Prof's numerous conversations with him, he sent him some 2,000 minutes during the war, an average of roughly one a day. So they had to be brief. Winston insisted, and Prof was a willing accessory. I can picture him sitting in his armchair with a big blotting pad on his knee, on which lay a draft minute to Churchill. He would spend hour after hour going through draft after draft, cutting out redundant words, unnecessary sentences, inessential parts of the argument and many qualifications. At first this last type of shortening worried me – and my colleagues – quite a bit. But we soon realised how right Prof was when he told us 'l'art d'être ennuyeux c'est tout dire', even though it could mean that weeks of our work ended up as a half-page minute to the PM.

Sometimes I also had to spend weeks persuading Prof that some idea he had come up with – or some prejudice he had expressed – was wrong. It was no good rushing him. The only technique that worked was to wear him down. I would go and see him day after day – he was always willing, and quite often free, to talk for hours – with more and more fresh evidence, usually quantitative; and at least as often as not he would come round to my way of thinking. The only infuriating thing was that, on occasion, when I thought I had convinced him, he would arrange a meeting with the Minister or officials concerned and then, to my horror, go right back to square one and come up with the views that I thought I had weaned him from after long patient argument. But it was usually possible to salvage the situation; and although we had these long arguments about many things, and our views on many others were very different, I cannot remember a cross word passing between us during all the time we worked together, or indeed in the eighteen years during which I knew him so intimately.

The same cannot be said about his relationship with many others; but, although there were exceptions, he was much more likely to be rude to his peers than he was to subordinates. An endearing feature was his loyalty to his staff. It would hardly be an exaggeration to say that 'My Branch Right or Wrong' was his motto; and he liked to talk contemptuously about 'they', meaning, it almost seemed, everyone not in the Branch – except, of course, Churchill.

Prof had a wonderful flair for orders of magnitude and Churchill greatly appreciated this; a minute to him was hardly respectable unless it contained some. I too was keen on them and not bad at working them out. There was a regrettable tendency in Whitehall to spend much time on trivial matters and hardly any on some really important ones. Once, when Prof discovered that debts were piling up at £1 million a day in India, he sent my colleague Tom Wilson (a jovial Ulsterman who became an

Oxford don and then a Professor in Glasgow) to the Treasury to find out more about this. He could get virtually no breakdown of the figure. On the same afternoon I spent hours at the Treasury trying to get an extra half-a-crown a week for one of our typists.

Prof found this kind of thing intolerable; and whenever there was a problem to be solved he would always look for, and concentrate on, measures that would have a big effect. Take coal. After the fall of France and the collapse of our export markets in 1940, many miners were taken out of the pits and put into the Forces or munitions factories. We then had recurring threats of a coal crisis. At first we reckoned, rightly as it turned out, that the cries of woe by the Ministers responsible were overdone, but later became convinced – again rightly – that the danger was more serious than many thought. Prof and I would then (as well as on the earlier occasions when we were sceptical but wished to resist demands for the return of miners from the Forces) list all the possible ways of increasing supply of, or reducing demand for, coal we could think of, make quantitative estimates of their effects, and recommend to the PM that Ministers should go for those that might contribute, say, a million tons or more, and not waste time on those worth only a few thousand. (I recall Prof's indignation when somebody started sticking up posters all over London telling us to turn off dripping taps – even cold ones. The idea was that it would reduce the power required by waterworks and thus save coal used in its generation. Prof quickly calculated that the saving would be far less than the power used in making the posters – to say nothing of their import content.)

I doubt if we attempted to assess in advance the effects of the PM's decision – at one stage – to address a mass meeting in Central Hall, Westminster, of miners' delegates from all over the country. It was a splendid occasion. They arrived hours before he was due to speak and sang hymns and songs from the valleys. Then the great man appeared on the platform. I had probably prepared a brief on the coal situation but, when the tumultuous applause had died down, he began: 'War is made with steel, and steel is made with coal. I come to talk to you today not about coal but about war'. He then gave a brilliant account of how the war was going and the problems that lay ahead. They loved it, and returned to their villages no doubt greatly inspired. We then watched carefully our charts of coal output per man-shift, absenteeism and the like. I believe they showed a significant improvement for a time, but could not put my hand on my heart and say that this was sustained for very long.

Be that as it may, the approach of the Prof and the PM was successful. Despite several threats of a coal crisis, we never had one (though I am not for a moment suggesting that this was wholly due to them). In addition to concentrating on important measures, Churchill took a detailed interest in the subject (as he did in many others), poring regularly over our charts – we kept up-to-date at least thirty that were relevant to the coal situation. Also, he was prepared to overrule Ministers directly concerned with a problem if convinced by Prof that this was necessary.

How different from the way in which Attlee handled the threat of a coal crisis when Prime Minister. The danger, unless drastic steps were taken, of a serious crisis in the winter of 1946/47 was clear for all to see well in advance – even to me, though I was no longer in Government service, and had only the published statistics to go on. It was certainly foreseen by Douglas Jay when he was Attlee's personal economic adviser from September 1945 until July 1946. He kept on warning the PM, who in turn prodded his Minister of Fuel and Power, Emanuel Shinwell (later the much revered and loved Lord 'Manny' Shinwell). But he refused to take the threat seriously and inadequate measures were taken. In desperation, just before he left, Jay persuaded Attlee to have a meeting with him and Shinwell, at which the latter, when asked if he agreed with Jay's forecasts, replied, according to Jay: 'Prime Minister, you should not let yourself be led up the garden path by the statistics. You should look at the imponderables'. (I am quoting here from Douglas Jay's book, *Change and Fortune*, 1980, p. 149.) Attlee stuck by his Minister, kept him in the same post, and a coal crisis hit us with a bang in February.

I am sure it would not have happened had Churchill been Prime Minister – or, by the way, had Attlee made Harold Wilson Minister of Fuel and Power instead of Shinwell. For during the war statistics of fuel and power and their interpretation had been pretty primitive until Wilson (whom I first got to know when he was a don at Oxford before the war and I used to visit my Alma Mater from Leeds to keep in touch with economists there) became Director of Economics and Statistics at the Ministry. Though still a very young man, he really got things under control and the quality of papers emanating from the department improved out of all recognition.

Though Attlee seems to have delegated much more to his Ministers than Churchill, his style as Prime Minister was not perhaps so extreme as that of Stanley Baldwin. I have the following story on the authority of Sheila Lochhead (née MacDonald), an old Somerville friend of my wife, and daughter of Baldwin's predecessor, Ramsey MacDonald. When her brother Malcolm was Secretary of State for the Colonies during Baldwin's Premiership, he got so worried about the Palestine question that he decided to consult the PM. Now apparently Baldwin was a great delegator, thinking it right to conserve his energies for really important matters like the abdication of the Monarch, and spent much of his time playing patience. When Malcolm knocked on his door in No. 10 he was thus engaged but welcomed his visitor warmly and asked what he could do for him. When he said he was very concerned about the Palestine situation and asked what the Prime Minister thought about it, Baldwin replied: 'Frankly, Malcolm, I don't.'

Another example of Prof's concentration on really big things – and of his tenacity (some would say obstinacy) – concerned timber. Shipping space soon became a major bottleneck and it was essential to cut out all unnecessary imports. Timber imports accounted for a very important part of the total, and Prof waged a relentless battle to get them reduced: by substituting materials that could be produced at home or needed less shipping space if imported, by felling our forests and in other ways. There was much opposition – from those who argued that the changes proposed were inconvenient or more expensive and from many others. Such opposition made Prof even more persistent; he got really furious when timber imports were higher than had been directed; and we thought out more and more ways of reducing them until even I – who fully agreed with the general aim – began to think he might be pushing things too far. (Even Churchill, at one stage, got concerned about keeping at least some of our finest trees standing.) But the campaign was remarkably successful and timber imports were reduced to under one-fifth of their pre-war level.

We were equally concerned with economising shipping space used by the Services. Early in 1942 I discovered that lorries were being driven onto ships on their wheels, so that they could not be packed on top of each other and very few could be carried on each ship, and taken that way on long trips, including that round the Cape of Good Hope – the Mediterranean being closed by enemy action – to Egypt. This seemed to me incredibly wasteful and I made enquiries. I discovered that a good many more vehicles could be put in a ship simply by taking their wheels off and putting them in boxes, that still more could be carried if further dismantled and that, if they were completely knocked down (CKD) and an assembly plant built at the other end, six to ten times as many could be packed in a ship. I also worked out how much shipping would be saved in terms of imports into Britain if the lorries were dismantled – and it was a lot. (By this time, after hours of patient discussion with the two main statistical advisers in the Ministry of War Transport – they were in fact distinguished actuaries, Sir William Elderton and P N Harvey – I had persuaded them, reluctantly, to agree rules of thumb for doing sums of this kind.)

Prof told the PM, but he was slow to react. So he sent him one of the tiny handful of minutes typed in red ink that went in during the war. The red ink must have had an effect because only a few days later Churchill asked the Ministers concerned to discuss the matter with Prof. There was strong opposition from the military because of the inconvenience they claimed would be caused. But, after much argument and counter-argument, Churchill directed that the lorries were to be dismantled and boxed to the greatest possible extent – with monthly reports sent to him so that he could check that it was being done (a common, and useful, habit of his). Quite often he sent replies to these reports (drafted by us) back to the Ministers concerned and the Chiefs of Staff, which were complimentary, or critical or at least questioning, according to whether progress appeared satisfactory or the reverse; and this continued for the next couple of years. The results achieved were remarkable and much shipping was saved.

Not long after going to the Admiralty I had to comment on – and willingly helped to demolish – papers by Sir John Simon, then Chancellor of the Exchequer, and Lord Stamp (who was killed in an air-raid in 1941); the latter had been called in by Chamberlain in the summer of 1939 to examine the war plans of Government Departments. They argued against a rapid building up of our war effort, pointing out the balance of payments difficulties (resulting, for example, from the diversion of output for export to arms production), the losses involved if we sold our investments abroad too quickly at bargain prices, the dangers of skilled labour shortages and so, presumably, of inflation, and so on. But they implicitly made a crucial assumption which Churchill and Prof regarded – and how right they were – as highly dangerous, namely that we could *afford* a slow build-up because we could shelter indefinitely behind the 'Maginot Line' built by the French to ward off a German offensive.

So, for roughly the first two to two-and-a-half years of the war we pressed for a rapid transfer of resources from civil to military use (while trying hard to prevent waste in the latter, and ensuring that the civilians' food diet was not too drastically restricted, a matter about which the PM felt strongly), even if this meant taking risks, on, for example, the balance of payments. At the same time we urged the need for measures to overcome the economic difficulties that would admittedly arise. In the event, both objectives were achieved. We had a rapid military build-up. We had no serious inflationary problems once the Ministries concerned (often helped by their economists and by those in the Economic Section of the War Cabinet Offices who had rooms just above us) had developed schemes for rationing, allocation of materials, price control, food subsidies, direction of labour and so on, to complement strict financial policies. We had effectively no balance of payments problem, at least after Lend-Lease began (although this came only in the nick of time when our gold and dollar reserves were nearly exhausted; and the huge increase in sterling balances built up by countries prepared to be paid by us in sterling left a troublesome post-war legacy).

Then, early in 1942, Prof – and I – felt increasingly that we had now got about the right balance between the civilian and military sides of the economy and that further transfers could be counter-productive. Roughly half our resources were going to the war effort, and civilian consumption had been severely curtailed. Prof got increasingly irritated by a long series of 'austerity' measures inspired largely by Sir Stafford Cripps, who had returned to London in February after being our Ambassador in Moscow and felt that our people should be subjected to sacrifices more like those in Russia – largely, it would seem, for 'moral' reasons rather than to set free resources for the war effort. 'We are told', wrote Prof to the PM, 'that the public is suffering from a sense of frustration because it does not see how it can help win the war and that depriving it of things it likes will cure this. I question this analysis.'

The measures taken or proposed included: further cuts in dog-racing, newspapers, the clothes ration, bus services, retail deliveries, restaurant meals; abolishing the basic petrol ration; no more white bread; much higher taxes on entertainment, drink and tobacco; soap rationing; complete prohibition of the manufacture of such things as jewellery, artificial flowers, manicure sets, leather suitcases, cigarette cases and holders. I worked out for Prof how much manpower and shipping space (our two major bottlenecks) they would save in total. The result was trivial in each case. In reporting my figures to the PM he added: 'Is it for such small profits that we should expose the nation's will to win to the Death of a Thousand Cuts?' Any direct gain to the war effort could be far outweighed by the effects on civilian morale, the ability of people to get to work and so on; not to mention the bureaucratic cost of the regulations involved. This was agreed and from then on the supposedly belligerent Churchill, helped by the supposedly ascetic Prof, were powerful champions of the civilian against the military, whose demands they knew were often exaggerated and wasteful. (This, incidentally, was something about which our friends in the Economic Section upstairs knew little or nothing, whereas we had masses of military information.)

Another major issue involving the distribution of resources – this time shipping – between civilian and military use arose in 1942. The Allies were planning to recapture North Africa, starting in the autumn with an attack from Egypt in the east combined with a more or less simultaneous landing from a huge Armada in Morocco and Algeria. This was making enormous demands on merchant shipping, leaving less and less for importing into the UK, despite the economies by now being achieved through boxing lorries sent to Egypt. Our forecasts of imports, already cut to the bone, were alarming. They implied that our stocks of imported food and materials would quite possibly fall to dangerously low levels before very long. This would have meant people going really short of food, and factories producing munitions and the bare necessities of life having to close down through lack of materials, with their workers thrown out of a job. It is hardly an exaggeration to say that we could have lost the war on the home front. Meanwhile we knew from our detailed statistics that the military equipment in Egypt, together with that already on the way, was, to put it mildly, amply sufficient; we used to say that some of it was enough to fight a hundred years' war.

I kept warning the Prof and he kept warning the PM, but in vain; he seemed too preoccupied with the military operations. So Prof asked me how much the Services' use of shipping must be cut to set free the minimum required for essential imports. During the summer getting on for 120 ships had been sailing each month for Egypt (and other parts of the 'Indian Ocean' area). By the late autumn the number had been somewhat reduced but I worked out that it would have to be cut much further, to 60. I told Prof he would never get away with such a dramatic reduction and had better suggest 80. He replied that, on the contrary, he would put in 40–50, which would be argued up by the military to my figure of 60, which he believed. To my amazement, Churchill eventually accepted the figure of 40 and issued a directive to this effect. I was, not surprisingly, a trifle apprehensive, for we certainly had stuck our necks out. But all went well. The pincer movement in North Africa proceeded, unimpeded by shortage of military material, to a triumphant conclusion; imports – after falling to a terrifyingly low level for about four months – started arriving in increasing quantities just in time; our stocks – after plummeting in an equally alarming way – levelled off just above the minimum safety level before starting to recover slowly.

This was the most momentous macro-economic decision in which I have been involved, although I did not at the time think of it in those terms. I believe also that the Prof's Branch, with its comprehensive information on both civilian and military matters, as well as the statistical expertise it had acquired, especially on shipping, was the only body in Whitehall in a position to give a responsible recommendation, in quantitative terms, on the matter.

*

Members of the Branch spent part of their time on inter-departmental committees of officials. One I attended allocated scarce materials between Departments. It was chaired by a junior Minister and served by a secretariat headed by Professor Arnold (later Sir Arnold) Plant, on secondment from the London School of Economics. Demands from Departments invariably added up to more than the total available. I admired the technique of Colonel (later Lord) Llewellin, the presiding Minister for a time. He would arrange a meeting for, say, 11 am, and make sure he had no lunch date that day. Some of the officials were less far-sighted and soon after 1 o'clock they started to slip away one after another, conceding the reduction the Chairman had asked for in their Department's allocation. He was prepared to stay on indefinitely until the books were squared. I sometimes wondered what happened to the officials when they got back to their Departments; but suspected that there were few reprimands because they had usually added a bit on to their 'demand', fully expecting it to be cut. An important part of the Prof's Branch's work was, incidentally, examining critically the 'requirements' of Departments, not only for materials but for shipping space, manpower and many other things; and more often than not we found them excessive.

Another Committee I went to was on the German oil situation. One of our first jobs was to estimate German oil consumption. Part of this was consumption by the German Navy and we naturally asked the Admiralty for a paper on this. They set about it in the following sort of way. Branch A wrote down how many warships of each type the Germans had. This was passed to Branch B which said what kind of engines they had. Branch C then gave estimates of the number of hours they spent at sea each month, and Branch D their average speed. Branch E, armed with all this information, estimated their total oil consumption. I clearly could not comment on the technical details, but I knew the consumption of the Royal Navy and the Admiralty's first estimate showed German consumption of the same order of magnitude. When I suggested that this was implausible since their Navy was considerably smaller and, apart from U-boats, largely confined to port for most of the time, they quickly reduced their figure dramatically. But I was not satisfied so they cut it dramatically again. I am not sure if I went back a third time but I finally settled for a figure less than one-fifth of our naval consumption. This illustrates the common sense approach we often had to use when assessing the estimates of 'experts'.

When it became fairly clear that we would win the war, more of our time was devoted to post-war problems. The main domestic one with which I was concerned was how to prevent large-scale unemployment. I was helped by my pre-war studies, described in Chapter 1, on the trade cycle of the 1930s for the British Association, and on the location of industry for the Barlow Commission (in dealing with the problem of depressed areas); also by work I had done in preparing lectures in Leeds on industrial fluctuations. In addition, I now did new work on what had happened in the transition from war to peace after the First World War. I spent many hours discussing all this with Prof. He needed a lot of convincing on certain matters, and asked many searching questions, particularly on some of the ideas arising out of Keynes' *General Theory*.

But I convinced him and the outcome was a Cabinet paper which he circulated early in 1944. This was well received by the Cabinet and elsewhere in Whitehall; in particular, the businessmen in Government service appreciated the numerous orders of magnitude which it inevitably contained. A few weeks later Prof sent a revised version, which he thought might serve as a summary of the White Paper on Employment Policy which the Government proposed to publish, to Norman Brook (later Lord Normanbrook). He was then Permanent Secretary to Lord Woolton who, in November 1943, had been given the newly created post of Minister of Reconstruction to deal with post-war problems. Prof also joined a Ministerial Committee dealing with the matter.

Re-reading, and comparing, Prof's paper and the White Paper eventually published on 26 May 1944, it is striking how much of the former re-appears, in one form or another, in the latter. I cannot say how far it was a case of great minds thinking alike – meaning the minds of Prof and myself on the one hand, and on the other those of people like Lionel (later Lord) Robbins and James (later Professor) Meade of the Economic Section, with whom I collaborated harmoniously. But I believe we made a significant contribution. Though naturally biased, I believe Prof's paper was more readable than the White Paper. But, of course, it is one thing to write a personal paper and quite another to produce one taking account of the conflicting views and interests of numerous Departments and Ministers. The White Paper was certainly a remarkable document, not only because it was the first time any government had accepted responsibility for maintaining a high and stable level of employment, but because it recognised (despite what critics who seem never to have read it sometimes said about it many years later) that the objective could be frustrated by adverse developments in the rest of the world – and by inflation. It emphasised that 'action taken by the Government to maintain expenditure will be fruitless unless wages and prices are kept reasonably stable.' Therefore, 'it will be essential that employers and workers should exercise moderation in wage matters so that increased expenditure . . . may go to increase the volume of employment.' It also recognised that 'the success of the policy . . . will ultimately depend on the understanding and support of the community as a whole . . . For employment cannot be created by Act of Parliament or by Government action alone.' Long afterwards, when in the Treasury and then the CBI, I used to have fun with my colleagues by quoting such passages and asking them 'who said that?' Quite often the answer was 'Barber' or 'Healey' or 'Howe' or 'Lawson'.

The famous Beveridge Report on 'Social Insurance and Allied Services' was published in December 1942. It was the report of an inter-departmental committee of which Sir William (later Lord) Beveridge was Chairman, and he was greatly helped by Norman Chester, a good friend of mine who later became a Fellow and then Warden of Nuffield College. Beveridge had hoped the Government would ask him to prepare a follow-up on employment policy, but when they showed no inclination to do so, he decided to write his own report.

So a race was on between Beveridge and the Government. The Government won by six months – with its White Paper. Beveridge's (much longer) book on *Full Employment in a Free Society* was not published until November 1944, accompanied by an almost simultaneous publication entitled *The Economics of Full Employment* by members of the Oxford University Institute of Statistics – mainly 'aliens' who could not work in Government service – who had helped him. (He was at the time Master of University College and must have written much of his book in Oxford.) But he felt that the Government had an unfair advantage. He had, he tells us in his Preface, sent his report to the printer on 18 May 1944. That was eight days before the White Paper was published, but it suffered the delays of private publication whereas the Government could rush through their Paper, as they had his report on social insurance which was printed eleven days after signature. In retrospect, all this seems rather petty, and I had a great admiration for Beveridge's earlier work. As an undergraduate I had read avidly the 1930 edition of his *Unemployment: A Problem of Industry*, the first edition having been published in 1909; I thought it a model of quantitative economic analysis.

While greatly interested in domestic aspects of post-war policy, probably more of my work with Prof was on the external side (which was also crucial for employment policy, as he emphasised in his Cabinet paper). Much of this work I developed later after returning to academic life. One advantage of my in-and-out career – moving between university and public service – has been the intellectual stimulus given by one to the other: spells in public service suggested problems that could best be investigated in depth in Academe, while also being relevant to real policy issues; research and teaching in universities gave me ideas that could be tried out in the harsh real world.

I had no difficulty in persuading Prof of the mammoth post-war balance of payments problem, given the extent to which we had sold overseas assets, incurred huge debts abroad, and cut our exports to the bone, and even allowing for all possibilities of substituting home production for imports. All this meant that, to pay for essential imports, we had the Herculean task of raising exports from around 30% of their pre-war level to at least 150%. Prof and I were also, as it turned out, very much at one on the external policies we should follow to deal with this situation.

The PM was – naturally – preoccupied with winning the war first, and reluctant to devote mental energy to post-war problems, as evidenced by a note he wrote on a minute from the Prof on some aspect of external economic policy: 'I cannot comprehend the issue and have neither the life nor strength to learn.' (This is the only minute I can recall which had such a reception; for, as I have said, Prof took tremendous care not to trouble the PM with anything not absolutely essential, and his minutes were always a model of clarity.) But the PM could not opt out of these problems if only because of the insistence of our American friends. In December 1940 he had sent a long letter to Roosevelt explaining the military situation and how the US could further help, but also that we could not for long continue paying cash for American supplies. The President's response was sympathetic and swift. Only three months later he had persuaded Congress to pass the Lend-Lease Bill, which Churchill described as 'the most unsordid act in the history of any nation'. This transformed the situation by enabling the Americans to 'lend' or 'lease' supplies to us without payment. Congress, however, insisted on some benefit in return, in addition to our contribution to the defence of the US. Clearly the return in kind after the war of the vast variety of articles supplied would be impracticable, and insistence on money payments would be to repeat the mistakes made after the First World War. So the idea developed that as a 'consideration' for Lend-Lease assistance we and other recipients should promise to cooperate after the war in the restoration of multilateral, non-discriminatory trade; and for many in the US, in the State Department particularly, this meant above all the abolition of Imperial Preference, under which Empire countries gave preferential treatment in their tariff systems to each other.

These issues came up at the famous meeting in August 1941 between

Churchill and Roosevelt in Placentia Bay in Newfoundland (which I had visited as a schoolboy). Prof was in the select party that accompanied the PM; I did not go. Much of the discussion was on military matters. But another important task was drafting the 'Atlantic Charter' – a remarkable joint declaration of post-war aims. Roosevelt wanted to amend Churchill's first draft by inserting, in a clause on economic matters, a phrase 'without discrimination' which might be held to question the continuation of Imperial Preference. This was resisted by Churchill who, realising what a political hot potato it was, suggested an alternative draft which was accepted by Roosevelt, despite protests by Sumner Welles, representing the State Department.

But this was not the end of the story. Shortly before, discussions had begun in Washington on a 'Mutual Aid Agreement' on principles governing Lend-Lease supplies. Article Seven of the draft, dealing with the 'consideration' for such supplies, went much further than the economic clauses in the Atlantic Charter. Negotiations lasted eight months and Redvers Opie, then economic adviser to the British Embassy, played a notable part in securing a form of words acceptable to Britain. (He was a Fellow of Magdalen whose seminars I attended during my last two years at Oxford.) The final draft was specific about the '*elimination* (my italics) of all forms of discriminatory treatment in international commerce,' but Prof argued strongly – and I agreed – that we should sign without undue delay, despite the possible implications for Imperial Preference.

Not only did we recognise the importance of playing along with the Americans, on whom we should have to rely so much both during and after the war. We could also argue that, in signing Article Seven, we were not agreeing to abolish Imperial Preference but only to 'agreed action . . . directed to' this end; and the Article made it clear that progressive elimination of preferences would occur only in step with a reduction in US and other tariffs, highly important for a country needing a huge expansion in exports; and that our obligation on preferences lapsed if the US failed to combat a slump. Also, some important Empire countries seemed to attach little importance to Imperial Preference, and were already having bilateral discussions with the Americans, tending to whittle it away in return for US concessions; while I reckoned that it was much less important for UK exports than was often thought. I confirmed this later by detailed research in Oxford.

Meanwhile, proposals for post-war international arrangements were being worked out on both sides of the Atlantic. On the financial aspects Keynes, who had joined the Treasury in 1940 (and became Lord Keynes in 1942), produced his plan for an 'International Clearing Union'. It was published in 1943 at about the same time as a rather similar American plan, the brainchild of Harry Dexter White of the US Treasury. An agreed compromise was published in April 1944, the key provisions of which were embodied in the Articles of Agreement of the International Monetary Fund adopted at the Bretton Woods Conference in July 1944.

On the commercial side, plans were also being developed. James Meade was the main architect of a plan for a 'Commercial Union', not dissimilar from draft proposals then being developed in Washington; and discussions with US officials in 1943 revealed considerable agreement, including the need for an International Trade Organisation (ITO) to interpret the rules of a Charter on commercial policy. But the agreement was only between officials and on broad principles. Getting the politicians to agree, and translating the principles into specific obligations, was to prove much more difficult.

A plan was also worked out in London, based on another initiative of Keynes, for 'buffer stocks' to reduce fluctuations in primary commodity prices. It fell by the wayside, but I mention it briefly for two reasons. First, when Churchill heard it being talked about, he asked: 'What is all this about Butter Scotch?' Secondly, I advocated such a scheme later, both on a UN Committee in New York in the summer of 1951 and – unsuccessfully – not long after in Whitehall, when once again working for Prof.

I followed, and took part in, all these discussions and kept Prof fully informed. He was in general agreement with how things were going. His approach was, as usual, pragmatic rather than doctrinaire. He took a broad view of the national interest and was quick to see through special pleading of sectional interests. One of his guiding principles was that in a world without a code of rules for international economic behaviour there would be international anarchy and this would be disastrous for a country so dependent as Britain on international trade. He also liked the particular rules being worked out because they would require countries without balance of payment difficulties to follow liberal policies, while allowing countries with such difficulties – which would probably include the UK for a good many years – to impose import and exchange controls. Similarly, the IMF would allow us to devalue the pound if our trade was in fundamental disequilibrium while preventing competitive devaluation by countries in a healthier state, as had occurred in the 1930s.

But there was much opposition from Ministerial colleagues as well as from backbench MPs. I spent a lot of time during 1944 and 1945 helping Prof to comment on the torrent of paper from these critics that came across the PM's desk. They were mainly concerned about agriculture, Imperial Preference, the IMF and the outlawing of 'bilateralism.' Mr (later Lord) Hudson, Minister of Agriculture, kept on arguing that the proposals would not allow us to maintain a 'healthy and well-balanced agriculture.' Prof explained to the PM that the rules would allow farmers to be protected by import quotas so long as we had balance of payment difficulties and otherwise by moderate tariffs, State purchase of imports, and a levy of limited size on imported wheat, for example, which could finance large subsidies to home-grown wheat. If this were not enough we should also be allowed to give what subsidies we liked from the Exchequer. Hudson, fearing that Parliament might refuse such open assistance, wanted levy-subsidy schemes, or tariffs – which would conceal more effectively help given to farmers – to be unlimited in size. But, as Prof pointed out, this could be disastrous since other countries would then feel free to use the same methods to keep out our exports.

The main champions in the Government of Imperial Preference were Leo Amery, Secretary of State for India, and Lord Beaverbrook, the Canadian-born newspaper tycoon whose *Daily Express* was noted for its strong pro-Empire views. Churchill was bound to listen to the latter in particular, if only because of the remarkable job he had done as Minister of Aircraft Production in 1940 in speeding up the output, and repair, of fighter aircraft. This may well have tipped the balance in the Battle of Britain which, had we not won it, might have lost us the war. Now Beaverbrook looked like, and was, a wily old owl. Remembering Winston's opposition to Imperial Preference as a young Liberal – after he had crossed the floor of the House in 1904 – he knew it was little good tackling him head on. But he had been one of the very few to warn Churchill, when Chancellor of the Exchequer, against going back to the gold standard at the pre-1914 parity in 1925, a matter about which Winston was sensitive, having recognised later what a great mistake it had been to fix sterling at such a high level. So Beaverbrook was wont to try on a flanking attack on the proposals for an IMF, saying in effect that it was 'the gold standard all over again,' hoping thereby to discredit, by association in the PM's mind, the proposals that might affect Imperial Preference. I have already described our defence of these proposals. On the IMF, it was easy for Prof to point out that we could in practice choose an initial parity for sterling that was competitive and that the IMF was much more flexible than the old gold standard.

Finally they were those who argued that, instead of entering into agreements to promote freer, multilateral trade, we should reserve the right to use our bargaining power as a large importer to force supplying countries to buy our exports, saying that we would buy from them only to the extent that they bought from us. I did a lot of quantitative work on this which showed that much of our trade was in fact done with countries not greatly dependent on our market or dependent even more on that of the US – which could certainly, if we embarked on this approach, beat us at our own game.

One reason I decided not to stay in Government service after the war was that I was told I would not be allowed to publish a paper I wrote on this even though it contained no recommendations for policy. (I published it in 1947, with a greatly expanded version in 1949, after returning to Oxford.) The paper did, however, certainly contain an *implication* for policy which Prof and I used a great deal in Whitehall, namely that to embark on the type of policy described, far from increasing our exports, might well reduce them by putting a large part at risk. Prof pointed out in a Cabinet Paper that: 'It is easy to exaggerate the strength of our position as the largest importer in the world. Without foreign wheat we should starve; our suppliers could well postpone their need for machinery, etc, or get it from other sources – and they know it.'

There was the additional danger that to go for a system of *bilateral* balancing of trade would endanger the large part of our exports dependent on *multilateral* trade, under which we used large surpluses in our transactions with some countries to pay for deficits with others. After the war I worked out that, before the widespread growth of bilateralism in the 1930s, between two-fifths and one-half of our exports depended on the willingness of countries in the first category to run 'unfavourable' balances with us. In a bilateral world a large part of our exports would thus be vulnerable.

Despite all the arguments we deployed – and many in Whitehall agreed with us – it was apparent by the spring of 1944 that many Conservatives disliked intensely the plans being negotiated with the Americans, particularly those on commercial policy that might affect Imperial Preference. The PM therefore decided in April 1944 to address a large meeting of the Party faithful. I was not there of course, but the account I had went something like this.

Churchill started by saying: 'It all began with the Atlantic Charter.' Then, perhaps because he had forgotten what the meeting was about or perhaps deliberately, he immediately went on to recall at length the military questions he had discussed with Roosevelt at their meeting off Newfoundland. I am sure this was fascinating, but after a time his audience must have become restive and he said: 'But we are here to discuss economic questions.' Then, apparently forgetting that he was now the revered Leader of the Conservative Party and not a young Liberal MP fighting the 1906 Election, he went on: 'It's all about dear food; we beat you on that before and we'll beat you again.' I do not know how the rest of the meeting went. But in the event, while negotiations with the Americans and others on the IMF continued apace, those on commercial policy were slowed down. They did not start again in earnest until 1945 and had not made much progress by the time the Prof's Branch was disbanded in July, following the defeat of the Conservatives in the General Election.

3

MISSIONS ABROAD: 1943–45

DURING 1943–45 I made several trips abroad, some with Prof, some without. When he told me to prepare – in great secrecy – for the first, to Washington with Churchill to meet Roosevelt in May 1943, I had to fill several boxes with papers and charts we might need. Since this was impossible without a few colleagues seeing what I was doing, Prof said to tell them we were going to a country retreat to do some serious work in peace and quiet. I doubt if anyone believed this and since have formed the view that it is better, when you want something kept secret, to come clean with the minimum number who must know, and say they will be shot if they leak; because if you concoct some cock-and-bull story people feel freer to speculate and talk to others; and may well hit on the truth.

We left London by train on the night of 4 May and boarded the *Queen Mary* on the Clyde next day. Nine years earlier I had been at the launching ceremony in John Brown's Clydebank Yard when Queen Mary, accompanied by King George V, gave her name to the great ship. Many at the time regarded her as an uneconomic white elephant, little dreaming what a vital part she – and her sister ship the *Queen Elizabeth* – were to play during the war, carrying vast numbers of troops across the Atlantic.

For the voyage I took Apsley Cherry-Garrard's *The Worst Journey in the World*, about the epic trip he and two companions made in appalling conditions – to collect Emperor Penguin eggs – from and back to Scott's Antarctic Headquarters during the winter of 1911. I thought this might remind me, in case I got scared of the U-boats, or seasick, how much more dangerous, and uncomfortable, journeys could be. In fact we had a reasonably smooth passage and, although we had instructions to carry lifebelts at all times, I like to think we were not in great danger. I knew, it is true, from the figures we had, that the number of operational U-boats was near an all-time peak, and what a massacre of merchant ships they had carried out during the past year-and-a-half. But it looked as if their offensive might have passed its peak, and the Battle of the Atlantic begun to turn in our favour. Also, the *Queen Mary* could travel much faster than submarines and I was told that, provided we zig-zagged sufficiently, we could evade them. (On a later trip, when taken into the map room, I was alarmed to see an apparently almost solid line of U-boats blocking our path, until I realised that the pegs showing their estimated positions were, given the scale of the map, each equivalent to several miles long.) For the last couple of days we were surrounded by the US Navy, which led Churchill to telegraph Roosevelt: 'We all greatly appreciate the high value you evidently set on our continued survival'. But up till then our only escort seemed to be a British cruiser, to which coded signals were flashed, and which was periodically replaced by a sister ship before going off a considerable distance to radio the signals to London, so that the Germans could not easily work out our position.

Most of the ship was infested with bed-bugs. The part used by the Prime Minister's party – including myself – had been 'de-bugged'; but two Very Important Passengers were in the other part: Sir William and Lady Beveridge. Sir William had quite recently married Mrs Janet Mair, of whom he had been a close friend and colleague for many years, following the death of her first husband. He was on his way to tell the Americans about his Report on Social Insurance. Lady Beveridge suffered badly from the bugs. One day Churchill invited them both to lunch. Afterwards I was told by his personal aide Commander Thompson ('Tommy') that the PM, who had placed Lady Beveridge on his right, had complained to him that she seemed mainly interested in moaning about being bitten in the neck by bugs (which hardly accords with the account of the lunch in her book *Beveridge and his Plan*); to which Tommy, who had lived since boyhood in a naval environment accustomed to earthy speaking, had replied: 'I don't believe it was bugs. Old Bill must have forgotten to take his false teeth out last night.'

Although I had crossed the Atlantic before, to Newfoundland, this was my first visit to the United States and I was fascinated by all the new things I saw, and by the differences between our austere Britain and a country that had been able to mount a huge war effort without significantly affecting living standards. After arrival in New York we took a special train to Washington. I recall the blissful pleasure of downing glass after glass of orange juice, not having tasted a drop, or indeed seen an orange, for years. In Washington I bought a pack of pipe tobacco for 15 cents which would have cost the equivalent of 70 cents at home. I told this to the shop girl, and when I came back a few minutes later to buy a newspaper, found her prostrate across the counter, gasping: '70 cents; 70 cents'. This was probably more effective in getting across the sacrifices we were making in the Allied cause than all the charts and statistics I had brought to convince our American friends.

We spent just over a fortnight in the US, including a weekend in New York where some kind Americans I had never met before helped me paint the town red. The British were amazingly popular at the time. In the early hours of Sunday morning I was surprised how many newspaper sellers there seemed to be in the streets. They turned out to be ordinary New Yorkers carrying home early editions of their Sunday papers. These, with all their sections and supplements, contained an enormous number of pages, so that one or two of them looked like dozens of ours at home, which were then, to save imports, drastically limited in size.

On my first night in Washington I found that my windows would not open. I had never in my life slept in a room with all the windows closed, and was sure it would suffocate me, so drastic action was necessary. I found that the windows *could* be opened but that the top and bottom parts had been nailed together. So I took the nails out, threw open a window and went to bed. I was soon aroused by a banging on my door and found an irate manager saying I had completely disrupted the hotel's recently installed air-conditioning system. I have long since got used to sleeping without a window open, especially after Prof worked out for me what an unbelievably long time a human being could survive in quite a small hermetically sealed space.

Churchill's telegram to Roosevelt suggesting the Conference had said that the problems of military strategy he wished to discuss would have to be considered in the light of 'the shipping stringency'. We had a lot we wanted from the Americans in this field, especially more ships and a change in the pattern of their shipbuilding programme to prevent a severe fall in carrying capacity in the first half of 1944; and most of my work, apart from expounding on our massive transfer of resources from civil to military use, was on shipping matters, with my opposite numbers in the US. When I suggested to one of them an interesting calculation that might be done, he got quite excited and said he must get a team to work on it for a fortnight. This was quite possible given the amazing numbers brought to Washington to run the war effort; but it was the sort of calculation I had to, and could, do myself in an afternoon on the back of a few envelopes.

I flew back to London in a converted bomber via Gander, in Newfoundland, and Prestwick. The journey lasted twenty-four hours, including eighteen in the air. We had to wear oxygen masks a good deal of the time and the heating system was such that when those at the front were comfortable those at the back were freezing; and when the latter were comfortable the former roasted. In London we were made members of a Club of those who had flown the Atlantic, still quite a small number. I was luckier than some who had to lie in the bomb-bays of unconverted bombers, hoping they would not be opened by mistake.

In August 1943, Prof and I set off for another meeting between Churchill and Roosevelt, this time in Quebec. We again sailed on the *Queen Mary*, but disembarked in Halifax and took the train to Quebec. The main subject on the agenda was the proposed cross-Channel descent on France which began ten months later. My services were not much in demand. The PM stayed on in Canada for a few days after the Conference and then went to Washington to continue his discussions. I had hoped Prof and I might also stay on for a while and that I might get some trout fishing, as some of the military chiefs did. But Prof decided that duty called and we set off for home as soon as the Conference was over.

We flew again by Gander. There we were told there was fog over London so we would have to wait a few hours to give it a chance to clear. But Prof was impatient, especially as Anthony Eden, then Foreign Secretary, had left not long before in another plane, and insisted on starting. As our plane approached London, I felt it swing to the left, then to the right, then to the left again. The two pilots were presumably wondering whether the fog had cleared sufficiently to make it safe to land in London. I also knew that the girlfriend of one was in London and the other's in Glasgow; and in my imagination pictured them struggling with the joystick as we swung one way and then the other. We finally turned north, flew to Prestwick, and came by sleeper to London, arriving much later than we would have done had Prof been a little less impatient in Gander.

On 5 September 1944 we once more set sail from the Clyde on the *Queen Mary* for the second Quebec Conference. I think it was on this trip that I made a real fool of myself. Assuming we were taking a northerly route, I stood on the starboard side with some colleagues, proudly showing off my knowledge of the west coast of Scotland by pointing out various landmarks – until I realised, to my horror, that we were looking at the east coast of Ireland and proceeding to the Atlantic round the south of that island. We landed, as before, at Halifax and went by train to Quebec, where we learned that Roosevelt had got there shortly before and had waited at the station to greet Winston. Many of our party rushed off to where they thought they might catch a glimpse of the great man but, not being convinced, I thought I would ask a man sitting in the back of an open car nearby if he knew where the President was. When I got within a few yards, I noticed several others in and around the car and they were pointing guns at me. I then realised that the man in the back was the President himself. He smiled and I beat an embarrassed retreat. He was to die only seven months later.

At this Conference I had plenty to occupy me. One of the main things Prof and I had to do – helped by Hugh (later Sir Hugh) Weeks, who had come to represent the Ministry of Production – was to get a satisfactory directive signed by Roosevelt and Churchill on the amount of Lend-Lease aid, and on what conditions, we should get from the Americans during what was called 'Stage II' – between the German surrender and the end of the war with Japan. We were told to assume it would last eighteen months, but in the event it was little more than three, following the dropping of atom bombs on Japan. I of course knew nothing about this weapon; and even those who did, like Churchill and Prof, were not certain if and when it would become operational.

Our job was to persuade the Americans that, although the defeat of Germany would enable us to cut down our war effort and transfer resources to civilian production, we would still require substantial Lend-Lease aid, in the form both of munitions – for the war against Japan – and of other goods. This would be necessary to help us make a modest start in repairing war damage, restoring our severely restricted civilian standards and raising our exports, which had been reduced to a small fraction of the pre-war level and could not possibly, within the space of a year or two, pay for essential imports. This last point was politically sensitive in the US, especially where there was a possibility that we might export, in competition with American producers, goods similar to those supplied to us on Lend-Lease. There was much semantic wrangling and we were pleased to get into the final version of the Quebec Agreement that we would not expect to get on Lend-Lease goods 'identical' to those we exported – a much better word, from our point of view, than 'similar'.

I had done a lot of work on all this before leaving London. We did not expect to find the Americans easy to persuade but in addition, during the voyage, we found the PM reluctant to raise the matter with Roosevelt. However, soon after we arrived, he sent a message to him saying it was one of the most important topics to be discussed. We also learned that Henry Morgenthau, US Secretary to the Treasury, was coming to Quebec with a companion. When we had lunch with them on their arrival, on Wednesday 13 September, the companion turned out to be Harry Dexter White, the main co-architect, with Keynes, of the International Monetary

Fund. But White, whose loyalty was subsequently questioned, with assertions – I do not know with what justification – that he was a 'communist spy', had not come to Quebec to discuss the IMF. Nor had he come only to discuss Lend-Lease in Stage II, on which, however, he was well-briefed and difficult to argue with – partly because he talked most of the time. He was more interested in a plan for the post-war 'pastoralisation' of Germany, leaving her with virtually no industry and a very depressed standard of living. This he had sold to Morgenthau – it was called the 'Morgenthau Plan' – and, through him, to Roosevelt. Churchill violently opposed it but, as we had so much else we wanted from the Americans, agreed to consider it. This meant that, in addition to negotiating on Stage II, I had to listen politely to long lectures from White on what I regarded as a crazy plan. (These lectures continued when I had gone on to Washington.) But it was worth it. After a few hectic days we got two rather good documents on Stage II signed by Roosevelt and Churchill, and on Saturday 16 September a congratulatory cable arrived from London.

Armed with these documents, Prof and I set off hopefully for Washington for discussions which would put flesh on the bones of the Agreement. Prof was reluctant to go, but his master insisted. In the event I spent about six weeks in Washington, but for nearly half the time Prof was away on trips to other parts of the US on 'scientific' business. When he was not there I did my best to safeguard his position during innumerable meetings, mainly with British officials – some resident in Washington, others who came over later from London for the negotiations – most of them much senior to myself.

A fortnight after we got to Washington Keynes arrived to represent the Chancellor. Prof thought this would be a good excuse for him to pull out and go home. He was persuaded to stay, but Keynes effectively took over the day-to-day running of the operation, especially as Prof was out of Washington for so much of the time; but he retained a powerful position as what Lord Halifax, our Ambassador, called a 'Plenipotentiary Extraordinary', and made some important contributions, both directly and – I like to think – through me on his behalf.

This was the only time in my life when I saw a lot of Keynes: virtually every day – and sometimes several times in a day – over a period of some four weeks. I was enormously impressed, and not least by his willingness to listen to a youngster like myself, provided I had something worth saying, just as readily as he would to his peers – and not simply, I believe, because I was often representing the Prof. I also witnessed examples of his well-known flexibility and willingness to change his mind. At a meeting on the morning following his arrival, after Prof had outlined his plan of attack for negotiating with the Americans, Keynes said this was utterly different from that envisaged in London and from the one he was instructed to follow. But in the afternoon, following a discussion he had with Morgenthau and White, he told us he was converted to the Prof's approach more or less in its entirety. Once, when Prof was away, he rejected at a morning meeting a proposal I made about how we should deal with a particular point. After lunch, when the meeting resumed, he said he had decided that the best approach was precisely what I had suggested in the morning. He had totally forgotten this, and I am not even sure that he realised he had completely changed his mind. I remained silent; but was pleased.

Although we were told that all Cabinet Ministers in the US Administration had received a copy of the Quebec Agreement, and would work in the required spirit, it soon became clear that a document signed by the President was not regarded by Washington officials as anything like so sacrosanct as one signed by the Prime Minister would be in Whitehall, one reason being that the former had to think more about Congress than the latter had to about Parliament. We found a lot of rivalry, and sometimes ill feeling, between US Departments, and much time was spent discussing tactics.

While I was in Washington, the Presidential Election campaign was in full swing and I was struck by its vitriolic tone. After four years of truce between parties and a Coalition Government at home I had forgotten how acrimonious politics could be. The publication of some of the things we were agreeing had to be delayed until after the Election; and indeed, had there been a change of President, much further negotiation would have been necessary. However, Roosevelt won the Election, with Harry S Truman – who was ridiculed by his opponents during the campaign as an insignificant little man – as his Vice-President. By this time – early November – Prof and I had flown home, but Keynes was still in Washington. What appeared to be a satisfactory agreement was reached and Churchill was optimistic when he announced it in the House of Commons late in November; but the President later met considerable opposition from members of his Administration and Chiefs of Staff.

During the later part of the war I did a lot of work for Prof on reparations from Germany and her post-war economy. Apart from the question of 'de-militarisation' he was much concerned with the economic aspects. He was keenly aware of our daunting balance of payments problems, especially the need for a huge increase in our exports, mainly of manufactures, when we had been forced, as a result of the war, to give up so many important markets overseas. It was therefore vital that the arrangements made for German reparations should in no way aggravate these problems, and so far as possible alleviate them.

He insisted, for example, that the Allies should not be allowed to take as reparations from Germany manufactures from current production. If countries like France or Belgium did this, we should incur a triple loss: we should have to re-stock and re-equip German factories in our zone of occupation to produce these manufactures – at our own expense; our European Allies would receive free from Germany manufactures which they would otherwise have had to buy from us for cash; and we should be restoring the industry of our principal pre-war competitor in export markets for manufactures. Why, asked Prof in a minute to Churchill, should we do this when 'the only notable compensation we can hope to receive from her (Germany) for all the evils she has inflicted on us is her export markets'? Reparations should therefore be confined to once-for-all deliveries of existing equipment, forced labour (in the case of the Russians), and raw materials (we should be happy, for example, to get from Germany some timber, of which we were desperately short). Removing existing equipment would reduce her manufacturing capacity, which Prof would not be unhappy to see since it would limit her ability to export manufactures in competition with us, though he would not wish to go nearly so far towards the 'pastoralisation' of Germany as had been proposed in the Morgenthau Plan.

Not long after the war with Germany ended I was asked to join a British delegation to Moscow to discuss these matters with the Russians and Americans. This was in accordance with an agreement at Yalta between Roosevelt, Churchill and Stalin that an Allied Reparations Commission should be set up – and work in Moscow. Our team was headed by Sir Walter (later Lord) Monckton, then Solicitor-General. A distinguished barrister, who had played a prominent role during the abdication crisis of 1936, he was a Balliol man and later became Visitor of the College. I liked him very much, especially when he wrote on a brief I had prepared for a discussion with his American counterpart in Moscow (on the share-out of reparations), which he was able to read only after the issue had been agreed over our heads by higher authorities: 'I don't often get a brief so admirably clear and concise, and it is a bit hard when I do, to have the case settled'. His Personal Assistant was Tony (later Lord) Greenwood, a contemporary of mine at Balliol who later became a member of Wilson's Cabinet; and his chief official was Sir David Waley from the Treasury (better known as 'Sidgy', short for Sigismund, his other first name). He too was a Balliol man so the old College was well represented.

The party, totalling about 35, flew off from Northolt on Monday 18
June in three Dakotas. We stopped in Berlin, still wholly under Russian
control, to refuel and take on a Russian navigator (to stop us flying over
secret installations). We had a chance to see the damage caused to
Germany, and especially Berlin, by bombing and shelling. The flight to
Berlin also confirmed that there was a lot of timber in the British zone of
occupation and fine motor roads running through the forests on which it
could be carried away as reparations – which I duly reported in my first
letter to Prof from Moscow.

On arrival we were welcomed by Mr Maisky, Deputy Minister for
Foreign Affairs, who had been Ambassador in London for a decade. Also
at the airport were Edwin Pauley, Head of the US delegation, and his
second-in-command, Isador Lubin. (Roosevelt had appointed Lubin to
the top post but when he died Truman gave it to Pauley, a producer of
petroleum. We soon found that the US team were sharply divided into
'Pauley's gang', consisting mainly of oil men, with little knowledge of the
reparations problem, and Lubin and his 'intellectuals', who had thought
deeply about it.) The first British plane to arrive was greeted by a military
guard of honour with fixed bayonets and there was some disappointment
when it turned out to contain largely typists and clerks. The second had
rather more important passengers like myself. By the time the third plane
arrived, containing Monckton, Maisky was getting a trifle impatient.

We drove to the Hotel Savoy where we were to stay. My room was quite
comfortable. It even had a bath but unfortunately without taps. However,
after I had given the maid the remains of the sandwiches I had brought for
the journey, I could get almost anything I wanted. So for a start I pointed
to the bath and indicated in sign language that I wanted to use it. She
scuttled backwards and forwards with bucket after bucket of absolutely
boiling water but I could not stop her, in her desire to please, filling it to
the brim, nor explain that I wanted some cold water added. So, as I had no
time to let it cool down, I could only dip my hands in and take them out
almost immediately to prevent them being scalded.

We soon discovered that the Russians were in no hurry to have serious
negotiations. On the day after we arrived – Tuesday – Maisky told
Monckton that, apart from a formal meeting on the Thursday (which I
attended and at which each delegation made a general statement and lots
of photographs were taken), there would be little opportunity for further
discussion until 'well after the weekend'. The reason given was that the
Victory celebrations were to begin on Friday. We also had trouble with
offices. The Americans, who arrived before us, had been hanging around
for a week trying in vain to get some. We were promised them for the

Wednesday but in fact had to wait until Friday and then found that they contained only eight tables for four times as many people – the rest, we were told, were being manufactured. So for the first few days we used our hotel rooms to work in; and Waley generously allowed his to be used as a general office. I have a vivid memory of several typists banging away while he sat placidly on his bed reading Ovid – he had got Firsts in Classical Mods and Greats. We also had difficulty getting cars, as well as a plane service for diplomatic bags to London; the Russians would not let us use RAF Mosquitoes because they had no room for a Russian navigator.

Maisky – an amiable, but exasperating, bearded character – kept on saying he would expound to us a detailed Russian plan for reparations, which we had agreed would form the basis for discussions, but kept putting it off and in the end we never got it at all. An imposing array of committees and sub-committees was set up, but they achieved virtually nothing. But although we made little progress with the Russians we did a lot of work inside our delegation – and to a lesser extent with the Americans – which came in useful later in the year. We also had ample time for recreation. We went several times to the ballet, always superb; when I asked a Russian if male ballet dancers were exempt from military service he could hardly believe that anyone could ask such a silly question – of course they were. Almost as good were the opera, folk dancing, and a puppet show. We did not go to the cinemas, outside which there were always large queues. One was showing 'Charlie's Aunt: The Latest American Comedy'! There were lots of cocktail parties; a picnic one Sunday when we swam in a river; and the inevitable sight-seeing tour of the Kremlin.

On the Sunday after we arrived we watched the Victory Parade in the Red Square. It lasted several hours. It was cold and pouring all the time, and having a hip flask of whisky which I unselfishly shared with colleagues made me popular that morning. One of our typists, who had mislaid the strictly personal, non-transferable, documents we had been given to secure admission, borrowed those of another typist who was ill; she got past the whole succession of security guards who checked us all carefully as we walked to the places reserved for us a stone's throw from the Lenin Mausoleum where Stalin and other Russian VIPs stood, reviewing the parade.

It was an impressive display of military might, immaculately carried out, with only one hitch when a tank broke down; not long after, a shot rang out from the direction in which it had been towed away. I was particularly interested in the march past of officer cadets. The first contingent looked like sixteen-year-olds; the second fifteen-year-olds; and the last could hardly have been more than thirteen. I just wondered whether it helped to become a young cadet if your father happened to be a Colonel or a General. I recalled this a few years later when on a UN Committee in New York and chatting with the Russian member over lunch in the canteen. When I asked what happened to a man's property when he died, he thought it a strange question. I explained that in my country the State often took part of it, to which he replied: 'What has the State got to do with it? It goes to his oldest son, of course'. He also told me that better-off people could pay for better education for their children.

In Moscow, when I was there, a high degree of inequality was plain for all to see: at one extreme a few prosperous, well-dressed people driving about in cars; at the other, very shabby, ill-fed creatures, either on foot or on unbelivably crowded trams. The underground Metro was even worse; one evening, for fun, we came back to our hotel on it after seeing some fantastic acrobatic dancing; we stood, packed tighter than sardines, and had to start pushing our way towards the door several stations before the one at which we hoped to get out. I also learned that pay differentials between ranks in the Russian Armed Forces were far greater than in the British.

After the war I often set my pupils in Oxford an essay on inequality in Britain; and when they had read it I told them, usually to their surprise, some of these things, and many others, about Russia – as well as the story about the Moscow Dynamo football team. When they visited England they naturally came to see Oxford and, when they asked where the University was, were shown to University College where the Master invited them to dinner in Hall with the undergraduates. One of the young Russians, who spoke a little English, seeing the food being taken up to the Dons at High Table, asked his neighbour: 'Do the teachers up there get the same as the students down here?' When the British undergraduate lied for his country and said they did, the Russian roared with laughter and said: 'Ach, in Russia it is not so; the teachers get much better food, so the students work hard hoping to become teachers'.

After three-and-a-half weeks in Moscow, I got a message from Prof to get ready to join him in Berlin for the Potsdam Conference between Churchill, Stalin and Truman. So on Saturday 14 July I flew off in the plane of Averell Harriman, then the US Ambassador in Moscow. He had been a close confidant of Roosevelt for many years and was a good friend of Britain; he was Ambassador in London in 1946 and I saw him later in Paris in the early days of the Marshall Plan. Harriman was not on the plane himself but flew to Potsdam later. He came to dinner there with the Prof and, when he asked who would win the General Election, all the

British present – including myself – were sure it would be Churchill.

In the plane were some other members of the British delegation and some of the US team, including Pauley, all on their way to Potsdam. It was a long journey and after a time we got hungry and thirsty. We could see at the back of the plane an attractive array of food and drink, but whenever the steward asked Pauley, the senior American on an American plane, if he should serve it he said not yet, because he was not feeling well; he never suggested that the rest of us might like to start. It was not till we had nearly reached Berlin that he relented; and by then we only had time to gulp a little down. I cannot say I was sorry when I heard later that he had run into a spot of trouble – I think over oil. Some of my British colleagues had a more hair-raising flight to Berlin in a Russian plane, with Russians lying on fuel tanks, unstrapped and smoking, while taking off from Moscow.

When I got to Potsdam I found that advance parties from London had been arriving since Thursday, and that the PM was coming on Sunday. A mass of paper on administrative arrangements informed me that Prof was also arriving on Sunday, with Tom Wilson, John Clarke, and Harvey, his 'man'; and that Mr Attlee, Leader of the Labour Party, would be in the same plane. The General Election had taken place ten days earlier, but the results would not be declared until just over ten days later when the votes of the Forces serving overseas had been counted. Attlee had been invited to Potsdam in case Labour won and he became Prime Minister. He did, and returned for the last few, crucial, days of the Conference.

While there I advised Prof on reparations, and on the related question of the effects on Germany's economy of ceding a large part of her pre-war territory, east of the Oder-Neisse line, to Poland; and the difference between taking the Western rather than the Eastern Neisse as the boundary. Harvey drew beautiful maps to illustrate my analysis, but I do not know whether they were used by Churchill; I think they might have been had he returned to Potsdam; he certainly would have fought Russian demands on these matters more vigorously than Attlee appears to have done.

The Conference – code-named 'Terminal' – took place against a background of strong suspicion by Churchill about Russian intentions in Central Europe and concern about their attempts to impose Communist-type regimes in countries they had 'liberated'; and also uncertainty about the attitude of the new, inexperienced, President of the United States, whom he met for the first time at Potsdam. Churchill would have liked the meeting to have taken place earlier, and before the American and British Forces had withdrawn to previously agreed zones of occupation, thereby giving control of a large and vital part of Germany to the Russians, which greatly increased their bargaining power. But Truman would not agree to delaying the withdrawal of US and UK troops, nor Stalin to hold the conference earlier. Much of the discussion while Churchill was there was about Polish questions, but many others were raised though few decisions were reached. Churchill's tactics were to leave them on the table and have a show-down on at least the most crucial issues after we knew the results of our election, which he – and Stalin – expected would return him to power. During the Conference news arrived that an experiment had shown the atom bomb to be operational, and Truman and Churchill agreed that the former should tell Stalin; but I, of course, knew nothing of this.

We were housed in comfortable villas. The Conference area – some distance from the centre of Berlin – had largely escaped the ravages of war. One day, while walking there with some colleagues, we passed three men walking more slowly in the same direction. The man in the middle looked small and unimpressive, but when one of my companions said 'do you know who that is?' and I said I did not, he replied: 'Truman'.

We had time for some fun. In our villa there was a model of an Egyptian mummy and one evening, when John Clarke was out, Tom Wilson and I put it in his bed and replaced the electric bulb in his room with a dimmer one. The mummy's face was heavily made up and had very red lips. Lying on the pillow with the sheets pulled up over the body, the whole thing looked just like a beautiful girl. When John came back he got a bit of a shock, but took it well.

We went to see Hitler's Chancellery in Berlin. It was a complete shambles and no one seemed to have got round to clearing it up. So we helped ourselves to souvenirs. I still have such useless, but in some ways intriguing, bric-à-brac as: a piece of Hitler's marble-topped desk; a medal for war service in 1939; a card of invitation to breakfast with the Führer; place cards for Frau Keitel and Frau Schacht; a menu for a meal at the 'Reichskanzlerhaus' on 26 July 1931, well before Hitler had become Chancellor; a scroll awarding to one Helene Meinhart the Cross of Honour of German Motherhood (Third Class), purporting to be signed by Hitler and dated 20 May 1945, several weeks after he is believed to have committed suicide (the name of the lady and the date had been inserted by typewriter).

On Wednesday 25 July the Prof (with Clarke and Harvey) returned to London – as did Churchill – to hear the Election results on the following day. Tom Wilson and I were told to stay in Germany and fully expected the others to be back soon. As there was little we could do in Potsdam we decided to improve the shining hour and early on the Wednesday got a lift in a mail plane to Bad Oeynhausen, the headquarters of the British zone of occupation, where we spent the day learning about the zone's grim economic problems. On the Thursday we were taken on a car tour of the Ruhr. The damage was beyond belief, even to one who had spent most of the war in London. But another thing sticks even more in my memory: driving through a city razed to the ground we saw emerging from a basement under the rubble a young woman in an immaculate, spotless white dress with white gloves. How could she have managed it in these conditions? Being in a Brigadier's car (but without a radio) we called in at all the military posts on our way to find out how the Election was going. It soon became clear that Labour was winning but we carried on and completed our 230 mile trip in six hours, the slow going through the ruins being offset by 80 mph stretches on the superb autobahnen. After dinner we heard on a very crackly radio that Attlee was already Prime Minister.

On Friday, lacking instructions, we thought we should try to go back to Berlin, and after a long wait at the airfield found space in a mail plane. At Potsdam we found a telegram from the Prof telling us to come back to London. This we did on Saturday (28 July), to find that his Branch had already been abolished by Sir Edward (later Lord) Bridges, Secretary of the Cabinet; but that, for pay and rations, we were now on the strength of the Economic Section of the Cabinet Offices. We had a farewell dinner for the Branch on the following Wednesday at which I had the privilege of singing the Prof's praises.

During August, apart from getting a CBE in Churchill's resignation Honours, I continued to work on reparations and the level of German industry, and early in September was off to Berlin again to discuss these matters with the Russians, the Americans and, this time, the French. On arrival I was asked by a British official at the airport who was filling in forms what my rank was. I said I was a civilian and did not have one. When he said I must have, I asked him what ranks he had. He said: 'Lieutenant, Captain, Major, Colonel, Brigadier . . .' At that point I stopped him and said: 'Okay, I'll take that one', and he at once wrote it down in my documents. I believe he would have put down anything I wanted, but discovered later that I had pitched it about right. So for two and a half glorious months I was a Brigadier, although the title was never used, and you could not tell from the khaki uniform of a civilian officer that I wore because it bore no marks of rank. It is true that I carried a card showing my rank, and had I got into a heated dispute with a colleague at the bar I suppose one of us could have said 'I'll see you,' and demanded that we each produced our cards; but this never happened to me.

This time we were billeted nearer the centre of the city than Potsdam. I was in a house that had been only slightly damaged, although I discovered just before leaving that I had been sleeping immediately beneath an unignited incendiary bomb lodged in the ceiling. There was a very comfortable, and rather select, Mess nearby where I ate and drank in style (aided by splendid French wines looted by the Germans). It was presided over by Sir Percy Mills, a big shot in the Control Commission, who later helped Harold Macmillan, while Minister of Housing under Churchill, build 300,000 houses a year in the early 1950s. He was a gruff fellow and conversation round the dinner table was more animated when he was absent. We were not supposed to 'fraternise' with Germans so could not easily find out how they felt, but I had long conversations with the lady looking after the house where I lived. However, the difference between our almost luxurious life-style and that of the Germans, often living in ruins and half starved, was glaring; one lasting memory is of a frantic scramble by a number of them for a few potatoes that had fallen off a lorry. But they were docile and one had no sense of danger. Once, when returning from a party in the early hours, I lost my way and spent a long time trying to find my billet. But, though concerned about the teasing I expected at breakfast for getting home so late, the thought of being mugged never entered my head.

The Potsdam Agreement had been signed by Stalin, Truman and Attlee on 2 August. Apart from prohibiting the production of armaments, aircraft and sea-going ships, it laid down, among many other things, that Germany should be allowed to produce 'goods and services required to meet the needs of the occupying forces and displaced persons in Germany and essential to maintain in Germany average living standards not exceeding the average of the standards of living of European countries' (excluding the UK and USSR). This was the main limitation on the capital equipment that could be taken from Germany as reparations; and I was one of a tiny British team which had to try and agree with our three Allies what it meant in detailed, quantitative, terms. Our leading economist – fifteen years my senior – was Austin (later Professor Sir Austin) Robinson, of Cambridge, with whom I had worked in London and Washington during the war and in Moscow earlier in the year. We had only a couple of young, but able, economists to help us; and there were a few non-economists we could call on when necessary. We had done a lot of work on the subject in London and Moscow and I can say, in all modesty, that we were better prepared than any of the other three teams.

Our task was formidable – some would say impossible. It bristled with conceptual, statistical and other difficulties, including great uncertainties, not least about the post-war population of Germany, allowing for frontier changes, the influx of displaced persons from the east, and war deaths. One also needed an outline of a plan for the whole economy, which the British team had a shot at, covering employment, the balance of payments and so on. This was no easy task, especially as it was far from clear that all the decisions at Potsdam were capable of simultaneous fulfilment: would it, for example, be possible to balance Germany's international payments if there were to be a drastic scaling down of her heavy industries coupled with the loss of a quarter of her farm land in the east? There was also the diplomatic problem of getting quadripartite agreement, the Russians being by far the biggest stumbling block. They wanted a lower level for German industry than the Western powers – partly because this would give them the right to take more equipment out of the Western zones as reparations, and also because, even if the Germans' standard of living were limited to the European average, it would still be above the Russians'.

A Level of Industry Committee was set up, and under it a Technical Staff which did most of the work. There was no simultaneous translation in those days and a typical discussion went something like this. The American, say, would present his case for choosing a figure of X for the post-war level of industry Y. This would be translated into French and then Russian. The French would follow and their presentation would be translated into English and Russian. The British proposal in turn would be translated into French and Russian. The Russian would then repeat, at length, what he understood to be the proposals of each of the others, sometimes agree with the lowest of the three, but more often disagree with them all, and propose a much lower figure. All this would be translated into English and French. The American would then say what he understood the Russian proposal to be, that he disagreed, and repeat his own proposal – all translated into French and Russian. Then the French . . . but need I go on? It hardly made for rapid progress; the only advantage was that it gave one time to think (or sleep).

When one had heard the same arguments several times, and often several times again on the Level of Industry Committee, which consisted to a considerable extent of the same people, one began to sympathise with the interpreters at Versailles in 1919. After the Peace Conference had been dragging on for some time, they are reputed to have met for a drink and drawn up a numbered list of all the arguments that had been used and were likely to be used; and thought how nice it would be, after a delegate had been speaking for an hour, to get up and simply say: 'Mr A used arguments 7, 36 and 52.'

We found it helped matters to circulate our papers in both English and Russian, and the Russians appreciated this; but on one occasion, our Russian version of a British paper was for some reason translated back into English by the Russians, the result being similar to what happens in the party game 'Chinese Whispers'. At the second meeting of the Technical Staff we spent most of the time discussing the Minutes of the first, with the Western members arguing that they should be a true record of what was said, and the Russians that they should say what the members would have liked to have said. Even more frustrating was the Russians' failure to turn up for meetings, which were supposed to take place about three times a week, without explanation or apology. This happened seven times in just over five weeks. When they came they were almost invariably very late; we then wasted a lot of time waiting to see whether they would come at all. The same was true of social occasions to which we invited Russians in the Mess; we got the impression that they came when relations at a high level between the British and Soviet Governments were good, but not otherwise. We did have a few hilarious evenings with them; one Russian had an extraordinary skill – opening a champagne bottle so that the cork shot up to the ceiling and fell back into his glass.

The Western delegations eventually got fed up with their cavalier treatment of official meetings and their failure to agree on so many issues, without reasoned arguments to support their case. So complaints were made at a higher level and the Russian team 'promoted to more important duties' and replaced by another from Moscow. At the first meeting of the Technical Staff after they arrived we were due to discuss a really major item – electric power. I had done a lot of work on this and led off with a comprehensive analysis concluding that, given our terms of reference, Germany should be left with a capacity of so many million KW. The Americans and French held their fire until they heard what the new Russian member would say. To our amazement he said my arguments seemed reasonable but that he would prefer a slightly lower figure which was, however, far higher than we had expected. It also happened to be the figure which the US member had been instructed to propose, and as I had pitched our opening bid a little on the high side, and the French were happy, we quickly reached quandripartite agreement. But alas, when it went a few days later to the higher (Level of Industry) Committee, the senior Russian delegate disowned his subordinate, whom we never saw again, and proposed a much lower figure.

Not long after this, despite pressure from the Treasury that I should stay on longer, I left Berlin; the period for which I had agreed to go had already been exceeded and I had much to get on with at home. Austin

Robinson had left a week or so earlier, and we were succeeded by Alec (later Sir Alec) Cairncross, whom we shall come across again in these memoirs. I spent a week or so in Whitehall writing a report on what had been happening in Berlin and suggesting how we should proceed; and then left the civil service – for the time being – to resume my academic career.

4

WELL before the war ended, I had started thinking about what to do afterwards. Edward Bridges and James Meade wanted me to stay in the Economic Section of the Cabinet Offices; and I was attracted, especially by the thought of helping to run an employment policy on the lines proposed in the White Paper. But, partly because my freedom to publish would be severely restricted, as described earlier, I opted for academic life. I could have gone back to Leeds, which I had enjoyed, but was sure I would rather go to Oxford, if I could make it, and preferably to Balliol, my old College.

I had serious approaches from Cambridge to which I was invited one day. I had a long walk and interesting talk with Piero Sraffa (a charming and distinguished economist who spent years editing, with Maurice Dobb, the writings of Ricardo), and I am pretty sure he would have recommended me for a University Lectureship. Later that day I was offered a Fellowship by a Cambridge College, which had had a look at me before the war when I was taken there one week-end by a Professor at Leeds. No reason had been given but they were clearly looking for a Fellow and, as I heard nothing further, they must have turned me down; I suspect one reason was my lack of culture – I was unable to make intelligent comments on the medieval manuscripts in their library. Seven years later I was better known as an economist so I suppose they were prepared to overlook this. When they invited me, I said I would prefer to go back to my old College, or at least my old University, and asked if they would mind waiting. They said they would not; indeed, they would not want a Fellow without this sense of loyalty to his Alma Mater.

Around this time I paid a good many visits to Balliol who wanted to elect an Economics Fellow to help Maurice Allen after his demobilisation from the Army. I gathered I had considerable support, but also a strong rival in the shape of Tommy (later Lord) Balogh, who had been teaching at the College during the war; he did not have a Government job presumably because he was regarded as too much of an 'alien', having come to Britain from Hungary in the early 1930s. He was strongly supported by the Master, still Sandy Lindsay as in my student days. The battle swayed to and fro. Then one day in August 1945, after Potsdam but before I returned to Berlin, my Balliol supporters told me I had almost certainly got the job.

Now I had another Oxford iron in the fire. Prof was a Professorial Fellow of Wadham, as well as being a Student of Christ Church, where he lived (an anomalous situation resulting from a financial rearrangement of the endowment of his chair in 1921). He had strongly recommended me for a Fellowship at Wadham. On the evening of the day I had received such good news from my Balliol friends, I had dinner in Wadham and, being so elated and relaxed, must have been in such sparkling form that the Warden – Maurice Bowra – offered me a Fellowship shortly afterwards. I said I would gladly accept if Balliol did not elect me. While in Berlin I heard they had elected Balogh after all. I was disappointed, but in the event am very glad I went to Wadham.

I was allotted a lovely, enormous room, with windows overlooking both main and back quads, and a small bedroom attached. It was big enough for me to have many piles of papers on the floor when working or, when tidied up, to hold a large number of students. I finished my work in Whitehall in time to spend a week there in December 1945, meeting my new colleagues and helping with the entrance exams. I then had barely a month to brush up my economics before being plunged into a heavy load of tutorial teaching; the College had greatly increased its number of students since before the war, and economics was a popular subject. Fortunately, because of the war, less than usual that was new had been written since I had been at Leeds; and I was *au fait* with many policy questions through my work with Prof.

It was hard work, but I enjoyed those early days of teaching mainly ex-Service men. They were more mature in their approach to economics than undergraduates straight from school and mostly keen to learn about the problems facing the country and the world. I did not lecture for the first few terms, but when I started – on Britain's foreign trade problem – Wadham Hall was filled to overflowing; even the gallery was crammed, and people were sitting on the floor all round me on the raised part of the Hall where the High Table was placed for dinner. I think an important reason was that I was talking, not about theory, but about crucial live issues; and Sir Hubert Henderson, Drummond Professor of Political

Economy, who also lectured on problems of the real world, had huge audiences too. He did not, however, have a strong voice and relied on a microphone. One day he had prepared a lecture criticising policy on electricity, but just as he was starting there was a power cut – not unusual in those days – so his words of wisdom were largely inaudible to most of his would-be listeners.

The Wadham Governing Body was a cosy little affair when I arrived, with ten members (compared with over forty at my last count). Much of the day-to-day running of the College was conducted by an even smaller body comprising the Warden and the six 'Fellows engaged in education', which excluded Professorial Fellows! We met in the Senior Common Room at 8.45 am on Wednesdays during term for 'tutors' breakfasts', read our newspapers while consuming a gigantic meal of cereal, fish, mixed grill, toast and coffee, then polished off our business in time to begin tutorials at 10 o'clock. Once a term – sometimes more often – there was a full College meeting of the whole Governing Body. It also was usually on a Wednesday – at 2 pm – followed by an enormous tea, and then – after perhaps an hour or two of teaching – a sumptuous dinner. It is just as well that this succession of meals did not occur more often. Even so, I wonder how my digestion survived – though it never worried Bowra. Nor do I know how the College produced such fare when food was strictly rationed – exaggerated accounts of which led generous American academic institutions to send food parcels to be shared among the starving Fellows.

Maurice chaired meetings with extraordinary expedition, and was a stickler for punctuality. He would arrive early for College meetings, watch the clock closely and – so it seemed to me – start five seconds before two o'clock. In 1948/49 I spent a period in Paris, where international meetings mostly began at least half an hour after the scheduled time. On my return I was four minutes late for my first College meeting and found the business virtually completed.

The small band of tutors were a friendly and interesting lot. The two with whom I did business concerning PPE were Freddie (later Sir Alfred) Ayer, who became one of the foremost philosophers of his generation; and, on the politics side, Bill (later Sir William) Deakin, who had carried out courageous war-time missions in Yugoslavia and later became the first Warden of St Antony's College. The law tutor was Bill (later Sir William) Hart, who became Clerk to the GLC. Then there was Jack Thompson, the maths tutor, a great friend who died in harness in 1975. He had incredibly high academic standards. At tutors' meetings, when we reviewed the progress of each undergraduate, he would say things like 'Snooks – he'll get a First of course, but he's not up to much'. He was also for twenty years Estates Bursar, with an uncanny knack of making acute investment decisions which did wonders for the College's finances.

Last but not least there was Keeley, the physicist, a lovable character. He had been a Fellow for over twenty years and had helped Prof build up the reputation of the Clarendon Laboratory, at a low ebb when he took charge in 1919, to a level approaching that of the Cavendish at Cambridge, assisted by some brilliant Jewish scientists Prof brought over from Germany in the 1930s. Keeley had rooms opposite mine on the other side of the main quad and was still living there in 1987 at the age of ninety-three. Once, when in Court on a minor motoring charge, he began to defend himself with a lecture on momentum, velocity, mass and so on, until the Magistrate stopped him and said 'Mr Keeley, we want facts not physics'. But generally he was a man of few words, which enhanced the impact of what he said. I was told that during his first seven years he did not utter a word at College meetings. Then one day, when a colleague was making a speech which particularly infuriated him, he interrupted and said, in a very loud voice- 'Bosh'. The effect was devastating.

I recall only one other equally effective speech-stopper – when John (Lord) Simon became High Steward of Oxford University, and we gave a dinner in his honour as one of Wadham's famous sons. He had excelled as a lawyer and in politics, having been Home and Foreign Secretary, Chancellor of the Exchequer and Lord Chancellor. He was one of an outstanding generation of Wadham undergraduates in the early 1890s. They included F E Smith (later Lord Birkenhead), another future Lord Chancellor; C B Fry, the famous cricketer – and a classics scholar; F W Hirst, for many years Editor of *The Economist*; J F Stenning, who preceded Bowra as Warden; Lord Roche, a future High Court Judge; and C R Hone, who became Bishop of Wakefield. They not only excelled in later life but, while at Oxford, took it in their stride to become President of the Union, get Firsts in Schools, and find time both to have fun and to show such skill and enthusiasm in team games that Wadham, despite its small size, was one of the leading sporting Colleges.

The Warden and Fellows invited to dinner in Hall the surviving members of this remarkable group, and afterwards we made our way up the narrow winding stairs to the Common Room, specially designed – those veterans told us – to test the sobriety of Fellows. Over the port, Simon began to reminisce about his early days as a barrister. He told us, at length, how he would come home late in the evening, divide his briefs for the next day into the urgent and immediate, deal first with the former, tell his landlady to wake him at 6 am with a cold bath, after which he would deal with the latter – and he would have gone on and on had not F W Hirst, who could stand it no longer, interrupted and said: 'You know, I once knew a man who kept his secretary in a grandfather clock'. This remark, like Keeley's 'Bosh', completely silenced the poor guest of honour for the rest of the evening.

A few months after going to Wadham I got involved again in work for the Government. Having decided to nationalise a considerable number of industries, they felt a need to do something about some of the rest. So Sir Stafford Cripps, President of the Board of Trade, set up seventeen 'Working Parties' of employers, trade unionists and independents to study the problems of particular industries. I agreed to be an independent member of the Party on the 'Heavy Clothing Industry' (which for some reason included shirts) and we produced an unanimous report in eight months.

Apart from helping with statistics and such questions as how to reduce seasonal swings in output and employment, I had to do the kind of debunking for which economists are put on such Committees, as when a colleague proposed that we should estimate how many shirts were needed over the next ten years, compare this with our shirt-making capacity and, unless the former exceeded the latter, forbid the introduction of any new firms or machines.

The Working Parties were in some ways the forerunners of the 'Little Neddies' later set up under the NEDC. But one important difference was that they produced one-off reports and then ceased to exist whereas most of their successors continued for many years and could monitor the action being taken, or not taken, on their recommendations, and take new initiatives in the light of changing circumstances.

Soon after I went to Wadham I got to know, and like increasingly, Evan Durbin, who had a house in Oxford. He had got a First in PPE, taught economics at the LSE in the 1930s, and during the latter part of the war was Attlee's Personal Assistant. He was a 'Gaitskellite' long before the term was invented; he and Gaitskell went up to New College in the same term and became life-long friends, sharing similar philosophies on the economics of a democratic socialist policy for Britain. He became an MP in 1945, a Junior Minister in 1947, and was tragically drowned off a Cornish beach in 1948, when only 42, after rescuing his daughter and a friend from the undertow.

In the spring of 1946 Evan asked me to write a chapter on foreign trade for a book he was editing on the UK economy. This fitted in well with my research plans. I had already published the article on Britain's bargaining power – or rather lack of it – which I could not have done had I stayed in Government service. I now wanted to write a lot more on our foreign trade problem, based partly on my war-time work. In the event the publishers got into difficulties and Evan's book was never published, though I am glad to say I got my fee for the chapter. I also got one when it was published in the *Economic Journal* for March 1947. It was a very long Article of forty-five pages, entitled 'Britain's Foreign Trade Problem,' and had the distinction of being one of only two in that issue, the other being a memoir by Austin Robinson of Keynes, who had died in 1946. As I can trace no other peace-time issue of the *Journal* with so few Articles, this illustrates the interest in the problem at the time. It must be one reason I got a third fee, from the BBC, for four twenty-minute talks on 'The World's Our Market', covering much the same ground in layman's language.

There were still more economies of scale from the piece I wrote for Evan. My lectures on Britain's foreign trade problem were based on it. I also summarised it at a meeting in Wadham of the Association of University Teachers of Economics (AUTE) in January 1947. I had been to three such meetings while at Leeds – in Exeter, Hull and Birmingham. When, many years later, I chaired a session at the 1985 meeting of the AUTE (by then held jointly with the Royal Economic Society), I reminded the audience that meetings before the war were, in one sense at least, cosy little affairs, with thirty to forty present, one-tenth of the attendance in 1985. They were, however, often less cosy in that they could be very cold, being held early in the New Year rather than in the Easter vac as they have been for a long time now.

The January 1947 meeting was still cosy in so far as those present could sit comfortably round the relatively small Junior Common Room at Wadham; but, my goodness, the weather was cold, and the College had been virtually empty, and unheated, since the undergraduates went down for the Christmas vac four weeks earlier. By this time, while continuing my academic duties, I had become Domestic Bursar, so was able to give instructions that everywhere to be used should be well fired for forty-eight hours before the Conference began. This sufficed to make the Junior Common Room warm enough for meetings; but it was not practicable to keep fires going day and night in all the conferees' rooms. The Conference started on the evening of Friday 3 January, and after dinner and the discussion that followed I went back to a relatively warm home. When I came into College on Saturday morning, the first person I saw in the quad was Arthur (later Sir Arthur) Lewis, that great black economist from St

Lucia, who was currently teaching at the LSE. He was soon to become Professor at Manchester and then to hold a succession of distinguished posts in various parts of the world, publish many well-known works, and win a Nobel Prize. He looked enormous, encompassed in thick sweaters, a heavy overcoat and a massive muffler. I greeted him cheerily: 'Hello, Arthur; I hope you had a good night'. He looked at me through bleary eyes, sneezed loudly, and said in a croaky voice: 'Donald, at last I understand the secret of the British Empire'.

Not long after, I once more found myself working part-time for the Government; but this time, unlike the clothing job, very much in line with my research interests. I mentioned in Chapter 2 the agreement between UK and US officials in 1943 on the need for an International Trade Organisation (ITO) to interpret the rules of a Charter on commercial policy; but that little progress was made at Ministerial level for some time. However, by the autumn of 1946 it was thought useful to have talks in London, under UN auspices, on setting up such an organisation; and negotiations on this and on a General Agreement on Tariffs and Trade (GATT) began in Geneva in April 1947. The Government wished to have contingency plans in case the negotiations broke down, and early in 1947 asked a group of five economists to examine the alternatives, in great secrecy, the code name of the study being OTI (ITO in reverse). The five included four in Cambridge and one in Oxford – myself. As the meetings would be mostly in Cambridge, and as I already had more than enough to do, I accepted on condition that the Government provide a chauffeur-driven car to take me between the two towns.

The benign Chairman of the group was Professor Dennis (later Sir Dennis) Robertson, whose delightful literary style was invaluable in writing introductions and epilogues. He had been Keynes' pupil and then collaborator, but later a critic of his *General Theory*. This caused him to have a rough time at the hands of some fiercely pro-Keynesian dons at Cambridge, where there were cliques of economists who got on much less well in their personal relations than did most Oxford economists, though the latter held at least as divergent views. Then there was Richard (later Lord) Kahn, who worked closely for many years with Joan Robinson. During our exercise he wrote lengthy, largely theoretical, papers on, for example, the characteristics of countries that would fit well into a group aiming at freer mutual trade. Another member was Austin Robinson, mentioned in the last Chapter, who put me up at his College – Sidney Sussex – during the nights I spent at Cambridge. His instinct, and mine – unlike Kahn's – was to look first at the figures; and in my case this meant to a considerable extent developing work I had already done. Finally there was John (later Sir John) Habakkuk, an economic historian who became a Professor in Oxford, then Principal of Jesus College, and Vice-Chancellor.

We wrote three voluminous reports. The first analysed the conditions under which departure from non-discrimination in international trade might be desirable (such as discrimination against imports from the US so long as severe dollar shortage persisted). I learned a lot from our discussions and published my own analysis later in an article called 'Notes on Non-Discrimination'. Our second report considered, as one way of overcoming our foreign trade problems, the formation of a permanent economic group of nations. We analysed this in general terms, and also the possibilities of particular groups, such as Empire countries, or these plus certain Continental countries and possibly their overseas territories. After assessing also the dangers of retaliation by outside countries and other possible consequences, we concluded that there was little future, at that time, in this type of approach.

Our third report, after reviewing other possible ways of improving the balance of payments, examined Britain's bargaining power as a large importer. Our conclusion was that it was not as great as often thought – hardly surprising since the analysis was a greatly amplified version of my earlier article on the subject. (I published the substance of it in the January 1949 issue of *Oxford Economic Papers*.) Finally, the report discussed the importance of multilateral trade. This too was largely my work, partly lifted from 'Britain's Foreign Trade Problem,' partly new work which I wrote up in 'Notes on Non-Discrimination'.

Although the group made no very specific recommendations, the general tenor of our reports was that, if we could not get an ITO, we should try to get something as like it as possible, under which countries could work towards freer, multilateral, non-discriminatory trade on a worldwide basis, but with let-outs for countries or groups of countries in balance of payments difficulties (which we recognised would have to be called in aid by many countries, including Britain, for a considerable period ahead). This is broadly what happened. The proposed ITO Charter was never ratified, and we were left with the GATT; but this did commit the US, the UK and others involved to the reductions in tariffs negotiated in Geneva in 1947, which were not insignificant, and to the most important provisions of the ITO Charter; and it provided a forum at which countries could meet to negotiate new tariff concessions, and adjust their differences under the Agreement.

My successful rival for the Balliol Fellowship, Tommy Balogh, held views on external economic policy diametrically opposed to mine. So when he had read my article on our foreign trade problem he wrote a comment which started politely by saying it was 'the most balanced plea hitherto published in favour of those international agreements which have been debated in the war-time discussions between this country and the United States', but arguing that my 'interesting analysis' and 'valuable statistical material' strengthened rather than demolished his view that these agreements would be disastrous for Britain. The Editors of the *Economic Journal* sent me his comment and I wrote a reply which I thought demolished his arguments. Both pieces were published in the *Journal* for March 1948.

Long before then we had met and got on pretty well, despite our differences on economic policy, and notwithstanding a strange episode on one of the first occasions we met. He had invited me to lunch in Balliol Senior Common Room for one o'clock and said it was most important I should be in his room at 12.50 so that we could be sure of good seats. This I duly did but found no Tommy there. He arrived at 1.20 and, when we went to the Common Room, the College servant in charge said that he (Balogh) had not booked us in for lunch. So we went to a restaurant, and at the end of the meal, after feeling desperately in all his pockets, he said he was dreadfully sorry, he had no money; so I had to pay.

We decided to start in the autumn term of 1947 a joint graduate seminar in international economics in my room in Wadham. It was well attended and an unusual, but I think useful, form of education. The students had to spend a good deal of time listening to Tommy and me arguing with each other; and I often had to come to the rescue of some of them whom he was criticising severely, even cruelly, although in the case of one little student from a far-flung Commonwealth country only after he had been nearly reduced to tears.

Balogh was sensitive, and careful, about his health and one day, when he thought he might have flu, attended the seminar in a heavy overcoat, with a rug over his knees and, for all I know, a fur hat (he liked to wear them outside at least); and kept taking his temperature every quarter of an hour. I am told he could be equally eccentric during tutorials – he taught my son for a time – and remember him behaving oddly at a lecture given by a Professor from the Continent whom he, personally, had invited for the purpose. The audience – rather a small one – was seated on benches behind desks in a Balliol lecture room. After ten minutes Tommy was getting visibly bored and restive; after another ten he began to read a newspaper; and after half an hour lay down on the bench and shut his eyes. A charitable explanation is that he found this the best way of absorbing the lecturer's words of wisdom.

In the mid-1950s, he turned his attention to development economics, and visited innumerable developing countries. So, as it happened, did Nicky (later Lord) Kaldor, another distinguished economist who taught first at the LSE and then at Cambridge. They had been born and educated in Budapest at roughly the same time and were great rivals, with a sort of love-hate relationship. One evening after dinner in the Nuffield Senior Common Room, when they both happened to be guests, they got into a passionate argument about some developing country, until one of them said: 'How dare you be so dogmatic when you've only been there for a fortnight?' To which the other replied: 'How dare you contradict me when you've never been there at all?'

On 5 June 1947 General Marshall, US Secretary of State, made a famous speech at Harvard which in effect inaugurated the Marshall Plan for Europe. Shortly afterwards, Oliver (later Lord) Franks asked what my reaction would be if invited to join a British Government team going to Paris to draw up with other Western European countries a provisional programme of European recovery and request for aid. Though attracted in many ways, I said I should find it much harder to say 'yes' than 'no', and in the end did not go. I realised what an economic mess Europe was in – not excluding Britain; it was about the time of the disastrous, premature, return to sterling convertibility. But I had barely finished my work on the OTI group, and felt I had done enough for my country for the time being and needed a holiday.

A year later, when I had a phone call from Robert Marjolin, Secretary-General of the Organisation for European Economic Co-operation (OEEC) in Paris, which had been set up in April 1948, asking me to work in the Secretariat for a year, I was much more receptive. The main trouble was that, while my previous outside jobs had not required leave of absence, this one did – and for no less than three terms. I had done only eight at Wadham. They had indeed been pretty hard ones, with up to twenty tutorials a week, plus the Domestic Bursarship, plus – for the University – lectures, seminars, supervision of graduates and, in 1948, examining in PPE, which was onerous: with a large number of candidates, all of whose papers were read by two examiners and all of whom had 'vivas', it took nearly two months. (When I examined in the Cambridge Tripos it took more like two weeks.) But all this had nothing like earned me a sabbatical; and it was then much more difficult to get leave from an academic institution than it has since become.

However, I thought I might be able to make a contribution in the job;

and even become a fluent French speaker. So I resolved to have a go. I knew that, if I could get Bowra to agree, the rest would be plain sailing, and decided to exploit his liking for speedy conduct of business. He was out of Oxford at the time, so the moment he returned – and before he could get his breath back so to speak – I marched into his room and said: 'Is there any reason why I shouldn't go to Paris for a year and work in the OEEC?' He could not think of a reason on the spur of the moment so, since delay in answering a question was abhorrent to him, said 'No'. I said 'thank you very much' and departed quickly before he could change his mind.

So off I went to Paris in the autumn of 1948. The idea that I should become fluent in French proved a pipe-dream. Apart from the Organisation's being run to a considerable extent by the British, and a strong American presence, the Continentals mostly wanted to practise their English. So I resorted to French lessons from a delightful little teacher of Austrian origin; he had been captured by the Russians in the First World War and kept for years in a camp on the Volga where the guards caught sturgeon, ate the flesh and gave the roes to the prisoners; if he never saw caviare again it would be too soon. I could converse a little with him in French because he spoke slowly and distinctly, but in ordinary conversation soon got lost, even after more than a year in France. Only once was I so indignant that I found myself almost fluent. It was when the franc was devalued against the dollar in September 1949 – by less than the pound was devalued – and my landlady came to my flat that evening and demanded an increase in the rent.

But if I failed to achieve one of my objectives, I suppose I must have had some success in another – contributing to European recovery – for round about May 1949 I came under strong pressure to stay on after my year was out. I realised this would help me to complete some things I was doing, but told the powers that be it was impossible as Wadham had already been unusually generous. But they were insistent and said that pressure would be brought on the College. So I wrote to Bowra explaining the position and concluding: 'One thing I hope you won't do is to write back to OEEC saying: "You can have him next term; and you can keep him" '. I had a prompt, friendly, but firm reply saying the College wanted me back in October and that 'if your present masters write to me, I shall tell them that we cannot let you stay away any longer'.

Then, in July, I got a letter from Maurice, which began:

I am in a quandary. Severe pressure is being put on me to say that you can stay away for another year. First a blackmailing Swede and his wife came to see me and said 'Haf you no lof for your country?' and threatened me with a hideous fate; now Sir Cripps writes in red ink to much the same effect. What am I to do?

'Sir Cripps' was of course Stafford Cripps, then Chancellor. The Swede was Per Jacobsen, then at the Bank for International Settlements in Basle, of whom I saw a lot during his frequent visits to Paris. He always gave me eighteen oysters to start off lunch and seems to have formed a favourable impression of me. He later became Managing Director of the IMF. He and Bowra were not only men of strong character but both – shall we say – portly, and their confrontation must have been worth seeing.

I replied to Bowra that I would completely understand if he said firmly I must come back; that the extra year mentioned in his letter was quite unreasonable; but that if I were given an extra term I should feel the College was doing me proud – and Cripps could hardly fail to give a special building grant to Wadham. My leave was extended until 1 January.

When I arrived in Paris and became the first Economics Director of the OEEC, the staff recruited so far was both small and, with some exceptions, mediocre, so one of my first tasks was to remedy this. Recruitment was proceeding at breakneck speed throughout the Secretariat, but I like to think I got better quality than some other Directorates. I naturally turned to former pupils and colleagues, and in due course got some first-class people, including Jack Parkinson, who was in the Prof's Branch during the war; Just Faaland, a Norwegian I supervised while he was a research student at Oxford; Maurice Scott, a Wadham pupil; Ann Romanis, who worked with me in Moscow and Berlin.

One of my most interesting appointments was someone I had never met before – John Fay. He was not an economist, but had been in the Board of Trade in London and one of the President's Private Secretaries. He turned up one day, having just spent a year or two in Washington, to see if there might be a job going in the OEEC. No one else seemed to want him, but I liked the look of him and took him on – that is how things happened in those early days. He was an unqualified success and spent the next thirty-five years in the OEEC and the Organisation for Economic Co-operation and Development (OECD), which replaced it in 1961 when the US and then other advanced countries joined. He lists as one of his recreations in *Who's Who*: 'helping economists to write English'. He certainly did that, but also much more, and became a leading figure in the organisations.

Another recruit was Mme Berger-Lieser, a lady of uncertain nationality who, I thought, would have made an excellent spy. She was immensely useful whenever I wanted a document not in our exiguous library. She seldom failed to come back with it within a few hours. I never knew how she did it, except that one of her techniques was to offer cigarettes to door-keepers, librarians and others who might be helpful.

Recruiting, however, took up a relatively small part of my time. I have seldom worked harder, especially during the last few months of 1948. We started first thing every morning with a short meeting of the top brass in the Secretariat – Robert Marjolin, his two Deputy Secretaries-General and the Directors, rather more than half-a-dozen of us in all (of whom three were British) – and went on till late in the evening or, not infrequently, the early hours of the morning. Usually we were just working in the office, but sometimes engaged in marathon drafting sessions with national representatives; during one, to sustain us, we each had a bottle of brandy on the table in front of us.

Then we had dinners given by Sir Edmund Hall-Patch, Permanent UK Representative on the OEEC and Chairman of its Executive Committee. At the end of a splendid meal, which always started at a late hour, when most of us were longing for bed, he would strike his glass with a fork and start a long discussion on the danger of Communism in Western Europe if we failed to achieve a decisive economic recovery in the next few years. He was an attractive and colourful character, a *bon viveur* who took his job extremely seriously. Having been brought up in Paris he was bilingual and had had an extraordinary career – as a musician, soldier, instructor in a riding-school, financial adviser, almost everything you can think of – before joining the public service. There was an abundance of stories circulating about him – no one being quite sure which were true. My favourite was that one evening, when on an assignment in the Far East, he was adjusting his white tie before going to dinner at the Palace when a young British Naval Officer rushed into his room, hauled him away unceremoniously, and pushed him on to a destroyer which forthwith sailed outside territorial waters. Our intelligence apparently had evidence that he was suspected of having an affair with a Princess and that powdered glass was to be put in his soup.

During my first week or two in Paris I spent a lot of time going to Committees, of which there were many – one day I reckoned that thirty meetings were taking place. I sampled them, going from one to another for half-an-hour or so each, rather like doing a round of cocktail parties, but soon realised that this was largely a waste of time because they were making little progress towards the Organisation's most urgent task of producing an 'Interim Report on the European Recovery Programme' by the end of the year. This was required by the Americans in return for Marshall Aid; it was to be the first stage in drawing up and executing a joint programme to achieve after 1952 'a satisfactory and stable level of economic activity no longer requiring outside assistance' – often called 'viability' for short.

So I decided to spend as little time as possible in Committees and as much as I could in my office preparing material and drafts for the Report. This involved both research based on published information, and analysing national programmes looking ahead to 1952–53, which each Government had been asked to provide. These were massive, detailed, documents and when bound together to form Volume II of the eventual Report ran to over a thousand pages. They were of very varying quality, the British being probably the best.

A somewhat similar exercise had been carried out a year earlier. At the meeting which Oliver Franks had asked me if I would like to attend, each country had been asked to complete a large form about its economic situation and needs, and all the delegates went home to have this done – except one. This was the Greek delegate, whom Robert Marjolin told me he saw sitting alone one day in the huge hall of the Palace where the meetings had been taking place. He had a pen in his hand and was mostly gazing at the ceiling, then every few minutes he would look down and write something on the paper resting on his knee. When Robert asked what he was doing he said 'filling in the form'; when further asked why he was not at home like all the others, he pointed out sadly that Athens was in a state of political and military turmoil and he could do it much better in Paris. I am not sure that the results were necessarily inferior to those of some of his colleagues who returned to their capitals.

Not surprisingly, the national programmes which arrived in Paris in the autumn of 1948 were mutually inconsistent in several respects and some of the projections seemed optimistic, but the exercise helped to point up the problems. Preparing the Report was a mammoth task. (Mrs) Kit Jones, later the highly efficient Secretary of the National Institute of Economic and Social Research, who was seconded for a month from the Economic Section of the Cabinet Offices to help us out, cannot recall ever getting away from the office before midnight. But somehow the Report was finished just in time and submitted to the US Economic Co-operation Administration (ECA) on 30 December in Paris where its Special Representative in Europe (Averell Harriman) had his Office.

During 1948 Western Europe made large strides in her economic recovery. Production increased greatly. Inflationary pressure was largely overcome in most countries. Exports to the outside world rose sharply. The deficit with the dollar area was reduced. It looked as if we were on course for 'viability' after 1952. But as 1949 progressed I got increasingly worried that things were going sour. I discussed this with Marjolin during the spring and early summer. I pointed out that OEEC exports to the US had fallen by a third since the end of 1948, partly as a result of the recession there, that the dollar gap had widened, that this was causing anxiety about the adequacy of American aid in 1949–50 and calling into question the 'viability' of Europe after 1952; whereas the Americans, partly because of their recession, were showing reluctance to back our plans for cutting imports from the US, and to tolerate at least temporary discrimination against them.

I proposed that we should therefore look again at some fundamental problems barely hinted at in our December Report, including US counter-recession policies; US tariffs and other trade barriers, which were restricting European exports to the US; US foreign investment, an increase in which could help European recovery; the price of gold; increasing trade between Eastern and Western Europe, which could reduce the latter's dependence on imports from the US; a realignment of currencies; and that OEEC should publish a new diagnosis of the situation, aimed primarily at American public opinion. I offered to produce a first draft quickly, having done much of the necessary work.

I got the go-ahead from Robert early in July, and produced a few weeks later a more tactful paper from a US point of view with more emphasis on how Marshall Aid had saved Europe from disaster and on what Europe herself had to do. It showed in quantitative terms how, if the right policies were followed on both sides of the Atlantic, we could before too long achieve one multilateral world; but that, if they were not, there would have to be large cuts in imports from the US and continuing discrimination against her, with a low standard of living in Western Europe, economic autarchy, unemployment and serious dangers of social unrest.

Copies of my paper were handed to a very limited number of people outside the Secretariat – Harriman and the Heads of the British and French Delegations. It was well received but there was agreement that it should be carefully guarded for the time being. I was hopeful, however, that I could get the essence of it into a published document, and before long, when the Organisation came to prepare its Second Report on the European Recovery Programme, I managed to do this to a very considerable extent. I spent much of my remaining time in Paris working for the Committee mainly responsible for this Report and doubt if I have ever before or since drafted or re-drafted so many thousand words per day over such an extended period. (The Committee was chaired by Eric Roll, who had come to Paris from the Treasury to join the UK Delegation; he appears later in these pages.)

Some of my arguments and analyses were watered down or even omitted, but this was hardly surprising when it was necessary to take account of the susceptibilities of eighteen European nations as well as the US. The Committee refused, for example, to say in so many words that the price of gold should be raised, when the existing $35 an ounce was a sacred cow in the US; but they agreed to say in the Report that the purchasing power of gold in America had been halved since before the war; that, largely because of this, gold output had fallen greatly; and that these changes had aggravated the dollar problem not only for gold producers but also indirectly for Western Europe. (Not long after returning to Oxford I gave a talk to the Marshall Society in Cambridge advocating a doubling of the gold price in terms of all currencies. I was taken aback when, in the ensuing discussion, one speaker after another – mostly dons who were good friends – denounced my proposal, not because it was intellectually vulnerable, but because it was immoral.)

I had no time to follow in detail the discussions on the freeing of international *payments* in Europe from the stranglehold of a myriad of bilateral agreements between countries recovering from the war and desperately short of reserves and foreign exchange earnings. That was in the capable hands of Frank (later Sir Frank) Figgures, on secondment from the British Treasury, who was Director of Trade and Finance. Although – or perhaps because – he was a lawyer by training, he dazzled us all in the Secretariat by his mastery of the succession of fiendishly complicated schemes put forward. Often, at our regular morning meetings, he would report on the latest stage of the negotiations. We would listen politely to a torrent of unintelligible technicalities and then say, in effect: 'Jolly good, Frank; carry on'. I did, however, play some part in the liberalisation of *trade* through dismantling import restrictions. In the summer of 1949, countries were asked to submit by October a list of articles which they would immediately import without quantitative restriction from other members; and further lists on which they were prepared to negotiate. We worked round the clock (missing a week-end tour of vineyards that had been arranged) analysing the returns, knowing that an important meeting of Ministers was taking place shortly. We calculated that the first list covered about one-third of private trade between members, the second a further one-fifth. Since it would have been slow and tedious to advance from this by conventional negotiations, I hit on the idea that reasonable, if rough, justice might be achieved if all countries agreed to 'liberalise' 50% of their imports at an early date; and, to make this more effective, that the 50% rule should be applied to food, raw materials and manufactures separately, so that a low percentage in manufactures, which was common in the lists submitted, could not be offset against a high percentage in raw materials, also common. To my amazement, this was agreed by the Ministers and was, to a very considerable extent, implemented, thereby making a significant start, by unconventional methods of which I am rather proud, in the freeing of trade.

I am also proud to have been the first Economics Director of an Organisation which, both while it was the OEEC and when it became the OECD, has developed into one of the most respected international bodies in the economic field. When I left Paris at the beginning of 1950 I was succeeded by Alec Cairncross – for the second time, the first being in Berlin in 1945 – and the post of Economics Director was later to be held by several other British economists. I had detailed correspondence with Alec during January about drafts which he sent me in Oxford of the 'Second Report', published early in February. I visited Paris in the Easter vac of 1950 and argued that the most urgent problem was to reduce the high unemployment then prevailing in Germany and Italy; and in the summer published an article in the *London and Cambridge Economic Service Bulletin* on 'Western European Economic Co-operation'. After that, I was not to be much concerned with Europe for a decade.

When in Paris I bought an Austin car imported from Britain and, when I left, brought it home on tourist plates, valid for a year. When this time limit was approaching I applied to the Board of Trade for an import licence which was refused. This was because there was a long queue of loyal British subjects waiting for cars, which were in very short supply on the home market, priority being given to exports; and it would be unfair for me to jump the queue just because I had spent some time in France. I then asked the French authorities for permission to take it back to France, but they refused. So I thought I would have to put it on a cross-Channel steamer and shove it into the sea on the way across. But happily, in the nick of time, I got my licence.

This seems to have been authorised by Sir John Woods, Permanent Secretary at the Board of Trade. Some time later he was opening a discussion in Nuffield, of which he was a Visiting Fellow, on the administration of controls and, wishing to illustrate the need to use common sense, told the story of my car – without, so he thought, mentioning my name. But he must have let it slip accidentally, and during the discussion Professor G D H Cole, also a Fellow, said: 'I don't think MacDougall should have got an import licence'. I was not at the meeting but had I been I doubt if this would have deterred Cole in the slightest. He was a prolific writer (with left wing tendencies) of political and economic works and also, with his wife Margaret, of Whodunnits, and when I moved from Wadham to Nuffield I sometimes sat next to him at College Meetings where he spent much of the time writing his latest book. At the first meeting after I got my Knighthood in 1953 an early item on the agenda was a proposal to congratulate me. After a few minutes he stopped writing and asked me in a whisper if we had reached the item. When I told him we had passed it he said: 'Oh dear, I wanted to record my dissent'. There was nothing personal about it; he just disapproved of Honours.

During 1950 the University established a Readership in International Economics and I was elected to it in the summer, the appointment to start at the turn of the year. It meant heavier University teaching than I had as a University Lecturer but I was limited to six hours a week of tutorials, and on balance this gave me much more time for research. The Readership was attached to Nuffield, and it was with sadness that I resigned my Fellowship at Wadham which I had come to love. But I continued to look after their economics teaching, and devoted my permitted six hours to Wadham pupils, until I finally left Academe in 1962. Only then did they appoint an Economics Fellow to succeed me: Eprime Eshag, of whom I soon became a close personal friend.

I kept in touch with the College and helped them when I could; and they made me an Honorary Fellow in 1964. Then in 1969, while I was at the Treasury, Keeley asked me to propose the toast of the College at a Wadham Society dinner in London. I gladly accepted, but when I arrived and looked at the table plan I was not on it. Keeley told me he had thought I was in Paris – he had misunderstood a 'phone conversation with my Secretary – and had got someone else to make the speech. This unselfish old member kindly gave way, and I began by describing the rumour that I was in Paris as greatly exaggerated.

I was sitting next to Maurice Bowra and, knowing that he was retiring in the following summer, devoted much of my speech to singing his praises. I was not qualified to dwell on his distinction as a scholar, so concentrated on his endearing qualities, his devotion to the College and his tremendous contribution to it. I also said that the resolution just passed by the undergraduates praying that, after his retirement, he should continue to have rooms in College (which he did) was an impressive tribute in those days of alienation between junior and senior members in many universities. I knew, however, that he would not wish me to be too serious for too long. He himself was deadly serious about things that really mattered; but his sparkling wit was legendary. So I peppered my speech with a few stories about him such as his remark when turning down a would-be entrant to Wadham: 'Young man, I think you would be happier in a larger or a smaller College'.

I knew he was pretty deaf and tried to speak loudly, distinctly and, as far as possible, in his direction, so I think he heard a good deal. Some Fellows who drove with him to Oxford after the dinner told me he said 'The old boy was pretty friendly, wasn't he?' He died, sadly, little more than eighteen months later, barely a year after retiring.

I am a firm believer in the complementarity of research and teaching. Research can clearly help teaching, but the reverse is also true. When teaching undergraduates economic theory, I liked to give practical examples where possible. We usually came in due course to the theory of comparative costs in international trade (first formulated by Ricardo over a century before), showing how a country with a lower *absolute* level of productivity (output per head) can compete with a country enjoying higher productivity, in products where the former has a *comparative* advantage. I illustrated this by figures for the US and the UK. Before the war, according to well-known calculations of Rostas, productivity in American industry was on average approximately double that in Britain (as also were wages); but there was a wide dispersion between industries. For example, America's productivity in making radios was 3½ times the British and she exported far more than we did despite her much higher wages; but her productivity in woollen and worsted was only a little above ours – we had a *comparative* advantage – and, with our lower wages, we dominated world markets.

But the point of the story is that the use of these odd examples in teaching prompted me to look at all Rostas's sample of products and I was astonished how well his figures, combined with statistics of exports, wages and prices, accorded with Ricardo's theory. This set me off on a long trail of research culminating in what turned out to be one of my best-known studies. My next discovery was how skilfully the US tariff (before the war, not after, when it had been greatly reduced) seemed to have been designed to offset our comparative advantage wherever we had one, and virtually exclude our goods from the US market even when we could wipe the floor with American competitors in third countries.

At this stage, I presented my preliminary findings at a meeting of the International Economic Association in Monaco in September 1950. (I recall Nicky Kaldor explaining excitedly one evening before going to the Casino a fool-proof way of winning; and how subdued he was at breakfast next morning.) I was urged to publish my paper straight away, as it was, in a learned journal. Particularly insistent was Lionel Robbins, Professor at the LSE, who not long after pressed me, unsuccessfully, to let my name go forward for the Chair recently vacated at the School by Hayek, the Austrian-born economist, who had just gone to Chicago and later won a Nobel Prize.

But I was not yet ready to publish, though willing to have a greatly abbreviated version in the conference proceedings. I had many loose ends to clear up and potentially exciting avenues to explore, particularly a possible new method my work had suggested of estimating the responsiveness of exports to relative price changes ('elasticities' in economic jargon) – then a matter of hot dispute, and not yet fully resolved – and also the importance of factors other than price (and of Imperial Preference, which turned out to be relatively unimportant). This was long before economists had access to computers and the calculations required were long and laborious; but I got funds which enabled me to employ as a research assistant Monica Verry – later Mrs Dowley – and eight students to help me during vacations. The results were published in two articles in the *Economic Journal* for December 1951 and September 1952 under the title 'British and American Exports: A Study Suggested by the Theory of Comparative Costs'.

I moved from Wadham to Nuffield during the Christmas vacation of 1950. I had in fact been elected to a 'Faculty Fellowship' of Nuffield in the summer of 1947; as the College was still being formally run by the University it was possible to combine this with my Official Fellowship at Wadham. Nuffield was then accommodated in North Oxford, and I remember going there for dinner in November 1947 to find Herbert Morrison, Lord President of the Council and a Visiting Fellow of the College, recounting with relish how Hugh Dalton, the Chancellor, before introducing an Autumn Budget that afternoon, had confided part of his proposals to a journalist whose paper was on sale with the news before he spoke. Poor Dalton, who does not appear to have been a particularly good friend of Morrison, resigned next day.

By the time I left Wadham, to become a 'Professorial' Fellow of Nuffield, part of the building had been completed on its present site and I was allotted a very pleasant room, opening on to a smaller one where I could house a research assistant, and with a room next door occupied by a secretary whom I shared with one or two other Fellows. All this made life much easier. For example, while at Wadham I wanted to publish my Cambridge talk on the price of gold and was only prevented by lack of typing facilities. This was now to be a thing of the past. But despite this, and the reduction in my undergraduate teaching, I was hardly idle. Apart from the supervision of Nuffield (graduate) Students and administrative tasks in the College, I had plenty to keep me occupied.

In the summer of 1951 I had three quite heavy tasks. I examined once more in PPE (the other economics examiner being Margaret Hall, my future wife). I then finished off, so far as I could, the two articles just described. Finally, I spent seven weeks in New York as one of five 'experts' writing a report for the UN on *Measures for International Economic Stability*, my colleagues being an American, an Australian, a Burmese and a Mexican.

In December 1949 another UN group, including Nicky Kaldor, had produced a report on *National and International Measures for Full Employment*, the international aspects of which had not commended themselves to Governments in debates of the Economic and Social Council. They therefore asked the Secretary General, Trygve Lie, to set up another group to formulate 'alternative practical ways' (I liked that) of reducing the international impact of recessions; and he appointed us. I think we did this rather well, with realistic suggestions for action by Governments, the IMF and the World Bank.

When we went to Washington for discussions with these two organisations it was unbearably hot and humid. It was hot enough in New York. My room in the UN building was, it is true, kept pleasantly cool until Labor Day – the first Monday in September – but someone seems to have decided that this was the end of summer, and when I went into my office on Tuesday one half of the air-conditioner was blowing out hot air. Someone else, however, must have thought this silly because the other half was blowing out freezing air. It was not very comfortable.

A few years earlier, during the Easter vac of 1948, I had done a similar job for the UN, but the organisation was then housed in a converted arms factory at Lake Success, on Long Island. One disadvantage was that the small offices in which we worked were separated by thin metal partitions, so that conversation in surrounding offices could be distracting, especially as one of my neighbours was Michal Kalecki, the brilliant Polish economist, the rasping nature of whose voice was aggravated rather than softened by the partition that separated us. The building had, however, the great advantage of being all on one floor. This entailed much walking but one had run into almost every one after a week or two. How different was the skyscraper in Manhattan into which the UN moved in 1951. Its numerous elevators went to sets of floors, and people working in different sets could go for months without seeing each other – hardly conducive to harmonious relations. I know from personal experience how rivalries and ill-feeling arose, whether for this or other reasons. I visited New York quite often and got to know many of the UN economists and statisticians; and I remember, for example, two sets of indices – of export prices – produced by two warring sections, one of which would not allow the other to use its indices in its publications; but I had no difficulty in getting hold of, or publishing, either or both. So I have always preferred horizontal to vertical offices, or at least those housed in a smaller rather than a larger number of floors.

One problem during my 1951 visit was that of dealing with the somewhat nerve-wracking behaviour of a brilliant, and delightful, colleague, Professor Trevor Swan of the Australian National University, of whom I was to see a lot more in Canberra in 1959. His trouble was an inability, or unwillingness, to put pen to paper until the last possible moment. He had agreed to write a key chapter of our report, but kept on saying he had not yet got round to it. But we need not have worried. Just before our deadline he spent forty-eight hours, virtually without sleep but sustained by the odd sip of brandy, producing a splendid chapter. (He paid a couple of visits to Oxford during the next few years and at the end of one of these, agreed to open a discussion at my weekly Seminar for Nuffield Students and Fellows. He did no apparent preparation until the evening before the Seminar fixed for the following morning. But, true to form, after a late dinner party, he stayed up most of the night and came up with a brilliant talk.)

I got back to Oxford just before term began, but with a good part of a course of lectures more or less prepared, based on our work in New York. Hardly any of them were, however, to be delivered.

5

BATTLING WITH ROBOT: 1951–53

ON THURSDAY of the second week of term there was a General Election. The next day, 26 October 1951, I was 39 and the Conservatives were back in power with Churchill, aged 76, Prime Minister. The Prof, after putting up a little resistance – for he was 65, not in very robust health, and enjoying Oxford life and his comfortable rooms in Christ Church – loyally agreed to serve his old friend as Paymaster General with a seat in the Cabinet, and got leave from the University. Prof asked me to join him. I also was reluctant, for I too was enjoying Oxford and loth to seek leave so soon after the start of my new appointments. But I got leave and accepted, largely out of a sense of loyalty; though, as it turned out, I was to experience some of the most interesting and exciting periods of my life which I would not have missed for anything.

We recruited a smaller staff than we had during the war, but it was of high quality. There were just three economists, working as such, besides myself: Jack Parkinson, who had worked with me during the war and in Paris, and subsequently had a distinguished academic career; Maurice Scott, whom I had taught at Wadham and examined when he got a First in PPE, who had also worked with me in Paris, and later became a Student of Christ Church and then a Fellow of Nuffield; and John Fforde, who had just completed a book on the US Federal Reserve System while a Student of Nuffield, and went back as a Fellow for a time before joining the Bank of England where he later became Chief Cashier – the chap who signs bank notes – and then an Executive Director. There were also two permanent Civil Servants trained in economics: John Clarke – another member of the war-time Branch – who, however, helped Prof almost wholly on non-economic matters, especially the organisation of the development of atomic energy; and Philip Searby, another of my Wadham pupils, who, on my recommendation, was Prof's Private Secretary for most of the period.

We had offices close to those we worked in during the war. My room overlooked Great George Street; the Prof's was just round the corner overlooking St. James's Park. 'Rab' (later Lord) Butler, who was appointed Chancellor, decided to go on living in his own house, and that he needed only the two bottom floors of 11 Downing Street for business and entertaining. He kindly offered Prof the use of the floors above. So Prof had a flat on one of these and I shared a flat on the top floor with Harvey, the Prof's extraordinary factotum, who did virtually everything for him – from typing to driving his car, helping him with his hobby on the theory of numbers, looking after his clothes, developing his photographs, cooking for him. I recall the loving care with which he prepared Prof's delicious vegetarian meals in that little kitchen I shared with him. He also drew beautiful charts; and the versatility of his artistic skill was remarkable: he drew a brilliant cartoon of me at the Potsdam Conference after I had had a bath, wearing only a towel round my waist and with two long hairs sticking out of my chest; and also made an impressive bust of the Prof in his little house behind Oxford railway station after his master had died. As a young man he had been a pugilist; and at the time Prof engaged him he was a waiter at the Randolph Hotel.

The three of us usually drove up from Oxford in Prof's car on Monday mornings, stayed at No. 11 during the week, and drove back to Oxford on Friday evenings, when Prof would sometimes stop on the way to visit his friend Lord Nuffield, at Nuffield Place near Henley. Prof frequently visited Churchill during weekends at Chequers or Chartwell.

Living in No. 11 had advantages, but also drawbacks. It was a good address, which usually impressed tradesmen, but could sometimes make them a trifle suspicious. The top floor was a magnificent view-point from which to watch Trooping the Colour on Horse Guards Parade. But there was a price to pay. For weeks before the ceremony one was woken up morning after morning at an unholy hour by the rehearsals – that make the occasion such an immaculate spectacle – during which military bands played the same tunes again and again, until one got thoroughly tired of them. Being next to No. 10 was another advantage. I could come in at any time of night through the No. 10 door after No. 11 had closed down. But another side of the coin was that, whenever some poor wretch was to be hanged the next morning – capital punishment was still in force – one was kept awake during the night by the chants of protesters in Downing Street.

When the Conservatives took office the gold and dollar reserves were falling rapidly and the balance of payments outlook was pretty alarming. Most of the gold and dollar reserves of the Sterling Area were then pooled in London. The Area included, besides the UK, all Commonwealth countries except Canada, and a few others such as Eire, Burma and some Middle East States. These held most of their national reserves in the form of sterling balances in London and in return enjoyed more or less free entry for their products into Britain while we (and they) were still restricting severely imports from the rest of the world.

Movements in the reserves thus reflected the balance of payments of both the UK and the rest of the Sterling Area; and both were heavily in deficit. There were various reasons, but in each case the deficit had quite a lot to do with the Korean War which had started in June 1950. This led the Labour Government to embark on a substantial rearmament programme and by the autumn of 1951 exports of engineering and other products were held up by shortages of steel and other materials and the diversion of capacity generally to arms production, while imports were swollen by stock-piling of strategically vital materials. The war was also an important factor in sparking off a speculative commodity price boom which greatly increased the incomes of many primary producing countries in the Sterling Area while it lasted. But when the boom burst, prices came tumbling down again and by the autumn of 1951 many of these countries were suffering a sharp reduction in export earnings, while still importing at a great rate out of high incomes earned during the boom.

The Government took action in a number of fields to deal with the situation. Restrictions on UK imports were further tightened soon after the Election and again early in 1952, and various measures taken to divert resources to exports. It was decided to have an early Budget and to make it a tough one. Commonwealth Finance Ministers were invited to a Conference in London in January at which governments in the rest of the Sterling Area agreed to tighten severely their restrictions on imports from outside the Area, and to take other measures to reduce their external deficits.

As another part of the policy it was decided to ask the Americans for, among other things, a million tons of steel, which was very scarce not only in Britain but throughout the world, and vital if we were to increase our exports. This was done during a visit by the PM to President Truman early in January. Prof was in the party and I went too. The only other Ministers were Anthony Eden (later Lord Avon), Foreign Secretary, and Lord Ismay, Secretary of State for Commonwealth Relations (because the visit was to include Canada). We sailed over on the dear old *Queen Mary*, embarking at Southampton on New Year's Eve (we had a party in the PM's cabin at midnight). It was nice to be crossing the Atlantic once again with Prof and Churchill, this time with no U-boats hoping to sink us. We were a little apprehensive when we heard that on the eastward trip which the QM had just completed – two days late – the weather was so appalling that the Christmas celebrations had to be cancelled as nearly all the passengers were sick. But the westward trip was not too bad, although I remember it being hard work pushing a rather large dancing partner up what seemed like a 45° incline when I was facing the port side and the ship was listing to starboard.

I was responsible for preparing Churchill's brief for the economic part of his talks with Truman and was delighted when, after he had read it, he sent me back a masterly summary of our economic plight in true Churchillian prose, full of metaphors about eating our seed corn, meaning not investing enough, and the like. Soon after we got to Washington we had a plenary meeting with Truman and I remember the shock I had when he came into the room. Compared with the unimpressive little person I had seen at Potsdam, and who had been depicted as even more insignificant by his opponents when Roosevelt's Vice-Presidential running-mate in 1944, he seemed to have grown in stature at least eighteen inches; and very impressive he was at the meeting. We had, of course, other meetings with less exalted personages and, thanks in considerable part to Prof, got our million tons of steel.

As a result of all these measures by the British Government and those which other Commonwealth governments had agreed to take, it was hoped that the Sterling Area deficit would be eliminated by the second half of 1952 and that the reserves would then stabilise before they had fallen to a dangerously low level. There was admittedly much uncertainty about these forecasts, and the continuing rapid fall in the reserves was extremely worrying, but it came as a great shock when, on 22 February, Butler suddenly informed a small group of Ministers (including Prof) that the reserves would fall very soon to a critically low level and proposed what would then have been revolutionary changes in our external arrangements.

Three main elements in Butler's plan were, in shorthand, as follows (I shall fill in the details later). First, a floating of the pound; this may not seem a revolutionary move to readers who have lived with floating rates for years, but it would have been so regarded at the time, when the IMF regime of fixed, but adjustable, rates was widely accepted. The resulting fall in the pound would also, in my view, have been disastrous, in the circumstances then prevailing – with, for example, serious supply shortages limiting exports and little scope for reduction in imports, already cut to the bone by direct controls. The second main element in the plan was convertibility – of a kind – of sterling into dollars. This again may now seem a mere return towards normality, but would then have been extremely risky, with most countries still short of dollars and anxious to acquire them by fair means or foul. Thirdly, the plan proposed a major blocking of overseas sterling balances held in London, which the modern reader will have less difficulty in regarding as revolutionary.

It is not easy for one who regarded the plan as crazy to give a coherent account of the rationale underlying it, or why it was put forward by Butler when his own paper, described later, emphasised so clearly the dangers and uncertainties. But a simple version might go something like this. First, to support the fixed sterling/dollar rate of exchange we were having to supply dollars in such large quantities out of the reserves that they were rapidly disappearing. So why not stop selling dollars and, as the Treasury put it, 'take the strain off the reserves and put it on the rate of exchange' – in other words, float the pound? But secondly, since no one would want to hold pounds that were both 'floating' – or much more likely sinking – and also inconvertible into dollars, we must make them convertible. But thirdly, since this could lead to a large scale conversion of sterling balances held in London by foreigners, we must block the great bulk of these. Put in this highly over-simplified way it all sounds quite plausible. It is only when one examines the argument in more depth that the serious consequences, both domestic and international, become apparent. I can only assume that the plan's proponents regarded these as being overridden by the apparently compelling logic of the simple argument.

The code name of the proposals was R O B O T – possibly to suggest that, under the plan, the economy would be run automatically, instead of by government control; if so, how wrong this would have been proved to be. Another theory is that R O B O T contained the initial letters of three of its main architects – Sir Leslie ROwan, Second Secretary at the Treasury (who had, incidentally, been one of Churchill's Private Secretaries during much of the war); Sir George BOlton, an Executive Director of the Bank of England; and OTto (later Sir Richard) Clarke, then an Under-Secretary at the Treasury.

I was dumbfounded when I learned that such a plan had been cooked up – especially by these three. Otto Clarke had for long been a chief protagonist of inconvertibility; both he and Bolton had strongly opposed floating rates; and when the PM and Prof had asked Lesie Rowan during the *Queen Mary*'s voyage to the US whether we should really be releasing the Egyptians' sterling balances when they were harassing British subjects, he had argued strongly that we could not possibly depart from our agreement to do so. Less than two months later he was advocating the blocking of most countries' balances. The Commonwealth Ministers, at their London meeting, had, it is true, set up a Working Party on Convertibility. This arose mainly, it seems, from pressure by the Australian delegation, in particular by Leslie (later Sir Leslie) Melville of the Commonwealth Bank. I remember walking up and down Piccadilly with him one evening during the meetings, and listening with surprise to his views on the subject. In the Conference, however, convertibility was regarded by nearly everyone as something which – though desirable and probably inevitable eventually – could not be achieved for a long time.

Towards the end of January, I wrote a paper suggesting that what the Australians really wanted was not so much convertibility as a strong pound sterling, of which convertibility would be a manifestation. I tried to show that this would require big structural changes in production and trade, such as a large increase in steel and engineering capacity, and suggested that a 'Statistical Exercise' should be conducted, looking ahead some four years, to see what *real* changes we should work for. This was accepted by everybody, including the Treasury, and a considerable amount of work was done by an inter-departmental working party under my chairmanship.

But this was rudely interrupted by Butler's bombshell of Friday, the 22nd of February.

The eight days from then until Friday 29 February were the most exciting I spent with the Prof. I suspect they were also one of the most exciting periods in his life. He played a crucial part in stopping the adoption of a plan which would, I believe, have had appalling economic and political consequences for the country. I have never seen Prof so worked up. He showed tremendous fighting spirit, but also had periods of extreme despondency. I spent a fair amount of time keeping his spirits up, especially on one occasion when the battle seemed to be going badly and he was convinced he would have to resign (as he certainly would have done had he lost); he apologised for having brought me from my Oxford job to London when it all looked like ending so soon and so disastrously. It must have been particularly worrying that, for much of the time, he was fighting, not only other Ministers, but also Churchill, to whom he was so tremendously loyal. And in the middle of it all he got a bout of 'flu.

The battle continued on variations of the same theme for about a year, but the critical defeat of the other side was on 29 February 1962. The episode embittered relations in Whitehall for a long time. Passions ran high, and civil servants of long standing said they could not remember any such row having occurred before. Apart from the acute disagreements on policy, there was strong resentment about the handling of the ROBOT proposals, without proper inter-departmental consultation. I have a feeling that one or two civil servants would have resigned had ROBOT gone through.

I think the best way of making this period – at least as I saw it – come alive is to quote extensively from a paper – call it a 'diary' if you will – which I dictated afterwards from notes written by hand, at the Prof's request, on the afternoon of Friday 29 February, immediately after the crisis was over – at least for the time being. This has been kept with the Prof's other papers since then. I have abbreviated here and there, mainly to avoid repetition, irrelevancies, and unnecessary technicalities. I have expanded a little here and there, for clarification, to remind the reader which job the *dramatis personae* were holding at the time, and to help him understand the environment in which we were working – so different in so many ways from the situation now existing. (I have often found it extraordinarily difficult to get these differences across to those whose adult life began a good deal later.) 'C' stands for Cherwell (the Prof). I start three days before the crisis broke.

Tuesday 19 February
Robert Hall (Director of the Economic Section of the Cabinet Office) asked me to see him at 2.45 pm. He had had authority from Butler to talk to me about the budget proposals. I had been working on these for the Prof, and explained my ideas to him; they agreed almost exactly with his. After seeing him I worked on this problem and gave the paper I had been preparing on it to C.

Wednesday 20 February
At 11 am C had a meeting with the Prime Minister and the Chancellor on the budget. The views of C and Butler largely coincided.

I had dinner with Robert Hall at the Travellers' Club. We then got into a quiet corner and talked about the budget. He also told me confidentially that a plan was in the offing to 'set the pound free'. This was the first time I had heard about the proposal. I said that my first reaction was against it, but that I would think about it further as a matter of urgency. Robert asked me not to tell C about this.

Thursday 21 February
I thought a great deal about what Robert had told me and decided definitely that it would be a bad move. In a talk with C, I led the conversation round to the subject. We talked about it in purely academic terms, but the discussion proved useful during the following days.

Friday 22 February
Early today Robert Hall warned me that the Bank/Treasury plan was

coming up at a meeting at 11 o'clock of a small group of Ministers. I had time to warn C only briefly. C went to the meeting and I went to lunch with Alec (later Sir Alexander) Spearman, Parliamentary Private Secretary to Peter (later Lord) Thorneycroft, President of the Board of Trade. Shortly after lunch began, at Queen Anne's Mansions, I was summoned by telephone to see C at No. 11. Finishing my lunch quickly I went across. He told me briefly about the meeting. Those present were the PM, C, Butler, Harry (later Lord) Crookshank (Leader of the House of Commons), Lord Woolton (Lord President), Maxwell Fyfe (later Lord Kilmuir, Home Secretary), and, I think, James (later Lord) Stuart (Secretary of State for Scotland) and possibly someone else. Butler had handed round a long memorandum on external financial policy which Ministers read hurriedly at the meeting. The PM, who had previously been told about the plan by Butler, was impatient and no one had time to read the paper at all carefully. (The PM, at some stage, also received a deputation from the Bank of England, headed by the Governor, advocating the plan. He reported that they were a fine, patriotic body of men, anxious to do what was right for the country.) It seems that there was no real intention to have a discussion of the Chancellor's proposals. It was largely a matter of informing Ministers in advance in the same way as they are informed of budget proposals shortly before a budget speech. In this case Ministers had to be informed some time before the proposed budget date (4 March) – when the plan would be announced – since telegrams had to be sent a day or two later to Commonwealth Governments to give them a week to decide their policies.

C was the only Minister who opposed the proposals. He said he would not be a party to them. The Chancellor said he would send round some of his officials to explain the scheme to C that afternoon; he was sure they would convince him of its wisdom. At the end of the meeting Butler took back copies of the memorandum from all the Ministers except C who insisted on keeping his as he wished to study it.

By the time C had told me all this, he had to go to a meeting about the resignation of Mr Hardie from the Chairmanship of the Iron and Steel Corporation. I cancelled a 'Statistical Exercise' meeting arranged for that afternoon and sat in C's room at No. 11 reading the paper and making notes on it.

The paper was called a 'Draft Memorandum by the Chancellor of the Exchequer'. (C, in the paper he prepared during the next few days, made some attempt to save Butler's face by saying that the latter's paper was 'admittedly only a draft'.) The main author had obviously been Otto Clarke. Butler had in fact said at the meeting how much he admired Otto's skill in writing it in twenty-four hours. (He had not spent six years on the *Financial*

News for nothing.) Long before I had finished it I was verging on hysteria. It was not merely the number of fallacies contained on nearly every page, but the frank and brutal way in which the consequences of the proposed action were stated. It seemed inconceivable that Ministers should accept, with virtually no examination, a set of proposals which the paper admitted could have disastrous and unpredictable consequences at home and abroad.

This method of presentation, as it turned out, was a very clever gamble that nearly came off. The psychological appeal was to the masochistic instinct of Ministers. The reserves had been running away at an alarming rate since the Government took office and there was an atmosphere of crisis and panic. The more appalling the consequences of the measures proposed, the more correct they must be. They also appealed to some Ministers' sense of duty and patriotism, even to the extent of putting country before party. I was told that Butler had admitted privately that they could mean the end of the Conservative Party for twenty years, and he seems to have repeated this at a meeting of Ministers described below.

The paper began by saying it was almost certain that our reserves would fall in the near future to a point at which we could no longer be in effective control of the situation, even if drastic internal measures were proposed in the budget. It was, therefore, necessary to take external measures which would conserve our reserves while we still had freedom of action. The remaining reserves could then be used as a *masse de manoeuvre*. If we delayed action much longer events would take control, and we should have a much more disastrous crisis.

The main features of the Chancellor's proposals (in somewhat over-simplified terms) were:-

(i)　A floating rate for sterling (it was then fixed at £1 = \$2.80, with a range of 2 cents on either side).

(ii)　The blocking of not less than 80% of the sterling balances held by members of the Sterling Area. (This proposal was dropped in the June attempt to introduce ROBOT.)

(iii)　The blocking of 90% of sterling balances held by non-members of the Sterling Area, other than those in the Dollar Area.

(iv)　Convertibility of sterling into dollars by non-residents of the Sterling Area, subject of course to the blocking of a large part of their sterling balances – a pretty important qualification.

(v)　Despite the convertibility granted to non-residents, residents of the Sterling Area (including Britain) would be no freer to convert their money into foreign currency than before. Exchange controls would be retained, as would quantitative restrictions on imports. (Not much Conservative freedom there!)

The Chancellor's paper admitted that the effect of convertibility on our exports might be serious: 'If (foreign countries) are short of dollars, they will tend to restrict their imports from us, and export as much as they can to us' (in order to earn a surplus with us which they can then convert into precious dollars). 'We must face the possibility that a substantial area of our export trade may be faced with conditions of great difficulty.'

(I believe that during the week the Treasury had discussions on this problem with the Board of Trade – once the latter had got to know more about the plan; and, according to the report I had, proposed trading arrangements that would have amounted to the most extreme form of Schachtian bilateralism, similar to that practised by Germany during the Hitler regime before the war.)

The Chancellor's paper admitted that convertibility might well kill the European Payments Union (from which we had just borrowed on a large scale) and set back seriously the freeing of trade within Europe.

The Sterling Area governments were to be given only a week to decide whether to accept the plan – which for them involved the blocking of the great bulk of their reserves and the tying of their currencies to a floating sterling. (As Prof pointed out in his paper, they would strongly resent receiving what amounted almost to an ultimatum only a month after their meeting in London at which they had been told absolutely nothing about such a revolutionary plan.) It was admitted that Pakistan, Ceylon, Burma and Iraq would probably leave the Sterling Area and that India and Australia might well do so. Only New Zealand, South Africa, Southern Rhodesia and Ireland were regarded as fairly safe. The United States were to be informed forty-eight hours before zero, but no modifications made to meet their criticisms. It was admitted that they 'would regard as anathema the opening of the London gold market at a floating rate' and 'the set-back to the liberalisation of trade within Europe as a deliberate and selfish act by the UK'. The International Monetary Fund (which forbad floating) was to be informed. It was admitted that the scheme might mean the end of the Fund; nevertheless it was proposed that we should borrow from it!

The paper admitted that, domestically, 'we cannot pretend to predict what its (the plan's) consequences will be . . . The basic idea of internal stability of prices and employment will not be maintainable . . . It will not be possible to avoid unemployment . . . The pressure will fall particularly on the cost of living.'

After C had returned from his meeting on Mr Hardie's resignation we saw at No. 11, as arranged at the morning meeting, first Robert Hall and later Leslie Rowan and Otto Clarke. Robert seemed to be on our side but still insisted that he must analyse the problem further. After talking to us he went back to finish a paper he was writing for the Chancellor on the subject. (He told me at some stage that when, earlier, he had first heard of the scheme, the Chancellor had told him that, if he advised against it, he would call the whole thing off, but Robert had said that it was a complicated problem which he must have more time to consider.) Leslie Rowan and Otto Clarke seemed very pleased and confident (presumably as a result of the morning meeting of Ministers). We discussed with them a good number of points and, in my opinion, made mince-meat of their arguments. C and I left late for Oxford by car and discussed the matter all the way home. C decided to write a paper. Robert Hall (who normally returned to Oxford on Friday evenings) spent the night in London.

Saturday 23 February
Between 4 and 6 pm I saw C in Christ Church and we discussed his first draft in detail.

Sunday 24 February
In the morning I visited Robert Hall on his allotment – he had by then returned to Oxford – and discovered that he was now definitely against the plan. At 3.30 I went to Christ Church to see C's second draft and we made some amendments to it. I then brought Robert round to see C. He read C's paper and liked it very much. We heard now:-

(i)   that Maurice Allen (my old tutor at Balliol, now an Adviser at the Bank of England, later an Executive Director) was against the plan;
(ii)   that Sir Herbert Brittain from the Treasury and Eric (later Sir Eric) Berthoud from the Foreign Office had gone to Lisbon to explain the plan to Eden who was attending a meeting of NATO;
(iii) that Robert Hall had sent a personal message to Sir Edwin (later Lord) Plowden (Chief Planning Officer in the Treasury), who was in Lisbon with Eden, and that he was flying back to London;
(iv)   that the Treasury were spending the week-end drafting telegrams to Commonwealth governments.

C's paper contained, I think, most of the main arguments used during the rest of the year. Its main points were as follows.

First, it cast doubt on Butler's gloomy view on the prospects for the reserves. It reminded Ministers that most of the measures taken, or to be taken, had not yet had time to improve the balance of payments. These included our own latest round of import cuts; the agreement by Sterling Area Ministers, some of whom had only recently got home, to cut their imports; the measures we had taken to switch production from defence, investment and consumption to exports.

The Commonwealth Ministers had reached agreement on measures which, at the Conference in January, had been regarded as a reasonable plan to deal with the situation. Why then suddenly adopt a completely different plan, with revolutionary aspects, when nothing much had happened to make the prospects worse? (In the event the reserves performed considerably better than had been forecast at the time of the Conference; and Governments in the rest of the Sterling Area took extremely severe measures to cut their imports, although the advocates of ROBOT were arguing that they would do virtually nothing.)

Even if the Chancellor's forecasts were right – C continued – this was no argument for ROBOT. The pound could safely be set free and made convertible from a position of strength. But to do this from a position of weakness would be extremely dangerous.

ROBOT, far from reducing our trade deficit, would increase it. The pound would undoubtedly fall, and with it our foreign exchange earnings; a given quantity of exports would earn less foreign currency, and we could not expect much, if any, increase in export volume, which was to a large extent limited by supply rather than demand. Where demand was the limiting factor, convertibility would indeed give countries a strong incentive to cut our exports to them in order to earn scarce dollars. It was most unlikely that imports, already severely restricted by direct controls, would be significantly reduced by a fall in the pound. Thus, with the trade deficit increasing, either the pound would fall disastrously low or, if it were supported out of the reserves, they would fall *more* than they otherwise would do, not less as the supporters of ROBOT would have us think. The '*masse de manoeuvre*' argument was thus fallacious.

After that it was easy for the Prof's paper to spell out the other serious repercussions of ROBOT at home and abroad – for they had nearly all been admitted in Butler's paper (from which he quoted liberally). Briefly they meant, at home, giving up the attempt to keep prices stable (because the fall in the pound would raise import prices) and to maintain employment (because really drastic deflationary measures might well be required to stop the pound going into a virtually uncontrollable nose-dive). Abroad they meant infuriating, in various ways so well described by Butler, the Europeans, the Americans and the Commonwealth.

The Prof's paper concluded by saying that if the outlook was as serious as the Chancellor believed – which he doubted – quite a different policy should be followed. We should cut our dollar imports still more severely and press the rest of the Sterling Area to do so – and quickly. We should borrow from the IMF, where we had considerable drawing rights available, on the strength of the American securities held by the Treasury which had been requisitioned during the war, and possibly on the strength of the aid we had been promised by the Americans. We should in any case raise Bank Rate and introduce a stiff budget to restore confidence abroad.

Monday 25 February to Friday 29 February
These five days were days of battle, with the fortunes swaying backwards and forwards. Prof attended six meetings of Ministers on the problem (including three of the full Cabinet). I spent my time partly with the Prof, partly preparing drafts, partly talking to a lot of civil servants – trying to win them over to our side and, when they were friendly, devising ways of persuading Ministers. No holds were barred. A lot was at stake. A handful of officials in the Treasury and the Bank had tried to spring a fast one in a most uncivilservicelike manner, and the resentment of other officials was often quite violent. Prof, apart from attending meetings of Ministers, saw a number of officials, lobbied individual Ministers, talked privately to the PM on several occasions and drafted minutes to him.

Monday 25 February
C and I left Oxford by car at what was for us the exceptionally early hour of 8.45 am, and talked about the matter all the way to London. On arrival, after checking a few facts in the paper, I took it to the Chancellor's Private Secretaries' Office to be duplicated. (Prof would not have it duplicated in his own office because of his insistence on the utmost secrecy – a matter to which I return later.) I found that a meeting on the plan was in progress in the Chancellor's room. I went along to his Private Office two or three times to find out what gossip I could for C on the pretext of finding out how the duplicating of the paper was getting on. I received black looks from Otto Clarke, Sam (later Sir Samuel) Goldman (Chief Statistician in the Overseas Finance Division) and Edmund (later Sir Edmund) Compton (a Third Secretary). Things looked better! I heard that Plowden was on our side, also Sir Arthur (later Lord) Salter, Minister of State for Economic Affairs in the Treasury. Though without a seat in the Cabinet he had full access to it when he found it necessary and seems to have attended Cabinet meetings on ROBOT. I got two copies of C's paper, one for the PM and one for C, before lunch.

After lunch C saw Plowden. I arranged to have dinner with Maurice

Allen. He came round to No. 11 at about 6 o'clock and told me about the set-up in the Bank. It appeared that Sir George Bolton and Thompson McCausland (an Adviser at the Bank) had sold the plan to the Governor (Cobbold – later Lord Cobbold). While I was talking to Maurice Allen upstairs at No. 11, the Chancellor rang up C, but the call for some reason came through to me. I went downstairs to talk to C, who said he would like to see Maurice Allen, but the latter, for obvious reasons, declined the invitation.

C went to dinner with Lady Birkenhead and returned at 10 o'clock for a talk with the PM and others about the former's speech on foreign affairs. I dined with Maurice Allen and later in the evening told C what I had heard from him.

Crookshank announced today in the House that the Budget date had been postponed from 4 to 11 March. At least, another week had been won!

Tuesday 26 February
In the morning C received a copy of a note that Oliver Lyttelton (later Lord Chandos, Secretary of State for the Colonies) had sent to the PM supporting the plan, with certain provisos regarding the interests of the Colonies. C left at 11 am for a meeting on the plan with the Chancellor and other Ministers, not including the PM. I sat in No. 11 and drafted a note for Prof to cover the copy of his paper which he proposed to send to the PM. This was largely a summary of the main paper, but also included a reply to Lyttelton's note pointing out that he ignored the fact that a cheaper pound would in present circumstances increase rather than diminish the trade deficit. He also ignored all the other adverse repercussions.

C, on his return from the 11 o'clock meeting, told me that Lord Leathers (Secretary of State for the Co-ordination of Transport, Fuel and Power) was a possible ally, that Swinton (the Government's Chief Spokesman on economic matters in the House of Lords) was wobbling, but that Salter had supported him, thus confirming the rumour I had heard the day before. (There was a story circulating later that when Churchill heard that Salter and Prof were in agreement in opposing ROBOT this convinced him that it must be a bad idea. Salter had beaten Prof in a by-election in 1937 when he became one of the two 'Burgesses' for Oxford when there were still University seats in Parliament; and it was well known that the two had for many years differed on most things.)

I had lunch with James Meade (Professor of Political Economy in Cambridge, later a Nobel Prize Winner) at the Reform Club and was summoned back early to see C at No. 11 before a meeting I had arranged for 2.30 to see Plowden with Robert Hall. Plowden told me what Sir Frank Lee

(Permanent Secretary at the Board of Trade) had said to him about C that morning. This suggested clearly that the other Ministers had not seen C's paper. I rang Frank from No. 11 and he confirmed that he had not had the paper; he invited me to come and see him at the Board of Trade at 5.30 or 6 o'clock.

I told C my suspicion that his paper had not been circulated. He phoned Butler's Private Office at once. They confirmed that the paper had not gone out and gave the excuse that his quotations from the Chancellor's paper were no longer accurate, since it had been revised! C was justifiably angry. Butler phoned him later and more or less apologised.

I saw C's covering note to the Prime Minister (my first draft had been very little altered) and also a personal note to the PM. This explained that at the morning meeting Salter was strongly against the plan and also Swinton (his name was inserted later in ink by the Prof – for reasons that will be apparent in a moment). The Chancellor had also told them at the meeting that his economic advisers were violently opposed to it and admitted that it might spell the ruin of the Tory Party. C went on to tell the PM:

The plan I gather emanates from the Bank of England; opinion there is divided but it seems that two very persuasive gentlemen have sold it to the Governor (this was based on my information from Maurice Allen) who is now pressing very hard to get it accepted. In the Treasury a brilliant but volatile Under-Secretary (this of course was Otto Clarke) seems to have persuaded Leslie Rowan to back it. Otherwise I do not think it has much professional support.

After talking to C, I went to see Frank Lee as arranged at the Board of Trade. He was accompanied by one or two of his officials including Sir James Helmore and David Caplan. They appeared to know rather little about the plan – and even less about its implications and possible consequences – and were obviously furious that they had been consulted only cursorily. They seemed to be wholly on our side. I also heard that Swinton might be too, and returned to No. 11 and told C. He at once telephoned Swinton, who came round to No. 11 to read C's paper. He appeared to be very strongly on our side, but woolly. I remember him saying emphatically: 'Prof, we'll stop it'.

I then went to dinner at the Reform Club and met Arthur (later Sir Arthur) Snelling, an official at the Commonwealth Relations Office who had accompanied Keynes on war-time missions to North America. After dinner, we got into a room by ourselves and had a very long discussion about the plan. He was in favour of it but did not seem to have heard any of the counter-arguments. I gave him a long lecture on the subject.

When I got back to No. 11, I found that C was in bed with influenza.

Wednesday 27 February

Nevertheless, early in the morning I was summoned to C while still in my dressing-gown. He had arranged to see the PM at 10 o'clock and *show* him the papers. (The PM was far more interested in his speech for a foreign affairs debate.) I told C about Snelling. After C left, I phoned him and discovered that his Permanent Secretary, Sir Percival Liesching, had had C's paper; this was satisfactory. I got the impression that Snelling had been considerably rattled by my arguments on the previous evening.

At 11 am there was a Cabinet meeting on the BBC Charter and at 12.30 pm another meeting on the plan, consisting of the PM, C, Salter, Butler, Swinton (who was weakening), Lyttelton, etc.

I had lunch with Ted Heath (then one of the Government Whips) at the Reform Club and was summoned back early to see C who was very gloomy about the morning meeting. He wrote a note to Eden and saw Leathers who took a very sound line (we gathered later that Butler thought he had sold the plan to Leathers and was upset when at the next meeting he opposed it).

There was at that time a disturbing rumour that the PM was having dinner with Eden and Butler that evening, but it subsequently turned out to be Eden and Field Marshal Lord Alexander, who was just being appointed Minister of Defence.

I saw Plowden again and heard from Robert Hall that Lionel (later Lord) Robbins (Professor of Economics at the LSE, who had been Director of the Economic Section of the Cabinet Offices during the war) had been told about the plan on the authority of Sir Edward (later Lord) Bridges, Permanent Secretary to the Treasury. Lionel had been very strongly against it. I suggested to Plowden that Robbins should see Thorneycroft. I knew that they were friends having been at a dinner some months previously given by Spearman, at which both were present. Plowden immediately phoned Frank Lee – Thorneycroft's Permanent Secretary – to try to arrange such a meeting.

We discussed other Ministers who might be approached. Plowden suggested that the way to approach Eden was to concentrate on the dangers of the plan to the middle class and the risk of antagonising organised labour. He also thought that Walter Monckton (Minister of Labour and National Service) would be worried about the unemployment aspects, and that Ismay, Secretary of State for Commonwealth Relations, might be approached. When I got back C rang Ismay, who promised to read his paper on the following morning.

Thursday 28 February

C attended another restricted meeting of Ministers on the plan at, I think,

11 am. He told me that Leathers had been sound, but he was still not very hopeful.

After lunch with Norman Chester (then a Fellow of Nuffield) I had my hair cut and did not get back until after 3 o'clock. C had visitors. The PM came round to our part of the office to see about accommodation for Alexander. C had an opportunity to tell him some interesting things. Between 5.30 and 7 I held a meeting of the Statistical Exercise Working Party (in an attempt to reassure officials not in the know that nothing unusual was going on). At 7 o'clock I saw C. He was extremely anxious. He had received another note from Lyttelton to the PM criticising his (Prof's) paper, and Lyttelton had sent copies to Butler, Woolton, Maxwell Fyfe and James Stuart. C drafted a minute on this to the PM which I do not think was ever sent in, but was used at the next meeting. Lyttelton's note was largely incomprehensible.

We then went over to No. 11. I ate some biscuits and C had dinner at 9.30. Bridges came to see him at 9.45 and at 10 o'clock they went to a meeting of the Cabinet to discuss the plan. I went to supper feeling very gloomy. After supper I returned to the office, and then to No. 11, where I studied some figures of prices etc. after the 1949 devaluation.

The Cabinet broke up at mid-night, and I saw C on his return. He was very much more cheerful. He had had support from Leathers, Salter, Eden (who had previously, I think, been rather neutral), Maxwell Fyfe, and Woolton in rather vague terms. There had also been some support from the PM. Thorneycroft had suggested a compromise. Swinton had completely ratted. There had been a rather 'pathetic' speech from Butler who seemed to realise that things were going badly for him.

Friday 29 February

I was up early and saw C in bed. I went over to the office to tell Plowden and Robert Hall the good news. C came into the office where I saw him and he then walked over to No. 10 for another meeting of the Cabinet.

At 12.30 pm I went again to No. 11 to see C after the Cabinet and received very good news indeed. ROBOT had effectively been rejected, at least for the time being. It had been agreed that we should wait until April to see what happened. The Chancellor had proposed March, but the Prime Minister had said April. Lord Salisbury (Lord Privy Seal) had weighed in and made a very sound speech arguing that the people were not yet ready for such a drastic change in our economic life.

From what C told me, the following was the line-up at the Cabinet:

For ROBOT:
Butler, Lyttelton, Swinton and, I think, Crookshank.

Against:
C, Leathers, Salter, PM, Eden, Maxwell Fyfe, Salisbury, Macmillan (Minister of Housing and Local Government).

Wobbly:
Monckton, Woolton, Thorneycroft, Ismay.

I don't know:
Lord Simonds (Lord Chancellor), Stuart.

(Woolton I put down at the time as a fence-sitter but he later, in July, urged that ROBOT be accepted – see below – and described himself as a supporter of it in February.)

It is amusing that the line-up of Ministers and officials for and against the plan tended to be a Cambridge versus Oxford affair, with one or two notable exceptions: for example, Plowden, a Cambridge man, was strongly on our side and Swinton, an Oxford man, on the other. I have no sociological or indeed any other explanation.

The Cabinet met again at 3 o'clock on Friday to consider the details of the alternative to ROBOT. I wrote notes on the history of the past ten days and, when the Cabinet was over, C and I drove to Oxford. We talked very little about economics.

There I shall end my day-by-day, blow-by-blow account, but before going on to the rest of the story, a brief word about secrecy. Prof insisted on the utmost secrecy throughout this period and, indeed, for many months thereafter. No one else in the Branch (except Harvey) was allowed to have an inkling of what was going on, although it was obvious that something odd was happening. It was probably – at least in the early stages – thought to be connected with the budget. Relevant papers were always kept in the safe. I worked on papers only in Prof's room in the office, or in No. 11. Typing was done only by Harvey, and in the case of the paper that Prof circulated it was duplicated by Butler's people. Needless to say, the lunches I had with James Meade, Ted Heath and Norman Chester during the critical week were pre-arranged, and there was no discussion of ROBOT.

Robert Hall told me, shortly afterwards, that Hugh Gaitskell (Chancel‑lor in the previous administration) had given him his version of why the budget had been postponed. It was that Prof had criticised the Chancellor's national income calculations as unduly pessimistic and so leading to too tough a budget. I had been instructed to do alternative calculations. To give time for this and for new proposals to be framed, the budget had been delayed for a week. Robert told Gaitskell that he scored 'beta minus' (meaning lower second class honours in Oxford exams). This suggested that there was little knowledge outside of what was going on, or at least of the personalities involved. I rather think that the extremely complimentary remarks Gaitskell made in the House of Commons on 11 November 1952 about the Prof stopping convertibility referred to the June attempt, described below. (In the same speech, Gaitskell suggested that Salter was a main advocate of ROBOT – the reverse of the truth.)

Prof, however, was continually saying he thought other Ministers, and the Bank, were being indiscreet; and officials in some other departments were much less careful than we were. I was shocked, when trying to find out whether Prof's paper had been circulated, on being told that it was lying, unattended, on Liesching's desk. Nearly everyone in the Economic Section of the Cabinet Offices seemed to know about it. They were busy writing papers and suggesting alternative plans. These had such names as 'Jukes's Folly', 'Downie's Desperation' and 'Butt's Abortion'. John Jukes, Jack Downie and David Butt were then members of the Section under Robert Hall. Downie died at a tragically early age not very long afterwards; Butt had been in the Prof's Branch during the war; Jukes became my Deputy in the Department of Economic Affairs some twelve years later.

(In March, when the first ROBOT crisis was over, the Economic Section produced a rather extreme alternative to ROBOT to which I had to object strongly, though our discussion was a friendly one between anti-ROBOT allies. Most of the Section disagreed with my criticisms. But Robert accepted them – at least my tactical objection that it would be extremely dangerous to put forward such contentious, and in some respects revolutionary, proposals as the alternative to ROBOT, since this could so easily play into the hands of our opponents – and he did not give the paper a wide circulation.)

It is fairly clear that, during the last week in February, many people in financial circles thought that something on the lines of ROBOT might be under consideration. The press reported several rumours that the Chancellor would announce in the Budget changes in external policy, including the unpegging of the pound and some form of convertibility. On the day of the Budget, shortly after Butler's speech, Per Jacobsen phoned me from the Bank for International Settlements in Basle to ask what was in it. When I told him, he asked whether there was any announcement about the pound. We discovered later, incidentally, that he was against any such move at that time.

During the ten days after the Cabinet rejected ROBOT, the loss of reserves continued at a high rate until the budget. There was then a very great change. Allowing for special factors, a chart of the reserves shows a steady and almost precipitous fall from the summer of 1951 until the budget, then a dramatic flattening, with the reserves remaining roughly constant for the following six months, before beginning to rise quite clearly in the autumn.

I mentioned earlier that my office overlooked Great George Street. I seem to remember that every evening a small detachment of soldiers – sometimes, I think, Scots Guards headed by a piper – marched past my window on their way from the Wellington Barracks to the Bank of England to guard the gold reserves; and I swear – though it cannot be true – that on the evening of Budget day the detachment was doubled.

The Budget also had a dramatic effect on the exchange rate. The pound had been at $2.78, at which the Bank was obliged to support it, almost continuously since early January. There was little change on budget day, though after the Speech there were a few transactions substantially above the support rate. But on the following day the rise began in earnest. I watched the tape frequently, and by Friday (three days after the budget) the rate rose at one time to nearly $2.81 – then an unbelievably rapid change, though not uncommon in the floating rate era after 1972. The budget undoubtedly had a striking effect on confidence in the pound, an important factor being the rise in Bank Rate, which was announced in the Speech, from 2½% to 4%. There was also probably a good deal of 'bear' covering by those who had expected an unpegging of the pound to be announced in the Budget Speech.

Heroic – and successful – efforts were made to get in as many dollars as possible before the end of March so as to have a good figure for the quarterly announcement. At that time the reserve figures were published only quarterly. During the second quarter we continued to watch the figures anxiously. We were most concerned that the wisdom of rejecting ROBOT should be vindicated and that there should be no excuse for another attempt. Fortunately the reserves kept up and by the middle of the year were well above the level to which the Chancellor implied they would fall, when he proposed ROBOT, if it were not accepted. This presumably explains why, although the Cabinet had decided to reconsider the matter in April, Butler did not bring it up.

The ill-feeling that the dispute had aroused made frank and easy co-operation with many Treasury officials very difficult. We often felt that their obsession with ROBOT as the one and only panacea stopped other important work being done, just as we had felt that the time devoted to ROBOT during the February crisis might have been more usefully spent working out a better excess profits levy (which Churchill – misguidedly in my view – had promised during the Election campaign to prevent 'profiteering' from rearmament). This turned out to be full of snags which caused a lot of trouble in Parliament. Relations improved, however, as time went on. They were helped by a minute sent by the Prof to the PM on 2 May. This was in response to a note by Butler to Churchill, who sent it on to Prof, with this covering note: '*Lord C.* Please give your whole mind to this. The Chancellor shows a great mastery of the subject. Do not consume our limited associated strength for the sake of argument. Let me know your whole mind on the matter'. In reply Prof sent the PM a comprehensive review of the economic situation and what needed to be done about it, and was at pains to emphasise the wide range of agreement which he believed existed between himself and the Chancellor. We heard that Butler was very pleased by the conciliatory tone of this note (which was sent on to him by the PM) and at finding so much apparent agreement between Prof and himself – although Treasury officials were reluctant to accept a good many of his proposals! The paper did, however, greatly raise the Prof's stock in the Treasury. When I saw Leslie Rowan and Otto Clarke to discuss a draft reply by the Chancellor to the PM, commenting on Prof's note, I was amicably received, though we had tough arguments on a number of matters.

But although relations improved, the threat of ROBOT was continually present – a sword of Damocles hanging over our heads. Butler could seldom resist allusion to it in any of his papers. We also suspected that work was proceeding in the Bank and Treasury and were pretty sure they were just biding their time and awaiting a favourable opportunity; we had several under-the-counter warnings to this effect. The PM also, in the early stages, had appeared to be hankering after ROBOT. So, not long after the Cabinet had rejected it, Prof felt it necessary to send him a minute explaining in child's language the guts of the problem and underlining in particular the internal political implications. This seems to have done a lot of good and Winston gradually got the arguments into his head and used them effectively in discussion.

This no doubt helped when suddenly, on Friday, 27 June, Butler tried it on again. He circulated a paper (dated 28 June for some reason), to be discussed by an informal group of Ministers at 10 pm on the Monday, prior to consideration by the Cabinet on Tuesday morning – the same 'rush' tactics as in February. But this time he fell at the first fence. Prof and I produced a counter-blast over the weekend and circulated it on Monday; and at the meeting that evening (chaired by the PM) Butler realised that ROBOT Mark II was a non-starter and the matter was dropped from the Cabinet's Tuesday agenda. (Shortly after, Harold Macmillan circulated a paper containing a very rude attack on ROBOT, which he described as a

'Banker's Ramp'. He also refused to accept a cut in housing that Butler had proposed. On this my sympathies were for once with Butler for reasons I explain later.)

Butler's paper again referred to warnings of an autumn crisis (which never came!) by the Governor of the Bank. But, whereas ROBOT Mark I had been presented in a brutal fashion, ROBOT Mark II (which was more or less the same) was put forward in exactly the reverse manner as if the February paper had never existed, and all its blood-curdling attributes had never been mentioned. The whole thing was presented almost as a relatively minor technical change. It was a good exercise in false perspective but seriously misjudged the gullibility of its readers.

One of the new arguments in Prof's paper was that it would be a bit hard on the Commonwealth to adopt unilaterally a course of action which pre-judged all the vital issues only ten days after Robert Menzies, the Australian Prime Minister, had persuaded the Cabinet to hold a Commonwealth Prime Ministers' Conference on economic affairs in November. This put the advocates of ROBOT in a quandary, and it may be significant that ROBOT Mark II was sprung on Ministers so soon after. For ROBOT was a revolutionary package which could only be pulled off in an atmosphere of panic and in the utmost secrecy. It would have been out of the question to spring it on a Commonwealth Conference – which would never have accepted it – or to have discussions about it, lasting months, in advance of a Conference. For the advocates of ROBOT, therefore, it was now or never. There might just be time to slip it through, under cover of an alleged autumn crisis, before preparations for the Conference got under way.

For some reason Woolton tried to persuade the PM to have ROBOT, in a minute of 21 July. This was answered by Prof on 23 July in a note to the PM. It was extraordinary that Woolton, with his economic training, and who had lived thirty years in the days of gold sovereigns, should have thought that the Victorian pound floated! Yet this is what his minute asserted. After Butler's second failure – and leaving aside Woolton's rather pathetic little one-man-band effort – no further attempt was made to push through a crude ROBOT operation. Attention shifted to preparations for the Commonwealth Conference, and it was here that the battle was fought. While there was little danger that anything so crude as ROBOT would get through such a Conference, the Treasury remained determined to get something as like it as possible.

By this time the other economists on Prof's staff, with his approval, were fully informed and involved; and we spent the summer and autumn in hard, and often bitter, discussions with other officials, preparing papers for Ministers. Prof attended a lot of Ministerial meetings, particularly of a special Cabinet committee on preparations for the Conference, prepared several papers for it, wrote minutes to the PM and carried on the tussle in the other usual ways. We now got a much more thorough discussion of the problems than was possible during the ROBOT crisis in February, though the fight continued to be tough.

But before coming on to the preparations for the Conference, it is necessary to go back a few months to describe a controversy that had been going on independently of that on ROBOT. Peter Thorneycroft had for some time been interested in reforming GATT. Alec Spearman had asked me round once or twice to discuss this and also to dinner with Thorneycroft himself, together with Frank Lee and Lionel Robbins. Thorneycroft thought it unlikely that the dollar problem would ever be solved, and therefore wanted some kind of more or less permanent non-dollar bloc. He was, however, against quantitative import restrictions, and so toyed with the idea of using tariffs as the main method of insulating such a bloc from the dollar area. This line of thinking led him to favour an extension of Imperial Preference and freedom from the relevant restrictive provisions of GATT. On this he was supported by a good many Conservative back-benchers, and some former Tory MPs.

It was all reminiscent of the war-time controversies, with Leo Amery (no longer in Parliament and approaching eighty, but still very spry) wanting a major intensification of Imperial Preference to make the Commonwealth much more self-sufficient; and Bob (later Lord) Boothby wanting a permanent non-dollar bloc comprising the Sterling Area (which excluded Canada) and Western Europe.

No one in Government, except Thorneycroft, took any of this very seriously. But a motion on the subject was put down in the Lords and Prof was asked to speak for the Government; most other Ministers were embarrassed by previous utterances. Although his speech was deliberately non-committal and vague, he poured a good deal of cold water on the proposals and many Conservatives regarded it as a blow to Empire trade. There were protests in the press (including a letter from Amery to *The Times*) and complaints from the Conservative Parliamentary Party, but these fairly quickly died down. In helping Prof to prepare this speech, and in other work I describe in a moment, I was greatly assisted by studies I had made of these matters during the war, and while in Oxford (and Cambridge) from 1946 to 1951.

As agreed in advance with his colleagues, Prof had concluded his speech by saying that the whole matter was the object of anxious study by the Government. This was a bit of an exaggeration and it was not until nearly a month later that a group of officials began work on the subject. I found myself writing two papers. One was on Commonwealth trade, where I was greatly helped by John Fforde, which showed how much the Commonwealth (and the Sterling Area) depended on the outside world and how vulnerable it would be to retaliation if it tried to move in too obvious a way towards self-sufficiency.

My second paper was on the longer-run dollar problem. This was a sequel to one by Robert Neild of the Economic Section (whom we shall come across later) which gave the impression that the problem was permanently insoluble. I argued that, while it would very probably persist for the next few years, it might well solve itself later. There was thus much to be said for continuing to work towards one multilateral world, rather than trying to set up a permanent non-dollar bloc; although, so long as dollar shortage persisted, discrimination against dollar goods would have to remain.

In the end Ministers decided, in July, after surprisingly little argument, that we should work towards 'one-world' as our ultimate objective, with multilateral trading, convertibility and a minimum of discrimination, covering the Sterling Area, Canada, Western Europe, the United States and the rest of the world. They rejected, as politically and economically impracticable, a 'two-world' system.

During the March–July period we had thus had a fight on two fronts: against the advocates of ROBOT on the one hand, and the 'two-worlders' on the other. By July, the latter had been defeated. The advocates of a crude ROBOT in something like its original form had also been defeated, though they were still fighting hard for it in a less extreme form. But at least there was agreement that the alternative to a ROBOT-type scheme was *not* a permanent non-dollar or Commonwealth bloc but a sincere attempt to move as fast as possible towards 'one-world' while avoiding a premature plunge. The dispute between Ministers thus became one on timing and on the necessary preconditions. Some, like Butler and Lyttelton, still favoured a dash to convertibility. Prof was a 'gradualist' and thought we should go convertible only when Britain's external position had become much stronger and world dollar shortage much less severe. However, the feeling in Whitehall was that we could not just carry on pragmatically, adapting existing policies as required. Something new and dramatic had to be done. The 'plungers' in the Treasury and the Bank were working on some modified form of ROBOT. It was essential for us to work out an alternative plan for 'gradualism' which was at least as attractive, and would stand up to intensive, critical examination.

This we did in the form of proposals for an 'Atlantic Payments Union' (APU), which Prof put to his colleagues in a paper dated 1 August 1952.

The idea had its origin three months earlier, when my old friends from Paris days, Robert Marjolin and Harry (later Sir Henry) Lintott, still Secretary-General and Deputy Secretary-General respectively of the OEEC, visited London. I dined with them and took them to tea with Prof in the House of Lords. The general line they wished to push in OEEC was that, after the US Presidential Election, the Western European countries should approach the Americans in an attempt to find a solution to the dollar problem. We should ask them, and the Canadians, to join the European Payments Union (covering the Continental countries, Britain and, through sterling, the rest of the Sterling Area) which would then become an 'Atlantic Payments Union'. We should offer at the outset to go convertible. I was attracted to this idea as a possible half-way house between the extremes of ROBOT and 'two-worlds' but argued strongly against offering convertibility at the outset. We should try to bring the US into a payments union in such a way that we retained discrimination against them from the start but moved gradually towards convertibility and non-discrimination, the speed depending on how rapidly dollar shortage was alleviated. Marjolin accepted this, and papers subsequently prepared by the OEEC Secretariat were consistent with it. His proposals, with my crucial amendment, formed the essence of our plan for an APU, though we had to work hard and long on the technical details before we had a paper which Prof could safely circulate to Ministers. Their initial reception was encouraging. This showed, I think, how much they wanted a scheme that could be presented as 'one-world' in nature, evolutionary rather than revolutionary, and cooperative rather than a unilateral 'take-it-or-leave-it' ultimatum.

But Treasury officials – including in particular Frank Figgures, another old colleague from my Paris days – spent much energy trying to find flaws in the complicated arrangements involved. We had some anxious moments when we thought the Treasury might have caught us out, but in the end I believe we found answers to all their technical objections; and although the APU proposal eventually fell by the wayside, I believe it had the merit of finally forcing the Treasury off a crude ROBOT scheme and on to a considerably less dangerous set of proposals called the 'Collective Approach' to convertibility.

Under this plan we should still go convertible (and float the pound) as soon as possible, but only if the US, the main European countries, Canada and the other main Commonwealth countries agreed; only if France, Belgium and Holland went convertible at the same time; only if there were rules to stop other countries cutting imports from us to get sterling which they could then convert into dollars; and only if the US provided a loan of some five billion dollars, and cut their tariffs – a formidable list of pre-conditions.

This new plan, and the way in which our APU proposals were to be put to the Commonwealth, were thrashed out during August and early September. For a short period I left John Fforde to bat for us and went to Scotland for a much-needed break. He batted nobly, but felt it necessary at one stage to interrupt my holiday and call me back to London to deal with our critics; and I worked well into the small hours of the morning re-drafting a paper with Arnold France of the Treasury (later Sir Arnold, and Chairman of the Board of Inland Revenue), before returning North. On another occasion, during the struggle over APU, Maurice Scott and I found ourselves sitting alone, for hours, on one side of a large table in the Treasury far outnumbered by a host of opponents on the other side trying, unsuccessfully, to browbeat us.

Despite the opposition of Prof and several other Ministers, it was decided to submit the Collective Approach, as one possible policy, to the Commonwealth officials who met in London in late September and early October to prepare for the Prime Ministers' conference. The plan got a fairly rough handling. Our APU was brought up only late in the day and in a way we regarded as rather unfair.

Later in October Prof circulated a paper which summarised the objections of Commonwealth officials to the Collective Approach; produced evidence that most European countries were highly critical of it; and argued that the US would be most unlikely to support it. He very much doubted in particular whether they would cough up anything like five billion dollars. He concluded that we should forget the Collective Approach and prepare a 'gradual approach' to put to the Commonwealth Prime Ministers in November. He failed to carry the day and was naturally disappointed, but not unduly alarmed, partly because, as he put it in a minute to the PM, 'I do not believe it (the Collective Approach) will come to anything'. But he feared that going ahead with such an impracticable plan could land us in a humiliating mess. At a Cabinet meeting on 3 November the PM concluded, nevertheless, that the UK should put the scheme forward with conviction to the Conference. This annoyed Prof a good deal as it did not seem to represent the general tone of the Cabinet debate; he regarded it as a put-up job between Butler and Churchill.

However, the Commonwealth Prime Ministers confirmed that many hard conditions had to be fulfilled before sterling could be made convertible. One of the most important was help from America; and when Eden and Butler visited the US in March 1953, the new Eisenhower Administration – just as Prof had forecast – told them they could not ask Congress for large scale financial assistance or to lower tariffs. As if to rub salt in the wound, they very much doubted whether we were yet strong enough to risk convertibility, and felt that the proposals for a Collective Approach were premature. That put paid to the plan.

So here endeth my account of the ROBOT saga. Despite the rejection of ROBOT, which its advocates argued was essential to avoid disaster, we were in fact just beginning what could prove to be, on balance, an uniquely favourable couple of decades of British economic history (though admittedly mediocre by international standards), with growth averaging around 3% a year, inflation just over 4%, and unemployment less than half a million. Had ROBOT been attempted, I very much doubt if this would have been possible. I am at least certain that the twenty years would have got off to a very bad start, with high unemployment and inflation, intensified controls, chaos in the international monetary system, and highly unfavourable reactions from our trading partners. Partly for these reasons I cannot accept the argument that we missed a golden opportunity by not floating the pound in 1952. I believe the IMF system of fixed, but adjustable, parities served us well during most of the period, although it helped to delay what I regarded as an essential devaluation of sterling a dozen years later, as described in Chapters 7 and 8. (At the end of Chapter 7 I explain more fully why my view then was quite consistent with my opposition to a fall in the pound in 1952, the situation being profoundly different.)

After returning to Nuffield I gave a radio talk in 1954 on 'The Risks of Convertibility' which was reproduced in *The Listener*. This led an elderly Scots lady, who was deeply interested in missionary work and lived in Argyll near my mother, to ask in a shocked voice: 'Is it true that Sir Donald is against conversion?' which she pronounced 'convurrsion'.

I stayed on with Prof until the summer of 1953. With all talk of early convertibility and floating rates out of the way we could concentrate on what we both regarded as much more important matters, on the lines of the 'Statistical Exercise' I had started in January 1952 on the changes required to strengthen the economy.

Prof spent much effort attempting to improve technological education, which he considered vital for our survival in a competitive world. We pressed for an increase in the investment plans of the steel industry, which we thought inadequate and likely to hamper growth through steel shortage. People at that time were strangely reluctant to assume that we would get any significant future growth in the economy; preventing a sharp decline such as we suffered in the 1930s would surely be a pretty good achievement. 'It would seem', Prof argued in a paper in January 1953, 'that we are deliberately planning for stagnation if not for unemployment'. We were concerned with measures to prevent coal shortage, a problem of which we had had plenty of experience in the war; and to economise on the heavy investment being made in power stations, through a more rational pricing policy for electricity.

We advocated – successfully – an expansionary budget in 1953 to take up slack in the economy. I wrote a paper for Prof at that time entitled 'Background to the Budget'. This was based in part on short-term forecasts which Maurice Allen and I cooked up one evening after dinner in the Reform Club. This was long before we had econometric models of the economy and forecasters had computers at their beck and call. Maurice and I sat down, each with a pencil and the back of an envelope, without any statistical reference books, and discussed what figures to put down, provisionally, for the main items of national expenditure – exports, consumer spending, investment, stock-building and so on. We then added them up, discussed their consistency, revised them and eventually – after a couple of hours – came up with forecasts of national output, the balance of payments and other relevant magnitudes. I have been unable to check, but doubt whether they were any worse than the considerably more elaborate, though still primitive by today's standards, forecasts of the Treasury.

One thing we failed to do was to prevent an excessive diversion of resources to housebuilding. At the Conservative Party Conference in 1950 the Labour Government's proposal to continue building at 200,000 a year was heavily criticised, but when a motion mentioning no specific figure was put to the vote there was orchestrated shouting from the floor demanding a target of 300,000 houses. Lord Woolton, Chairman of the Party, said: 'This is magnificent. You want a figure of 300,000 put in'; and this was carried without further discussion, and confirmed in the manifesto issued before the 1951 General Election.

Now it is true that housing was very short, but we had other pressing calls on our resources, particularly rearmament and the need to increase exports; and I think most economists in Whitehall regarded this commitment as a tiresome millstone round the economy's neck. But Winston was determined to hit the target. He appointed Harold Macmillan as Minister of Housing and Local Government to do the job. He in turn recruited, to help him, Sir Percy (later Lord) Mills – a tough businessman whom I had known in Berlin in 1945; and together, with the PM's support, they did it. 326,000 houses were completed in 1953 and 354,000 in 1954.

So there was no lack of economic problems to occupy us even with ROBOT and Commonwealth Conferences out of the way. But much of Prof's time was devoted to a non-economic, but controversial, matter – the organisation of the development of atomic energy – with which he had been deeply concerned ever since the war. The struggle appears to have been nearly as fierce as that over ROBOT, and here again he found himself at times in opposition to his friend Churchill. But those in a position to know are convinced that he won a famous victory, virtually single-handed, culminating in the setting up of the Atomic Energy Authority.

Finally, there was this question of a Knighthood. Prof had got Churchill to get me an OBE in 1942 and a CBE in 1945, both at an absurdly early age. Before I left in 1953 Prof was determined to get me a 'K'. With Churchill's aid and, as I understand, in the face of considerable opposition from the Civil Servants concerned – entirely understandable given my youth and relatively junior position – I was made a Knight Bachelor in the Coronation Honours. This honour comes, in order of precedence, below that of KCB which Civil Servants mostly get, but I like to think it rather distinguished – it certainly comes before KCB's in lists published in the newspapers.

When I heard what was going to happen I was naturally pleased, but not a little embarrassed because I was only forty and friends in the Civil Service considerably senior to me had not been so honoured. I searched frantically through *Who's Who* to see if anyone I knew had been knighted so young. I was delighted to find that Edwin Plowden had been under forty; and equally delighted when, thirty years later, I was able to write a letter of congratulation to Terry Burns telling him what a cad he was to have beaten my record as the youngest to have been knighted among Chief Economic Advisers to the Treasury (he was the fourth holder of that post after I left). Waiting with me in the queue of Knights-designate in Buckingham Palace in 1953 was Gordon Richards, the great jockey, with whom I had a most interesting chat. Six days later he won the Derby, after 27 attempts.

6

BACK TO OXFORD –
WITH MORE INTERLUDES:
1953–61

WHILE working in London I had kept closely in touch with Nuffield. I spent most Saturday mornings in my room there and started writing a book on discrimination in international trade, which fell by the wayside. I went to College meetings and discussions whenever I could. In 1952, my status changed. John Hicks (later Sir John and a Nobel Prize winner) became Drummond Professor of Political Economy in succession to Hubert Henderson who died early in the year. John had held a special Official Fellowship at Nuffield, with a higher stipend than that of others, and this fell vacant on his transfer to All Souls, to which the Drummond Chair was attached. I was offered, and accepted, this Fellowship; provided I got a University Lectureship as well (which I did) it was worth slightly more than my Readership, and involved less University teaching.

I imagine Roy Harrod was disappointed not to get the Drummond Chair, as he must have been in 1945 when Henderson was elected. But, characteristically, although their views on economics differed widely, he paid a handsome tribute to Henderson's work in a special memorial number of *Oxford Economic Papers*. Roy was elected to the Readership in International Economics which I vacated – a rather strange case of a guru succeeding his protégé – but kept his Studentship, and his beloved rooms, in Christ Church. (After retiring he had a building erected in the garden of his London house into which were transferred all his precious books and papers, and his bookcases and furniture, from his Christ Church study, and it soon became almost indistinguishable from it, not excluding its smell – of tobacco smoke from his pipe.)

When I returned to Oxford we started taking a graduate seminar on international economics together and continued to do so for over eight years. He had been unwilling to join the seminar should Balogh be involved, as before; but an awkward situation was avoided by the latter's deciding to take a class on another subject. The seminar was much altered with Roy rather than Tommy as my partner, partly because of their very different personalities, partly because Roy and I were in broad agreement in our approach to economics. We did have differences, for example on the timing of a return to convertibility – I was more cautious than he. But one matter on which we entirely agreed was the need for a large increase in the price of gold; and thereby hangs a tale.

One evening in Nuffield, Roy was sitting next to me during dessert. He was due shortly afterwards at the BBC's Oxford studio to take part in a transatlantic radio discussion on the gold price. I was responsible that night for circulating the decanters, and Roy kept on asking me to pass the port round again. After he had had a few glasses I felt obliged to remind him that he would soon need all his wits about him for his broadcast. He turned to me and said: 'Donald, you're a young man; when you're my age you'll realise that it's not what you say that matters but how you feel while you're saying it'. I have found this story and Roy's immortal remark a useful opening when a guest after-dinner speaker, the next sentence being to the effect that, whatever my audience may think about what I am saying, I certainly feel good while I am saying it, after such excellent hospitality.

In addition to my seminars with Harrod, I organised weekly seminars for Nuffield economics Students and Fellows. When I first came to Nuffield these were run by John Hicks and consisted to a greater extent than I cared for of Students covering the blackboard with mathematics. When I became responsible I tried to get more emphasis on applied problems and to have discussions opened as often as possible by people invited from the outside world.

My research plan on returning to Oxford was to write a book on Britain's economic problems in general. I started on the dollar problem, an analysis of which seemed essential background but which I expected to cover in a single chapter. How wrong I was. In the event it occupied most of my research time during the next few years, although I also spent quite a lot on other matters.

One was on whether we should do better under a regime of flexible exchange rates – then becoming an increasingly fashionable belief – rather than the existing 'adjustable peg' system of the IMF, under which countries maintained fixed parities as long as they reasonably could, but might change to a new fixed rate if in 'fundamental disequilibrium'. I favoured this system and argued the case during 1954 in newspapers, a bank review and a radio discussion with James Meade. In one article I summed up my arguments with the moral to be drawn from the miserable end of Hilaire Belloc's Jim, who ran away from his Nurse, and was eaten by a Lion:

> And always keep a-hold of Nurse
> For fear of finding something worse.

By the time the pound and most other major currencies were floated in the early 1970s I had become convinced that this was – regrettably – inevitable, in view, among other things, of the enormous growth of funds ready to slosh around the world from one currency to another. The large and violent swings in exchange rates during the following decade or so did, however, show that floating rates were far from the answer to a maiden's prayer that they were claimed to be by my opponents in the 1950s and 1960s.

During my first year back in Oxford I also worked on Imperial Preference with Mrs Rosemary Hutt. Before I went to London in 1951 she, then Miss Orton, had done most of the detailed statistical work on this subject for my article on British and American exports. She now did a prodigious job with the trade returns and tariff lists of a large number of Commonwealth countries, including Britain, and we made a much more detailed and sophisticated analysis. We published the results in the *Economic Journal* for June 1954 with the following opening sentences: 'Much has been written, and perhaps even more spoken aloud, on the subject of Imperial Preference. But the discussion has been to a large extent theoretical and political rather than quantitative.' I think our article – 'Imperial Preference: A Quantitative Analysis' – filled an important gap. We showed, among many other things, how preferences (on both exports and imports) had been greatly reduced since before the war. The importance of preferences for our export trade, already rather small before the war, was now even smaller. We also concluded that their effect on *total* sales of US manufacturers was 'entirely negligible' – not uninteresting given the fierce opposition to the system of many Americans during the war.

Despite this, I felt it vital to point out, in articles and lectures, how important *other* factors had been in helping our exports to the Colonial Empire and giving us in effect captive markets which were bound to be eroded as one country after another became independent after the war. Many civil servants and engineers in the old Empire were trained in Britain, and were often in fact British; British companies operating there tended to buy from businesses in the UK; local populations had acquired tastes for British goods; and most Empire countries, before independence, bought from us 50% or more of their total imports from the main industrial countries. This was hardly sustainable after independence. But while the transition from Empire to Commonwealth accounted for a good part of the post-war decline in our share of world exports of manufactures, our exporters deserve credit for the massive shift they achieved from Empire to European markets.

My first semi-public utterance on the dollar problem, based on work done in Whitehall and during my first few months back in Nuffield, was to a meeting of the Oxford University Political Economy Club of which I had been elected a member soon after the war. It followed a dinner of the Club on a Saturday evening in November 1953 in Worcester College, the host being Asa (later Lord) Briggs, when a Fellow and later Provost of the College. I have the minutes, and the list of the twenty-odd present is not uninteresting. They included Roy Harrod, John Hicks, Dennis Robertson (from Cambridge but an Honorary Member), Arthur (Lord) Salter, all already mentioned in these pages; Sir Henry Clay, a former Warden of Nuffield, Alexander Loveday, then Warden, and Norman Chester, his successor; and one of the guests was Professor Milton Friedman from Chicago, later recognised as the High Priest of 'monetarism' and a Nobel Prize winner. Hugh Gaitskell was elected an Honorary Member of the Club that evening – a distinction I achieved over 28 years later.

The minutes simply say that I put the question: 'Is the dollar problem soluble?' There is, according to tradition, no record of the discussion, but the tenor of my answer was that there was no decisive reason why it should not be – in time. I believe this came as a surprise to the majority of those present and that a good many were unconvinced. One of the older members – I think Henry Clay – said that if I was right this was the best news he had heard for a long time for his children and grandchildren. I think this gives a correct impression of conventional wisdom at the time.

I continued working on the subject and in March 1954 gave a further report of my findings in a lecture at the LSE, which was published in August in *Economica*, the LSE's journal. I outlined the main arguments that had been used to show that the dollar problem was chronic, added one or two of my own for good measure, then set out the counter-arguments, which seemed to me equally strong. I concluded, agnostically, that, 'in my opinion, it would require a very courageous man to forecast either chronic dollar shortage or its absence during the coming decades. I for one lack the necessary courage.' I cast doubt, on the basis of preliminary calculations, on the widespread current belief that productivity rose faster in the US than in the rest of the world, and later documented this doubt fully in *The Review of Economics and Statistics*, published by Harvard University. (In my work on this and other matters I was greatly helped, as I had been in the past and continued to be for several years, by Monica Dowley, who cheerfully tackled – single-handed – calculations of a size and complexity that would have daunted many a team of statisticians.)

I also poked a little polite fun at John Hicks' Inaugural Lecture (published in June 1953 in *Oxford Economic Papers*) which had been on the dollar problem, which he regarded as serious and long term. My criticisms (amplified later in my book on the subject) were partly of his theoretical analysis, but also of his empirical assumptions, some of which seemed at variance with the real world. For example, he argued that productivity in American agriculture increased relatively slowly; that the US was an exporter of agricultural products; and that this was bad for the rest of the world and would turn the terms of trade (the ratio of export to import prices) against it. I pointed out that, in fact, US productivity had gone up faster in agriculture than in industry, not more slowly; that the US was a net importer of agricultural products, not a net exporter; and that the terms of trade had moved against the US, not in her favour.

Despite such disagreements with Hicks, we were good friends. I enjoyed going to the discussion group he held after dinner each Monday in term in his flat in Woodstock Road. He started this early in 1948 and his letter inviting me to join the group said he had in mind 'particularly those who have started teaching in the last year or two' – a phrase I naughtily believed he concocted to exclude Tommy Balogh. At the end of each meeting Ursula his wife, also a well-known economist, produced a fruit cake and coffee. I enjoyed too visiting them in their lovely house in Blockley in the Cotswolds, where Ursula's green fingers made a beautiful garden which, however, at one stage gave John tetanus while he was pruning the roses.

After the LSE lecture I should have spent, say, a year completing my calculations, refining my arguments and producing a short book on the dollar problem with the same agnostic conclusion. But I got fascinated with the subject, and with all manner of related matters, and worked away at them for another two-and-a-half years. I also made long-term projections of the US balance of payments, on optimistic and pessimistic assumptions, looking in detail both at rates of inflation in the US and other countries and at possible 'structural' trends in trade and other transactions even if price levels moved broadly in line. These suggested that a favourable or neutral trend in the world's balance with the US was quite possible, but an adverse one more probable. Given that such a trend was unlikely to be smooth and more likely to manifest itself in 'bumps' I concluded, rather cautiously, not that the problem was chronic, but that there was 'a distinct possibility that the world will from time to time run into substantial deficit with the US'; and, after giving reasons why it might not always be possible to remove this quickly by exchange rate changes, that it was 'as likely as not that a widespread dollar problem will recur, say, a couple of times during the next twenty years'. I also discussed implications for policy.

The book – *The World Dollar Problem* – ran to some 600 pages, about one-third devoted to nearly fifty appendices. It went to the publishers in the autumn of 1956 and was published in July 1957. It received early, and widespread, publicity, partly because of the timing of publication. The world's balance with the US had been continuously in surplus while I was writing it. Although this was more than accounted for by US aid to other countries and their restrictions on dollar expenditure, one had been hearing less and less about the dollar problem. Then, while my book was going through the press, the rest of the world suddenly – and conveniently for sales – went into substantial deficit with the US. There was much renewed talk about the dollar problem which gave the book a good deal more topicality than it would otherwise have had.

I had several dozen reviews quite quickly, nearly all extremely complimentary. Had I written a play, the theatre where it was appearing would have had no difficulty finding flattering pithy phrases to hang outside: masterly survey; monumental treatise; classic study; indispensable reading; admirably lucid and thorough; a model of economic analysis; impressive; scholarly; rigorous yet readable; a challenge to Governments on both sides of the Atlantic. The *City Press* certainly brought me down to earth and stopped me getting too swollen headed. 'Interesting nonsense' was its comment; and 'not for a moment do we accept the views of Sir Donald MacDougall'. But otherwise there was surprisingly little criticism even by those from whom I might have expected it, like Ralph (later Lord) Harris, who that year became General Director of the Institute of Economic Affairs, and whose review in the *New Commonwealth* seemed to agree with me completely. No doubt he had forgotten this when he derided my 'false forecast' in *The Statist* in January 1964.

I took seriously the criticisms of three reviewers in particular. First, Roy Harrod – who had spent hours reading my drafts and given invaluable advice – would have preferred me to concentrate on my refutation of the traditional arguments of the chronic dollar shortage school, and to omit my quantitative projections. After a very friendly introduction he criticised my book as 'somewhat too pessimistic' and 'too defeatist'. Then there was Bob (Professor Robert) Triffin, of Yale, an old friend from Paris days – where we called him 'The Little King' after a cartoon of a chubby little monarch popular at that time – and an expert on international finance. He stressed 'the vast area of agreement on fundamentals which exists between us', but when it came to my long-term projections, while neither agreeing nor disagreeing with them, he was sceptical of the whole approach. Finally, Walther Lederer, of the US Department of Commerce, wrote a thoughtful review in the *Manchester Guardian*. He was a charming man of Austrian origin and had helped me greatly in preparing my book, knowing more about US balance of payments statistics than any other living soul (although by then I almost regarded myself as a close second). His criticism was not about my use of these statistics, but of a more general nature. I was pleased to get a letter not long after from Richard Fry, Financial Editor of the *Manchester Guardian* (and later of *The Guardian*) for a quarter of a century, saying: 'I have been reading your book on odd evenings at home, and I must say it is beginning to persuade me against my inclination'.

Around this time I had numerous requests to write articles on the dollar problem. I wrote one for the *Financial Times* a few weeks *before* my book was published, which included a trailer for it, incorporating the latest figures for the US balance of payments which Lederer had kindly given me in advance; my article was timed to appear immediately after the figures were released in Washington. I tried in these articles to play down the worsening in the world's balance with the US because it was much sharper than I had expected and I felt it might well be a flash in the pan. I was therefore annoyed when I wrote another article for the FT six months later in a suitably cautious tone, and some sub-editor changed my neutral title to 'Dollar Shortage Again'. (I have since got used to, and come to tolerate, the ways of sub-editors.)

I was right to be annoyed because, as I thought might happen, the world's balance with the US went sharply into surplus again in 1958 and 1959; and, although it began to worsen again later in 1959, and came back to within the limits I had projected in my book, people began to wonder whether there was not a dollar problem in reverse – that it was the Americans who had to worry about running into deficit with the rest of the world, not the other way round.

This led Professor Fritz Machlup of Princeton University to invite me in 1960 to write a reappraisal for their series of *Essays in International Finance*. I had been following the situation closely but thought that, before putting pen to paper, I should visit the US. This I did during the first few weeks of July and had talks with numerous officials, academics, bankers and others in Washington, New York and Boston.

After this trip I felt much more confident about writing my 70-odd page piece on *The Dollar Problem: A Reappraisal*. It was published in November. Essentially, I returned to the agnostic conclusion in my LSE lecture. Some kind friends have suggested that the huge rise in the dollar exchange rate in the first part of the 1980s, to a level against a basket of currencies far above that when I was writing my book, shows that I was right after all, except that the world's craving for dollars came rather later than I had expected; but I confess that this was hardly the kind of dollar problem I was thinking about.

My book was used a good deal for teaching for a few years, but as time went by, and the danger of a dollar problem seemed more and more unlikely, I believe it was used less and less. This is rather a pity, because it contains a good deal of empirical and theoretical analysis of general interest which is quite independent of the dollar problem.

A fortnight before my book was published the Prof died. This left a large void in my life because in some ways I had got to know him better than I have known any other man. I had seen him regularly since coming back to Nuffield in 1953, both on social occasions and when I used to pop into his rooms in Christ Church and chat about this and that – sometimes even economics. He told me that 'Rab' Butler, who remained Chancellor for over two years after we returned to Oxford, had asked him to persuade me to go back and help him in the Treasury. This was surprising, and rather pleasing, following our dispute over ROBOT; but it was out of the question to ask for yet more leave – and in any case I wanted to get on with my book.

Prof's death came as a shock. He had for some time been talking of having one foot in the grave, but always jocularly, and I had never taken him too seriously; and only about a week before he died I sat next to him at a Wadham Gaudy when he was in sparkling form. I had been asked to propose the toast of the College and prepared a speech containing some risqué jokes which I thought appropriate for the occasion. But just before dinner some Fellows told me this would not do, so I implored Prof to give me some good, clean stories to replace them. Instead, he regaled me with a succession of hilarious jokes, more ribald than any I had proposed to use. That was the last time I saw him. A day or two after his death his brother Charles arrived from Washington, where he lived. (One of his war-time duties was to call periodically on Roosevelt to place in his hands up to date volumes of the charts we drew in Prof's Branch – with Churchill's compliments.) He asked me round to Prof's rooms and invited me to take anything I liked from a collection of Prof's treasures laid out on a large table. I chose two of his numerous tennis trophies, dating from before the First World War when he (and his brother) won many tournaments on the Continent. One was a silver-topped claret jug with the following inscription:

Lawn Tennis – Tournier
Darmstadt 1902
1. Preis
Herren Doppelspiel
Ohne Vorgabe
F.A. Lindemann

The other was a silver cigarette box (in which I keep pens and pencils) inscribed:

F.A. L.
Academic Championship
1st Prize
Jena 1912

Prof also left me £1,000 in his will.

Readers of these memoirs so far will have got some flavour of Prof's personality, character and abilities as I saw them. I can recommend Harrod's memoir, *The Prof*, published in 1959, for a fascinating account of how Roy saw them; also the official biography, *The Prof in Two Worlds*, published in November 1961 by the second Lord Birkenhead (son of F E Smith, the illustrious son of Wadham mentioned earlier). He acknowledged most generously, in his preface, the help I gave him which he described as 'a labour of love for his old chief'.

I cannot so recommend C P Snow's description of Prof in *Science and Government*, published early in 1961, my review of which in *The Oxford Magazine* of 18 May 1961 was by far the most caustic I have ever written. The book, based on lectures in Harvard in 1960, was mainly about two disputes between Prof and another distinguished scientist, Sir Henry Tizard – on radar before the war and strategic bombing in 1942 – with Snow very much on Tizard's side. I had no personal evidence on these matters, though others well qualified to judge, including Professor R V Jones, Sir Charles Webster and Sir Robert Watson-Watt, had, shortly before I wrote my review, exposed in the press the highly distorted nature of Snow's story and shown him to be wrong on many factual matters (Birkenhead later reached the same conclusions). I did, however, feel qualified to comment on Prof's personality. To quote a few passages from my review:

I find the abominable Snow man quite unrecognisable. The 'savage', 'malevolent', 'sadistic' man in fact spent endless time doing kindnesses to others, though always by stealth. The 'brown eyes' which 'were usually sad', except when 'glowing with a gleeful sneer', in fact more often than not contained a cheerful, friendly twinkle.

The man who was accepted in 'Society' only because he was 'rich and determined' was a delightful companion and an outstanding conversationalist, versatile and amusing. It is evident that Sir Charles completely missed the point of the Prof's sense of humour, of his wit and of his satire.

It would be absurd to claim that Cherwell was universally liked, or that he had no failings. But too many who did not know him well saw only these and not his likeable qualities. And a man who was a close friend of Churchill for so many years can hardly have been the completely odious character portrayed by Sir Charles.

The book contains tiresome little inaccuracies which could easily have been avoided. For example, the statement that Lindemann 'was not an Englishman but became one' is wrong. He was born well after his father was naturalised, although his mother was taking the cure in Baden-Baden at the time. The man Snow claims to have had no interest in literature or in any other art was in fact a good pianist and widely read; his rooms were filled with serious books of many kinds; he was himself a practitioner of the literary art, having an exceptional command of crisp and telling phrase, and was critical of anything that fell short of his high standards of literary form.

Such mistakes do not increase one's confidence in the more important assertions on which Sir Charles bases his thesis. It seems that a scientific training does not always instil the habit of checking one's facts.

I had many grateful letters from Prof's friends about this review, and Birkenhead ordered a dozen copies of *The Oxford Magazine* to send, as he put it in a letter to me, 'to some of the misguided people who, I know, have been influenced by Snow'.

When I moved from Wadham to Nuffield the Warden was Alec Loveday, who had become an Official Fellow in 1946 and Warden in 1949. He had served for years in the League of Nations Secretariat on economic and statistical matters; and I feel that the excellence of the League's publications in this field – which in my view were generally better than those of its successor, the United Nations – must have been due in considerable part to him. I personally got on very well with him, which I regarded as a privilege because he did not hit it off with everybody. I continued to keep in touch with him after he retired in 1954, and when he knew he was dying he told me, made me promise not to tell anyone else, and gave me a cheque to be given to the Senior Common Room after his death. I found it macabre that cashing a dead man's cheque was so difficult, but in the end the S C R got his gift.

He was succeeded by Norman Chester, an old friend from war-time days who had become an Official Fellow in 1945, and must have been disappointed not to be chosen as Warden in 1949 when Henry Clay retired. He did, however, rule the College for nearly quarter of a century, and so had plenty of time to exercise an enormous influence on its development; and when I had the honour of proposing his health at a dinner in 1974 to celebrate his Knighthood I had no difficulty in showing that that influence had been very much for the good.

Norman was a bluff Lancastrian, with a distinctive, bushy, but always well-groomed, moustache. He had wide interests ranging far beyond his main field of public administration. These included Association Football, on which he was such an expert that Harold Wilson, when Prime Minister, made him Chairman of a Committee to inquire into its problems. Not least among his achievements was a reconciliation of Lord Nuffield to the College. For a time, he displayed a certain coolness towards it; he felt he had been cheated by the University in the negotiations leading to its foundation, and misled about the arrangements for preparing the original design of the building, which he rejected; he also disapproved of certain war-time activities of the College, particularly some of those directed by G D H Cole. But, thanks largely to Norman Chester's patient efforts, there was a gradual rapprochement, and the Founder arranged substantial additional finance for the College and began coming to dinner with us. It was pleasant and interesting to meet and chat with the grand old man. He certainly did not look his age – he was born in 1877 – but I sometimes found him a little sad.

The building was not completed for a long time after I came back in 1953, and I suffered from the thud of pile-drivers; but I had become used to noise while working during the war. My colleagues and I spent many hours discussing details of the buildings with the architects. We had particular trouble with the wine cellar. The Senior Common Room had been lent £3,000 by the College to build up a stock of wine, and I was put in charge. As at first we had no cellar I kept most of it with merchants in London. Then, when we looked at the first plans for a cellar under the Hall, I pointed out to the architects that it was next to the boilerhouse and asked if this was a good idea. At the next meeting they assured me it would be all right. I was unconvinced so at the following meeting they produced plans for an extra thick wall between cellar and boiler. I am unsure whether there were further such exchanges but eventually it was agreed to go ahead. When everything was built I asked how soon I could put wine in the cellar and was told 'straight away'. But to be on the safe side I decided first to put in a minimax thermometer which I observed daily; and, sure enough, the temperature rose from 40° to 50°, to 60°, to 70°, to 80° . . . The architects then said it would be necessary to instal refrigerating equipment but, as the cost would have been prohibitive, we had to abandon the cellar and build another elsewhere.

I enjoyed being in charge of the wine (and spirits) for many obvious reasons. But I had difficulty with my colleagues – even some of the economists – about pricing policy. Some Colleges were selling vintage port of great age to the Fellows at the original *historic* cost, often ludicrously low. I had to persuade our Fellows that, given inflation and the appreciation over time in the value of wines laid down, I had to charge *replacement* cost if they did not want our stock of wine gradually to dwindle away. In later life I used this example when arguing the need for inflation accounting.

I should have known that Oxford dons were not 'economic men' when it comes to wine. This had been shown by F Y Edgeworth, that great holder of the Drummond Chair for over thirty years, in my favourite footnote in economic literature in *The Economic Journal* of 1907. He had kept a meticulous record of 98 Sunday dinners during 1903–1906 in 'a certain Oxford College' – presumably All Souls, of which he was a Fellow – showing the numbers dining and consumption of wine per head. This showed no tendency for the latter to be greater the larger the company. He thus refuted both the view that larger parties, being more convivial, are associated with heavier drinking, and the hypothesis that, since the total cost of the wine was divided equally among those who had 'taken part in the potation' so that the cost to an individual of an extra glass was smaller the larger the party, he would tend to drink more – as might have been expected of an 'economic man'.

In due course the Duke of Edinburgh came to the College, primarily to present the Royal Charter. Twenty-four hours before, the place was a shambles, with builders' litter everywhere, but by the time he arrived it had been tidied up miraculously. This, however, had been achieved in part by dumping rubbish into convenient areas concealed by low walls and, would you believe it, Prince Philip unerringly walked up to one of these and looked over. After lunch, at which he made a characteristically entertaining speech, he was a little ahead of schedule so the Warden took him to look at the room of a Student studying Anglo-American relations. When they entered, without knocking, they fittingly found an American Student and an English girl embracing on the sofa.

Until the College became fully independent in 1958 the University managed our investments. When we took over responsibility (formally in June but effectively, to a large extent, earlier) we sold nearly all the agricultural land and concentrated mainly on equities. It was decided not to hand our investments over to a merchant bank to manage. I was appointed 'First Bursar' and Ian Little (who first made his name as a welfare economist and later turned his attention to developing countries) 'Second Bursar'. Under the guidance of an investment committee, which gave us much helpful advice but great freedom of action, we ran the portfolio. We chose Vickers da Costa as our brokers – we had both used them privately before – and worked mainly with Ralph Vickers, the senior partner. After a short while Ian and I took it in turn to do this for periods of usually six to twelve months each. This worked well, and was in fact necessary because during nearly half of the four years (1958–61) we worked together one or the other was out of the country.

We did rather well. We were lucky in our timing. The *Financial Times* index doubled during 1958 and 1959 before levelling off in 1960 and 1961. But we also beat the index by a handsome margin. This was partly because we got in early on the fashion of growth stocks – buying mainly those of companies whose profits had increased markedly over a period of years. In 1959 Vickers set up a Trust called Investing in Success Equities, Ltd ('Insects' for short) to operate mainly on this basis. I was a founding Director and Ian joined the Board later. Then, would you believe it, he published in November 1962 an article called 'Higgledy Piggledy Growth' which concluded, after careful statistical analysis, that there was no tendency whatsoever for companies whose earnings had shown above average growth in the past to do so in the future. Rather letting the side down one might think. But I had by then resigned my Directorship on going to Neddy; the Trust (and Nuffield) had already done extremely well; the 'growth cult' was dying; and 'Insects' was now adopting a much more sophisticated approach.

I had certainly done so while investing for Nuffield, using past growth as only one of many criteria in deciding what to buy or sell. We were very active, turning over a high proportion of our portfolio most years. Ralph Vickers would ring me up nearly every morning for what was sometimes an embarrassingly long talk. When I had pupils there they were at first impressed but later got impatient as they saw their allotted time with me slipping away. I got into the habit of taking the *Investors' Chronicle* home at weekends, looking at preliminary results, including those of quite small companies, and selecting a few for further examination. I would then come into College on Monday morning and look at the relevant 'Moodies' cards (alas no longer with us) which we kept up-to-date in the Bursary, and any other information about the companies I could lay my hands on, and discuss perhaps one or two with Ralph. I eventually bought a small fraction of those I had provisionally picked out at weekends. It was surprising, but gratifying, how often the market came round to the view that they were good buys a week or so after I had; I am sure that today, with the greatly increased expertise of brokers and institutions, the market is much quicker off the mark. One problem was getting Ralph to sell. His father, also a stock-broker, had told him 'always buy, never sell', and he took a lot of persuading that this was impossible with a fixed fund. So I had to do most of my selling while he was away, through junior members of the firm.

Our method of operating increased the proportion of smaller firms in the College's portfolio. I also reached two general conclusions. The first was that good stocks to buy seemed to be about as common in declining as in expanding industries; and indeed that going for the latter could be a mistake – as often as not there would be over-investment, pressure on margins and a fall in profits. The second was that playing the market as a whole was not worth while, given the size of fluctuations we had experienced since the war. Allowing for the impossibility of getting out exactly at the top and in again exactly at the bottom, for commission, stamp duty and the jobbers' turn, and for the impracticability of going liquid on more than a fraction of a College's total portfolio, it seemed most unlikely that one could make at best more than a few per cent on the latter; and that the time and nervous energy would be much better spent in selecting the right shares to buy and sell. This is what I did, and allowed my view of the market as a whole to influence only the timing of these transactions, and by not more than a week or two.

I became a bit of an expert for a time. Once I sent to the brokers forecasts of the next dividends on each of the 30 shares in the FT index. The partners were amused and wrote down their own forecasts. I believe I beat them all and got about the first 20 spot on; I only went wrong when we came to a company which declared a dividend not as a round percentage but in terms of pence, with decimal points.

It was all good fun but time consuming. I was usually quite glad when the time came to hand over to Ian for a spell; and indeed not sorry when I gave it up completely. I certainly could not have borne to be a stockbroker, or investing for an institution, all my life.

For six years after returning to Nuffield in 1953 I had no leave of absence from the College. I had some jaunts abroad but only during vacations. In the Easter vac of 1954 I went to a Conference in Lahore of, broadly speaking, the 'Chatham Houses' (Institutes of International Affairs) of the Commonwealth. The leader of the British delegation – about a dozen strong – was Hugh Gaitskell. This was the first time I really got to know him, both at preparatory meetings in London and at the Conference itself, where he not only showed his intellectual and debating abilities and grasp of economics and politics but was also the life and soul of the party on social occasions. We flew first to Delhi in Tourist Class, which was not very comfortable. But when the pilot discovered that our party included not only politicians (Tory and Labour), academics, journalists and similar riff-raff, but also a Marshal of the Royal Air Force – Sir John Slessor – we got VIP treatment. This was fortunate because the journey took nearly 30 hours.

My main recollections of the Conference are: my decision not to visit the Khyber pass on a Sunday when we had the day off, because I felt I must prepare for economic sessions on Monday and Tuesday – I have since learned to put pleasure before business; and how often, whether the Conference was due to discuss race relations, the United Nations, defence, the cold war, the sterling area, convertibility, the dollar problem, Commonwealth Preference, or whatever, we got round sooner or later to a heated argument between the Indians and Pakistanis about Kashmir.

In 1954 I had been invited by Professor Willard Thorp, of Amherst College in Massachusetts, to spend up to two months in the summer at the Merrill Center for Economics in Southampton, Long Island. This had been strongly recommended to me by Austin Robinson, Alec Cairncross, Hugh Gaitskell and Robert Marjolin, all of whom had been there in the summer of 1953 when it was first established, both for its intellectual and for its sybaritic attractions; but I declined partly because I had been away from my family quite enough during the past few years and also because I desperately wanted to get on with my book on the dollar. When, however, I was again asked in 1955, I had made sufficient progress on the book to feel that I would benefit by discussing some of my problems over there. So I agreed to go for four weeks in August.

I flew to New York overnight in great comfort in a sleeping bunk, then proceeded less comfortably in an excruciatingly slow train which took nearly three hours to cover barely a hundred miles to Southampton, at the far end of Long Island. There I found the luxurious house in which I was to stay; also a couple of dozen people, mainly economists, with whom I was to spend at least the next fortnight and, in many cases, the next four weeks; fresh faces arrived to replace those who left after my first two weeks. They were an impressive lot – many old friends but I made many new ones – including American and other academics and almost as many from international organisations, US Government agencies and the financial world, one of this last group being from the New York stockbrokers Merrill Lynch, who were footing the bill.

It was probably the most enjoyable and stimulating working holiday I have ever spent. It was also extremely well organised by Willard Thorp and his wife Clarise. We met for discussions for about 3 ½ hours in the morning and 2 ½ after dinner, for 4 ½ days in the week. The afternoons were free as were the weekends from Friday lunchtime. Austin Robinson had told me it was hard work, and tiring, but I did not find it so. I think he took it more seriously than I did and spent a lot of the afternoons working. Although I had to open quite a few discussions at short notice, it required little preparation as I was currently working on most of the subjects.

In the afternoons I usually went bathing in the big waves of the Atlantic shore. I also had a game of golf – the first for twenty years – with Professor Ingvar Svennilson from Sweden. He later invited me to lecture in Stockholm and meet academics, Government officials, bankers and the like. I spent a most pleasant week there, although it was one of the most teetotal in my life. In the plane coming back my next door neighbour was a businessman who complained that he had just had the most alcoholic week of his life; we had evidently been moving in different circles.

Each weekend I went to see friends – in Washington, Boston, Canada and New York. I fortunately found a quicker way than the train of getting to the other end of Long Island and back. It was on one of a couple of tiny amphibious planes operating a highly convenient service that summer. They took off and came down on water at Southampton and on land at La Guardia, near New York City. On each of my flights I sat next to the pilot and was the only passenger. Perhaps this was not surprising. Before landing at La Guardia he would ask me to look out and see whether the wheel on my side was down; and when coming down at Southampton to shout out if I saw sticks poking out of the water – there were many of these, securing fishermen's nets. Also, the radar was being repaired – there was hole in the cockpit where it should have been – so when we were approaching or leaving La Guardia, a busy airport, he asked me to keep a good lookout for other aircraft. Only once did I funk the flight – on a Sunday evening when there was a violent, and seemingly unending, thunderstorm; so I took the train.

Early in 1957 I was invited to a Conference in Jamaica in August on 'Economic Development in Underdeveloped Countries', organised by the Jamaican Government and the University College of the West Indies. I was keen to see the Caribbean and begin to learn some development economics; but the trouble was that so far I knew little or none. When, however, I confessed this to the organisers, and told them my paper would have to be very general, though I hoped it would provoke discussion, the invitation was not withdrawn. So I happily accepted.

I wrote a paper on the merits of bold and cautious development plans, with particular reference to the balance of payments. It did stimulate discussion, including comments from Dr K S Krishnaswamy, an Indian currently at the Economic Development Institute of the World Bank in Washington, who used India's development programmes to illustrate my analysis. During my wanderings round Jamaica both before and during the Conference – which included three long field trips as well as discussion sessions − I learned more about developing countries than I had done during my whole previous existence. I even felt able to give a radio interview − how irresponsible one can be when abroad. I also learned how keen, and good, Jamaicans are at speech-making. On our field trips someone had to make one at every agricultural project, sugar refinery, community hall, factory or whatever that we visited; I made several myself. And of course, when I called on the Minister of Finance before a lunch party, we had first to listen in his office to the one o'clock news to hear the latest Test Match score. But although they played cricket rather than baseball the American influence was evident. When we spent a lovely Sunday on the northern shore at Ocho Rios, little boys swarmed round us saying we could take their photograph for seven shillings; this seemed an odd sum until I realised it was approximately equal to a US dollar (£1 was then worth $2.80).

In January 1958 the dictatorship of Pérez Jiménez of Venezuela was overthrown. As a result I spent a couple of months of the following long vac in that country. It happened like this. A young political exile, Dr Carrillo, had been attending graduate classes in economics at Columbia University, particularly those of Professor Carl Shoup, an authority on public finance. On his return to Venezuela after the dictator's fall he helped persuade the Minister of Finance to ask Shoup to direct a study of the country's fiscal system − including, as background, a description of the economy. I was invited by Shoup, whom I had never met, to do the latter. The others in the team were Stanley Surrey and Oliver Oldmam, two tax law Professors from Harvard Law School; Lyle Fitch, First Deputy City Administrator in New York; and John Due, Professor of Economics at the University of Illinois − half a dozen of us in all.

I flew out *via* New York. At London airport I was sought out by a representative from Shell, who had somehow got to know what I was up to, and given masses of literature on Venezuela. Although our group was precluded, by its terms of reference, from recommending changes in the taxation of oil companies, we were bound to discuss − and in fact did − some of the relevant issues; and Shell had an obvious interest in any report on the country, where they had a large stake. (It was interesting how important the company was regarded by British residents in Venezuela. When I asked one what he would do if he got invitations to dinner on the same evening from the British Ambassador and the head of Shell, he unhesitatingly replied that he would accept the latter.) On arrival in New York in the early hours of the morning I was met by someone from Shell who whisked me through customs and immigration to a huge limousine in which I was driven to a palatial suite in the Waldorf-Astoria. It was a pity I had only a few hours to enjoy its luxury, complete with champagne and whisky which I dared not touch as I had a meeting after breakfast at Shell's New York office. They then drove me back to the airport to wait in their private set of rooms until my plane to Caracas was ready to leave; and there were still people there to look after me when the plane returned a couple of hours later as one of the engines had caught fire.

In Venezuela, before putting pen to paper, we spent a considerable time collecting information and impressions, in Caracas and on trips all over the country. One impression was of the youthfulness of many in powerful positions. A Professor I met was seriously afraid of failing students in case one should shortly afterwards become Minister of Education – which it seemed quite possible to do in one's twenties – and then fire him. Once, when I went to see the head of a bank – it may even have been the Central Bank – and asked the young man in the office I first entered if he would kindly tell him I had arrived, he stretched out his hand and said: 'I am he'.

Then there were the waste and corruption which had been massive under the previous regime. It was reckoned that one-third of public capital expenditure had gone on bribes. One example of waste and inefficiency that struck me was when we went to see an iron mountain near the Orinoco and a steel works being built nearby. The latter was getting nowhere, partly because a team of engineers from one country was checking on a team from another. The only thing completed was a very tall, thin, office building, which did not make much economic sense when the land for a hundred miles around was almost entirely empty and thus virtually a 'free good'; and only the top floor was in use – as a cocktail bar. We spent the night down there – not in the cocktail bar – the excuse being that our plane was being repaired; but the real reason was a rumour of a coup in Caracas against the Government, still precariously placed. All turned out to be well, although when we got back to the capital we were driven on a very circuitous route from the airport to our hotel, carefully avoiding the city centre.

Another impression was of the huge inequalities in living standards. This was the subject of the first chapter I wrote – and of the book eventually published by the team entitled *The Fiscal System of Venezuela*. This was, I am told, one of the first quantitative analyses of the distribution of incomes in Latin America. I was surprised by the amount of information I was able to unearth, partly because officials gave me figures on things like income tax returns and payrolls in far more detail than would have been possible in Britain with our rules on confidentiality. I even got figures for the very large incomes of named individuals, at least as declared to the authorities; and the incentive to understate was small because tax rates were so low. Some relevant surveys had also been made recently by a market research organisation, Caracas University and the Agricultural Ministry. The

Central Bank, which bravely produced national income estimates, was also helpful.

My study showed striking inequalities, both between individuals and between town and country, regions, and economic sectors. I reckoned that average income in Caracas was ten times that in rural areas; that, on average, oil workers' earnings were nearly twenty times those of agricultural workers, earnings of professional people around seventy times, and incomes of some large landowners and capitalists very much larger. A handful of families controlled many of the large businesses. A few thousand landlords owned most of the agricultural land, leaving a tiny fraction for the *campesino* eking out a living on a small family plot, of whom there were hundreds of thousands, and who, according to the University survey, 'tills the soil with his hands, aided sometimes with the traditional pico, planting stick, and machete; 66% of them have no other tools'.

After doing some complicated sums, using pretty heroic assumptions, I concluded that the lowest 45% of income receivers got one-tenth of the total, and the top 12% one-half (the results would have been more striking had I been able to estimate the share of, say, the top 3–4%). Moreover, public finance did not change this general picture: the tax system was only very mildly progressive, and its small effects were probably offset by a tendency for government expenditure to benefit the rich more than the poor. I also wrote the book's second chapter, on 'General Economic Considerations Relevant to Public Finance'. It covered the waterfront, but I make no attempt to summarise it. It was interesting to study an economy in which the Government got a stream of manna from heaven in the form of taxes and royalties from foreign oil companies; and I found it relevant when analysing, years later, the implications for Britain of North Sea Oil.

During my last weeks in Venezuela I worked furiously, completing my calculations and drafting and redrafting my chapters. I worked mainly in my hotel bedroom and later and later into the night. Before going to bed I would dictate what I had written on to tapes and put them into Carl Shoup's pigeon hole in the lobby. He always got up early and was moreover a saintly character. So as soon as he had breakfasted, he took these to our office in mid-town, some miles away, had them typed, and returned with the drafts just as I was emerging from my room around noon. Without his cooperation in this menial task, on top of his responsibilities as leader of our group, I could never have finished in time.

After I got back to Oxford in September 1958 I stayed put for most of the following year. My only journey abroad was to Addis Ababa, where the UN had just established an Economic Commission for Africa, with Mekki Abbas, a large Sudanese, as the first Executive Secretary. He had been a

Nuffield Student, working under the highly distinguished Africanist Margery (later Dame Margery) Perham, whose colleague as a Fellow I had the privilege to be for many years, and in partnership with whom I once very nearly won the College croquet tournament. Mekki invited me to advise on the setting up of the new organisation. This I did during the Easter vac of 1959, but could spend only a week.

I spent quite a lot of time during this academic year on the College investments, especially as Ian Little was in India for the whole period. I also got interested in inflation. I had been uneasy about the Government's restrictive measures in 1957 in an attempt to control it. I was sceptical of the arguments of economists like Professors Paish and Phillips (of 'Phillips curve' fame) that inflation could be prevented if we settled for an unemployment level only moderately higher than we had experienced since 1945; and that any attempt to change the attitude of pay negotiators was both unnecessary and a waste of time, because settlements were determined by the level of unemployment as though by an iron law. So I worked away at this and prepared a course of lectures which turned out to be largely a refutation of these arguments based on quantitative analysis of the evidence. I found myself unconvinced that reasonably full employment and reasonable price stability could necessarily be combined, at least without some form of policy for incomes, although I recognised that this bristled with economic, political and administrative difficulties.

For some years I had been pressed by the Australian National University (ANU) in Canberra, which was engaged wholly in research and had no undergraduates, to go there for a minimum of about six months as Visiting Professor of Economics and Finance. The Chair had been established with financial support from Australian banks, including the Commonwealth Bank. I was keen to see Australia and the duties were light, involving mainly doing my own research, discussing that of others, and giving a few lectures and seminars in Canberra and elsewhere. One trouble was that to be away for six months, even if I included the long vac, meant asking the College for a term's leave of absence. This I was loth to do until I had been back for a considerable spell after my two years with Prof in London. But I judged that by the summer of 1959, when I should have had six years without leave, it was reasonable to ask for the autumn term off. So, after several polite refusals of offers from Canberra, I agreed to go for roughly the second half of that year. This was to be the only period when I could correctly be called 'Professor', although I have declined a good many offers of Chairs in various parts of the world in my time.

I travelled in a westerly direction, seeing many old colleagues on the way, and on arrival at Sydney the Commonwealth Bank gave me red carpet treatment. The Governor, 'Nugget' Coombs, a tiny but wonderful man, soon became a great friend; he had somewhat left wing views for a banker and extremely wide interests, including economics generally, the theatre, ballet, the ANU, almost anything you can think of. The next day I flew to Canberra and was met by Trevor Swan, Head of the Economics Department, who had been a colleague on a UN committee in 1951, and taken to University House where I was to stay. It was extremely comfortable and tried to be like an Oxbridge College, though it took some getting used to; I remember having dinner at 6.15, preceded by sherry at 5.45 and followed by port at 7.15.

A few minutes' walk away I had a room in the Economics Department of the ANU, where I could sit and work, or pop in and chat with congenial colleagues who helped me enormously with my research and taught me a great deal about Australia. Trevor's room had to be seen to be believed. Against one wall was a huge pile of unopened letters, and I now understood why I had sometimes found it difficult to correspond with him. Another colleague was Ivor Pearce – an Englishman who later returned to a Chair in Southampton – from whom I learned much about the theory of international trade.

The standard of economists in Australia was high; but there were exceptions. One Professor, at a University that shall be nameless, had, as I had been warned, rather gone to seed and got out of touch. When he heard I was at Oxford he asked: 'Have you got Marshall's Chair?' and 'Do you see much of Keynes these days?' Apart from getting the University wrong he seemed unaware that Keynes was long since dead.

It was wonderful to be largely free from administration and teaching. But I did not by any means spend all my time researching and discussing economics in Canberra. I visited every State except Tasmania – and both islands of New Zealand. Nor did I visit only the capitals, but also saw much of the countryside, and smaller towns. I met hundreds of people, not only economists but other academics, civil servants, farmers, bankers, other businessmen, journalists and many others. I naturally had to sing for my supper. My repertoire of talks included the dollar, inflation in the UK (I compressed my Oxford course of lectures into one) and, later, international investment (on which I did new research). Perhaps my friendliest reception was in Wellington where the local paper reported that, in the discussion following a lecture I gave there: 'Sir Donald fielded questions with the informal ease of another Sir Donald on another field' (referring, of course, to Don Bradman, the cricketer).

But it was not all work. I had lots of fun. There was much social life, and once one got to know Australians one could joke about things like their allegedly classless society. Then there was the Melbourne Cup, the nation's greatest horse race, when I – and many friends – naturally backed a horse called 'Macdougal' (his mother had died when foaling and a Miss Macdougal had brought him up on a bottle – presumably of milk, not whisky). It won, at 10 to 1, and I was popular at Flemington Race Course that day. The horse's name was, it is true, not spelt my way, but I did meet a man called Donald MacDougall, spelt my way, in Queensland – the only time I have ever done so.

I even got some fishing, catching small trout near Canberra and much bigger ones in Lake Taupo in New Zealand. But they were not so big as they used to be. I saw a photograph of an angler taken many years before, surrounded by half a ton of trout that he had caught in the same place in one day. That was when, I was told, they averaged ten pounds, having grown rapidly after their introduction from Britain; by 1959 the average was more like three. I enjoyed even more being taken by a New Zealand Professor round his large garden, through which meandered a stream full of trout. Though a keen fisherman, he would not have dreamt of trying to catch one. They were his friends and, as he took me from pool to pool, he introduced me: 'Here is Jim; there is Joe'.

My research on international investment was stimulated by a controversy then raging in Australia. Many were arguing that private investment from abroad was bad for the country; commonly quoted was an American car company that had made quite a small initial investment and was now taking much larger sums each year out of the country. So I studied the problem, helped greatly by colleagues in Canberra and elsewhere, and wrote an article entitled 'The benefits and costs of private investment from abroad: a theoretical approach'. Though cautious in my published conclusions, I formed the view that investment from overseas was in general a good bet for Australia. The article appeared in *The Economic Record* (the Journal of the Economic Society of Australia and New Zealand), which also published my lecture on inflation in the UK. The former was reprinted in the *Bulletin of the Oxford University Institute of Statistics*. It turned out to be one of my better known studies and stimulated a good deal of further literature. As late as 1985 I received a paper from a Japanese economist saying it was based on mine; but as its thirty pages consisted largely of unintelligible mathematics I could neither check nor comment.

I left Canberra on Boxing Day 1959 and, after short stays in Singapore and Bangkok to see friends, spent a few days in New Delhi where I was cared for by Jagdish Bhagwati. I had supervised him when he was a Nuffield Student and he subsequently achieved a world-wide reputation in both international and development economics. On 31 December he took me to Agra to see the Taj Mahal. He had got hold of an aged Government car and a driver. We left Agra rather late and the car kept stopping. We somehow managed to start it again each time though once, when it stopped on a level crossing without gates, we had to push hard to get it across before a train came along. Eventually, as neither the driver, Jagdish nor I knew anything about cars, we sought help at a petrol-filling station; but the best the attendant could do was to direct us to a village some miles off the main road where he said there was an expert mechanic. We just made it and, although it was by then well past midnight, the whole village seemed to turn out, including all the children and the cows, to see what must have been an exciting event when cars were still a comparative rarity, at least in remote villages.

Some kind of light was found, the 'mechanic' turned up, rolled up his sleeves and opened the bonnet. He then took the leads off the plugs, changed them round and screwed them up again. Even I thought this was hardly the thing to do, but he stood up proudly, folded his arms and ordered the driver to start up. Of course nothing happened. Meanwhile Jagdish had gone off to see whether we could get a train back to Delhi and there was I, left alone, in the first Indian village I had ever seen, in the middle of the night. In time Jagdish returned, having had no success with trains. Then somehow, perhaps because God helps Scotsmen on New Year's Day, the car miraculously started and we limped back to Delhi, arriving not long before daybreak. Though tired, I was mightily relieved, especially when told that the area we had been travelling through was at the time infested by dacoits.

After I got home I took over the College investments again; and my main research during 1960 was reappraising the dollar problem, as described earlier. Then, early in 1961, I was off again to India. The MIT Center for International Studies had an India Project in New Delhi and I was invited to go there. Ian Little, Trevor Swan and others I knew had done so and recommended it strongly. The College gave me leave for the spring term and, by taking in part of the Easter vac, I was able to spend three months or so in the country, mostly in Delhi, though I also got around a good deal.

I knew quite a few Indians there already, and had introductions to others; and everyone was so friendly that I soon met many more. I was treated in a way that I think would have been impossible had I been of any nationality other than British. Although MIT had an office for me it was not long before I had found one in the Indian Government's Planning Commission as well. I spent most of my working time there, and felt I had really made it as an honorary Indian when my name appeared, along with others working in the Planning Commission, in the New Delhi telephone directory. I not only had my own office, but a room across the corridor, where my Secretary (male) and his assistants were housed. One day I spilt some coffee on the carpet. I rang the bell and in came, first, the man who sat outside my door all day in case I wanted something. He reported the problem to my Secretary who came to inspect the damage, followed by at least one of his assistants and the man who sat outside the door. They then departed and in due course all returned with, I suppose, the housekeeper and his assistant, the whole procession of half a dozen or so being completed by a little man – obviously of low caste – who actually wiped up the mess. (When I tried to wipe up a similar mess myself on another occasion I felt like 'the man who . . .' in a Bateman cartoon, surrounded by horrified looks.) I suppose it helped to alleviate India's huge unemployment problem, if not her problem of underemployment.

I had no idea what I was supposed to be working on, but after chatting around for a time decided to concentrate on the balance of payments. I was made a member of a Committee of civil servants considering policies to improve it. It was fascinating to compare the workings of such committees in Whitehall and New Delhi. Exaggerating to make my point, the former often spend a lot of time deciding which departments, committees and people shall do what and when, and comparatively little discussing the problem on hand. In New Delhi, discussion of the problem was all important and the intellectual standard extremely high; but then, after an hour or two, people tended to drift away – to have tea or something – and no one seemed very interested in deciding what should be done next.

The Committee did, however, somehow succeed in producing a report. Now Nehru was then Prime Minister and enjoyed talking to visiting economists, so I was summoned to see him shortly before I left. He was exceedingly friendly, so I took the liberty of telling him that he and his Cabinet would shortly be considering this report, and that I had just discovered that they had discussed a report containing many of the same recommendations two years earlier, and nothing seemed to have happened. He smiled and said: 'No, you are wrong; we discussed it *three* years ago, and nothing has happened'. He went on to say that, while the Indian character and way of life had much to commend them, they were not perhaps ideally suited to running an economy in the modern world.

Meanwhile, I had been writing my own piece on India's balance of payments. This appeared in two issues of *The Economic Weekly*, published in Bombay, in April 1961, and was reproduced in *The Bulletin of the Oxford University Institute of Statistics* a month later. It aroused a good deal of interest, particularly my conclusion that a massive increase in exports was necessary – much larger than many in India were then contemplating – if the current targets for growth and progress towards independence of foreign aid were to be achieved over the next decade (the period of the Third and Fourth Plans). Much of the increase in exports would, moreover, have to consist of manufactures other than the traditional ones of cotton and jute. I was doubtful whether my article would be of any lasting interest and so was gratified when asked in 1973 by an Indian publisher for permission to reproduce an abridged version in a volume of readings on India's economic policy.

I was shocked by the poverty I saw in India (and worried at how soon I got used to it). Picking my way one evening over the half-starved souls lying on the pavements of Bombay, it seemed to me that they were much worse off even than the wretched *campesinos* in Venezuela; and, since total income per head was far lower in India, the alleviation of poverty was a much more intractable problem.

7

NEDDY: 1962–64

AROUND this time I got a desire for another spell in the real world of economic policy making in the UK. Although partly no doubt a rationalisation of my wish to get back into the fun of the London whirl, I felt that perhaps the best way I could help the Third World was by trying to make advanced countries more prosperous so that they could buy more from the others and give them more aid. It was also dawning on me, as on others at the time, that our own dear old country was not doing all that well. We seemed largely to have conquered unemployment – how wrong this turned out to be – and our economic growth was faster than before the war; but it was much slower than in Germany, France, Italy and Japan. For some years we attributed their rapid growth to recovery after the war. But by the early 1960s this was no longer a plausible explanation, and there was a feeling we could do better if we really tried. I did not share the view of some that more growth was unnecessary. John Hicks once asked why I was so keen on it. 'Surely', he said, 'we're rich enough already.' I reminded him that his income, and mine, were several times that of the average Briton and many times the world average; and that I at least had no difficulty in spending mine. Nor did I agree with Fritz Schumacher, for years Economic Adviser to the Coal Board but with deep Buddhist sympathies, that three per cent per annum growth meant 'life becoming three per cent more complicated every year'. This view, like so many of Fritz's, was thought-provoking, but I argued that if this were so we had only ourselves to blame.

Towards the end of 1960, I thought I might have a chance of an attractive Government job because Robert Hall (then the husband of my future wife) who had been the top Government economist since 1947 – as Director of the Economic Section of the Cabinet Office and then 'Economic Adviser to HM Government' (stationed in the Treasury) – would reach the normal retiring age of 60 in the spring of 1961. Then one day – I think at an

East/West Conference in Prague organised by UNESCO in December 1960 – Alec Cairncross told me he was leaving his Chair in Glasgow to take a Government job in London. 'Nothing out of the ordinary', said Alec; but I suspected it was the job I was after – and I was right. I read the official announcement while in India and was bitterly disappointed. Alec had succeeded me twice: in Berlin in 1945 and Paris in 1949. This time it was his turn to be first; I was to succeed him later.

But I had no occasion to be disappointed. First, Alec was plunged in at the deep end in the Treasury shortly before what were then regarded as the rather savage deflationary measures of Selwyn Lloyd, the Chancellor, in July 1961 – with which I would not have liked to be associated. Secondly, not long after, I got a fascinating job as the first Economic Director of the National Economic Development Office (NEDO), which was to serve the newly created National Economic Development Council (NEDC). I am sure I had a more interesting and congenial time there and later in the Department of Economic Affairs (DEA) than if I had gone to the Treasury in 1961.

Although the NEDC did not hold its first meeting until well into 1962, the idea of forming a tripartite body, representing government, management and unions, to discuss ways of improving our economic performance, had been developing for some time. This was inspired in part by what was happening in France. We noticed that French growth had been rapid, that they had had a succession of four year 'Plans', and thought there might be some connection between the two. I had been to France, on a visit organised by the National Institute of Economic and Social Research, in a team of civil servants, businessmen, trade unionists, politicians and academics, and we were told by the Chief Planner, Monsieur Massé, that French planning – on a tripartite basis – had indeed increased their rate of growth.

Selwyn Lloyd mooted the idea in a Commons debate in July 1961, no doubt in part to show that, although his deflationary package would set back growth for a time, he favoured growth in the medium term. By December the general shape of Neddy had been more or less thrashed out, the employers' organisations had agreed to cooperate and although the TUC had not yet decided to come in (several times, when they seemed on the point of doing so, the Government somehow managed to do something to put them off) it was decided to appoint a Director-General.

This was Sir Robert Shone. He was an old friend, an economist who had spent most of his working life at the centre of things in the steel industry. We had worked together when I was with Prof during the war and in 1951–53. I arranged to have dinner with him in the Reform Club on New Year's Eve 1961 – having travelled down from a Christmas holiday in Scotland for the prupose. Although I had not yet been offered the job of Economic Director – and it was not in his gift – we talked for hours, on the assumption that I would get it, about our plans for Neddy. It was a wonderful evening. We were both full of enthusiasm and had great fun building castles in the air.

Not long after I was, to my delight, offered the job. Nuffield very generously gave me two years' leave of absence. It was subsequently extended; and, as it turned out, I had left Academe for the last time to help manage – or mismanage – the economy: first in Neddy; then in the Department of Economic Affairs (DEA) under successively George Brown, Michael Stewart and Peter Shore; then at the Treasury under Roy Jenkins, Iain Macleod and Tony Barber; and finally in the CBI – facing first a Conservative, then a Labour, then again a Conservative Government, and working under three Directors-General and six Presidents.

We moved into an office opposite Big Ben. I had a large, high ceilinged, very splendid – if rather dilapidated – room on the second floor on the corner of Bridge Street and the Embankment, with a balcony looking out over the Houses of Parliament and Westminster Bridge. I had visions of emerging onto it in 1966, when we had achieved growth of 4% a year between 1961 and 1966, which the NEDC adopted as a possible target at its first meeting, proclaiming to the cheering crowds: 'Four per cent. We've done it'. But it was not to be. First, we achieved just over 3%. Secondly, long before 1966, Neddy had moved to more modern quarters in Millbank Tower, where my room also had a magnificent view, spanning the vista from Westminster Abbey to St Paul's; but as it was on the fourteenth floor, and the windows would not open, I could not have made a proclamation to cheering crowds in Millbank far below (even if I had not by then gone to the DEA).

When Shone and I moved into the Bridge Street office early in 1962 we were joined by Frank Pickford, seconded from the Ministry of Labour to be Secretary of the Council. He was a prodigious worker, with a fine feeling for the English language, a fund of common sense and unfailing good humour. We began recruiting like mad, mainly from Universities and business, on a full-time and part-time basis; and before too long had a team of economists which, in terms of numbers, was within shooting distance of that in the Treasury – and of extremely high quality. In February the TUC agreed to join and the Council held its first meeting on 7 March 1962. The lift was not working, so members had quite a climb to the room where we met. This was regarded as symbolic of the run down state of the economy. Neddy would change all that. By 1966 all the lifts would be working all the time everywhere.

One idea behind the setting up of Neddy was what I call the 'confidence trick'. This consisted of thinking of a number for the growth of the economy over a period ahead rather greater than had been achieved in the past, and working out what it would involve for all concerned. Then everyone would work on the assumption that it was going to happen, and lo and behold it would happen. Given the projected growth of the labour force and the rate at which we thought output per head was rising we could hardly have chosen a lower figure than 4% a year, which implied only a small improvement in productivity growth. Some cautious souls would have preferred something nearer 3%; but many thought 4% not ambitious enough.

The exercise involved working out what 4% growth meant for broad aggregates like private consumption and investment, government spending, exports, imports and employment; and also, if we were to do the sort of 'indicative planning' we understood the French did, the implications for individual industries. We made only a primitive start on this in 1962 – for seventeen industries covering nearly two-fifths of the national product. They included the distributive trades, on which my future wife Margaret was an expert; and I persuaded her to work part-time in the Office, although she was very fully occupied in Oxford as a Fellow and Tutor at Somerville and a University Lecturer.

It was also hoped to achieve faster growth by better policies on the 'supply side' of the economy (although I do not think we used the term – now fashionable – at the time). We worked on a wide range of issues: education, industrial training, business schools, redundancy payments, earnings-related benefits, the tax system, regional policy, housing policies to help mobility, transferable pension rights.

Finally, it was thought we might get faster growth by better demand management. Here, believe it or not, the argument was between daring high pressure of demand chaps like myself who wanted to go for $1\frac{1}{2}\%$ unemployment and reactionary, low pressure of demand people like Professor Frank Paish, who wanted $2\frac{1}{2}\%$. We studied the effects of different levels of demand on such things as efficiency, investment, structural change, prices and incomes, the balance of payments. Much of the work was done by Dick Lipsey and Frank Brechling, who later became very well-known economists. Their first econometric results were repugnant to my commonsense. When I asked whether they had taken account of the outbreak of the Korean War in their time series, they regarded this as irrelevant. It was only when I had spotted several elementary arithmetical mistakes in their calculations that they were shaken; and after forty-eight hours of almost continuous work, produced revised results that looked much more plausible.

I tried to get into what became known as the 'Orange Book' (*Conditions Favourable to Faster Growth*, which the Council approved for publication in April 1963) that the objective should be to get back to 1½% unemployment. I thought this would be welcome to the TUC and might just about be acquiesced in by Government and the employers. But Frank Cousins, of the Transport and General Workers' Union, would have none of it: he could not be party to a report which admitted that a single person should ever be out of a job.

It was accepted that achieving the growth objective might involve unorthodox policies on the balance of payments; and the relevant chapter in the Orange Book discusses most such policies in an almost daring manner – exchange control, import restrictions, restrictions on overseas investment, use of reserves, borrowing from abroad and so on. But there is one notable omission. There is no discussion of exchange rate policy. Up till a very late stage the draft report did in fact have a very good section on this, written mainly by my old pupil Maurice Scott, whom I had been fortunate enough to get seconded from Christ Church, of which he was then a Student. The Treasury had seen successive drafts of everything we had written, but for some reason it was only shortly before our final drafts were due to be sent to Council members that they tumbled to the fact that we had dared to discuss the forbidden subject and vetoed the section. If you look at the terms of reference of NEDC, you will find that one of its objectives is 'to increase the rate of sound growth'. This seems innocent enough but I argued, unsuccessfully, with my Treasury friends for the omission of 'sound' because we all knew it was a code word for 'at £1 = $2.80', then the sacrosanct parity of sterling; for, though I hoped at the time that we might achieve a decent rate of growth without devaluing, I was by no means certain, and did not wish to rule out the option.

During 1962 the NEDC met regularly discussing many of the subjects I have been describing. The Chairman was at first Selwyn Lloyd. But in July 1962 he was dismissed by the Prime Minister, Harold Macmillan, presumably because he did not consider him sufficiently committed to economic expansion, and replaced as Chancellor – and Chairman of NEDC – by Reggie Maudling. Macmillan was encouraged in his desire for expansion by a stream of private letters from Roy Harrod – of which Roy sent me copies – all in his own handwriting. Now we all wanted expansion, but Roy also wanted import controls so that expansion would not lead to balance of payments difficulties which necessitated deflationary measures to slow demand; he was firmly against devaluation as one of the measures that might be used in such circumstances. After a while I suppose Macmillan got a little tired of this barrage of correspondence. Whatever the reason, he arranged a lunch party to which he invited just Roy, Alec Cairncross and myself. It was in Admiralty House, in Whitehall, where the Prime Minister was temporarily installed while repairs were being carried out in Downing Street. It was a delightful lunch. Harold was the most charming of hosts. Over coffee, Roy expounded his views with his customary clarity and vigour; and Alec and I the problems that might arise if we imposed import controls. Then Macmillan said: 'You know, I would like to do what you say, Roy, but they won't let me.' By 'they' he presumably meant his Cabinet colleagues.

I found this fascinating. It may have been a polite way of trying to satisfy Roy, hoping that his letters would become less frequent. But it may also illustrate a thought I have sometimes had that, after a Prime Minister has been in office for some years, he can tend to find economics a trifle boring – and even a little beneath him – and prefer to concentrate on the more glamorous tasks of foreign policy, especially when this means hob-nobbing with statesmen on overseas trips.

At the beginning of Maudling's Chairmanship of NEDC it appeared to some that his heart was not really in it. So at one meeting Oliver Franks, one of the two independent members, and sometimes the mouthpiece of the other – Professor (later Sir Henry) Phelps Brown (a distinguished economist and life-long friend of mine) – made a brave speech saying that the Council was getting nowhere and that it was the fault of the Chairman. From then on Maudling took the job much more seriously. But the real work during 1962 and early 1963 was done by the staff. I have seldom worked harder over such a prolonged period. Partly as a result I got glandular fever in the summer, but when convalescing spent some time pondering on possible changes that might increase our annual growth rate by at least 0.1%. If we could get enough of these, it should surely be possible to achieve 4% growth. I like to think that my musings and back-of-the-envelope calculations made some contribution to the Orange Book.

During the last month or so of drafting, Robert Shone, Frank Pickford and I spent morning, noon and night, along with Tom Fraser, appointed later in the year as Industrial Director, going over drafts line by line and comma by comma. To illustrate how hard we concentrated, I remember coming out of the office at two o'clock one morning and being amazed to find people milling around Parliament Square with paper hats and balloons. They had come down Whitehall from the celebrations in Trafalgar Square for, believe it or not, it was the first of January (1963) and a true Scot had forgotten all about it.

Not long after, when the drafts were more or less completed, I went to Scotland for a short break and on the way lay awake in the sleeper wondering whether we should have one or two documents. When I got to Glasgow I phoned Robert Shone and agreed that we should have two – the Green Book, *Growth of the UK Economy to 1966*, giving most of the figuring, and the Orange Book, containing the policies. I am sure this was right, because the policies were largely independent of the figuring and would remain valid even if we failed to achieve our particular growth objective. Then, in a period of just over two months, from late January to early April 1963, the Council devoted six *full* days, including two consecutive ones – a Sunday and Monday – to meetings at which they went through drafts of the Green and Orange Books virtually paragraph by paragraph and finally authorised their publication. On the Sunday Reggie Maudling came to the meeting in his bedroom slippers and at lunch-time shuffled along Bridge Street in them to a brief meal we all had in St Stephen's Tavern, half-way between Westminster Bridge and Whitehall.

There was much negotiating and horse-trading before the reports were agreed. Arthur Cockfield – then Managing Director of Boots and a member of Council – argued against a passage I wished to put in the Orange Book (having been convinced by Margaret Hall) recommending abolition of Resale Price Maintenance. I deduced – perhaps maliciously – that Boots gained from this practice being followed by other firms by making it easier for them to put these firms' branded products in their shops alongside competing Boots products at a lower price. Arthur won and my draft passage was deleted in return for a concession on some other matter – though I am glad to say that this was not the end of the story. Nor was it the last time I crossed swords with Cockfield.

This first year of Neddy's work illustrates how greatly things have changed. It showed how seriously Council members took their work; six full day meetings in little more than two months would now be inconceivable. It was possible too to get a consensus between a Conservative Government, the TUC and representatives of employers – and also, I believe, the Labour Opposition, led by Hugh Gaitskell. I had a long talk with him shortly before he died telling him what Neddy was likely to come up with, and he was in virtually complete agreement. What a contrast from the early 1980s when 'consensus' was a dirty word in some quarters.

The Government certainly implemented its side of the 'social contract' with the others represented on Council (although no one then used this term – it was applied a dozen years later to a bilateral understanding between a Labour Government and the unions, which was different in many important respects). Listening on the radio as the details of Maudling's Budget Speech of 3 April 1963 came over the air I was amazed – and sometimes amused – how closely he was following Neddy's recommendations. In addition to proposing an expansionary budget to take up slack and get growth going – in line with the Green Book, already published – he made proposal after proposal on the lines of the Orange Book – which the NEDC authorised for publication two days later. Even on small points he was not found wanting. George Woodcock, the TUC General Secretary, was buying a house at the time, and had complained at meeting after meeting how iniquitously high stamp duty was. So Maudling obligingly halved it – and for good measure abolished the tax, under 'Schedule A', on the notional income from owner-occupied dwellings.

The ability to get consensus reflected mainly a consensus in the country. But also important was the way the Council worked. It was Selwyn Lloyd's idea that it should operate under rules of Cabinet secrecy; and at press conferences after meetings, taken by Robert Shone and myself, we did not attribute opinions even to one of the three 'sides' of the Council, let alone to individuals (which later became quite common and led members, on occasion, to make statements intended mainly for public consumption). This enabled everyone to talk much more frankly, and did not, for example, inhibit the management side from ganging up with the trade unions against a Conservative Government – a sin which the CBI was later terrified of committing during at least parts of the Thatcher administrations – and telling them they had no idea how industry and commerce worked. I believe that frequently, if one had shut one's eyes, and did not know individual members' voices, it would have been impossible to tell from what was said whether an employer, a trade unionist, a Minister or an independent member was talking. It is symbolic that, whereas in later years the CBI team sat as one bloc and the TUC as another, a photograph of the first NEDC meeting shows little groups of employers interspersed with little groups of trade unionists round the table. On the whole, secrecy was well observed, with one striking exception early in 1963 when Peter Jenkins got hold of a draft of the Orange Book and published large chunks in *The Guardian*. The fact that his Editor thought it worth giving him so much space does, however, illustrate the interest in Neddy at the time.

Another contributory factor to the atmosphere is that only three officials were normally present at Council meetings in the early days (apart from the Secretary to take the minutes): Len Murray for the TUC, Ken Johnson of the Federation of British Industries (FBI) for the employers, and myself as Economic Director of the Office. (Later Tom Fraser joined us when he became Industrial Director.) There was indeed hardly room for more in the small room where the Council met in Bridge Street. The last time – in 1983 – when I counted the officials at a meeting in the more spacious Council Chamber in Millbank Tower, there were more like forty. There were more members too – with twice as many Ministers and more 'independents'. This seems ironical when the influence of NEDC had so significantly diminished.

Very early on, the non-government members made it clear that they wished discussions to be based on papers by the NEDO staff, not papers by the Treasury or other government departments. The Treasury was somewhat under a cloud in the public eye at the time and the popular view was caricatured one week in a TV satirical series then running – 'That Was The Week That Was' (TWTWTW) – which portrayed Treasury officials as old fuddy-duddies compared with the Brave New World of Neddy. At an early meeting the Treasury produced what was really quite a good paper on obstacles to economic growth. The Chancellor brought along Otto Clarke, a senior Treasury official (with whom I had clashed ten years earlier over ROBOT). For nearly an hour one after another of the non-ministerial members – all round the table – criticised sentences and paragraphs in the paper until George Woodcock said how embarrassing it must be for the author to be sitting there unable to reply. Whereupon Otto did not improve matters by saying: 'Oh, I am not the author'. It was a long time before a government official was again brought to a Council meeting. But by the early 1980s there were often nearly a score.

Officials have hardly ever, however, sat *at the table* and taken part in the discussion. The only major exception I can remember was when George Brown was Chairman of the Council in 1964–66. (The Chairmanship moved from the Chancellor to the Secretary of State for Economic Affairs on the change of government in October 1964, but later reverted to the Chancellor.) Quite frequently, when I was sitting behind him, George asked me to pull my chair up to the table and speak. Once, when a paper by the Office on VAT was under discussion, he asked me to give the pros and cons. He was in favour of VAT on political grounds being a good European, for if we joined the EEC – we were not then applying for membership – we would have to introduce the tax; but he knew I had reported against it as a member of the Richardson Committee, described later. After my little speech, in which I could not entirely conceal my bias, he thanked me, in a somewhat sarcastic tone of voice, for such an objective analysis.

In George Brown's time, press conferences after NEDC meetings were also very different from the sober, cautious affairs I described a few pages back. George usually insisted on being there himself. I sometimes had to drag him down from the sumptuous lunches we had in those days on the thirtieth floor of Millbank Tower – once he refused to come until he had kissed every one of the waitresses – to meet industrial correspondents waiting with growing restlessness half-way down the building. George would then sit, hardly attempting to conceal his impatience, while the Director-General gave an account of the morning's meeting, and then hold a press conference of his own covering every conceivable subject; and the discussion often became heated and sometimes hilarious.

In Neddy's first year, Britain was indeed applying for EEC membership (before de Gaulle's first veto). Whether we should join was a matter of acute controversy which I had found myself discussing continuously in Oxford and elsewhere during 1961; and I agreed to write an article on the question for a Dutch Bank Review. This was published in December 1961, shortly *before* I joined NEDO. I expected to hear no more of it, for I supposed that the Review would have, at most, a very limited circulation in Britain. Also, I had gone to great lengths to make the article impartial and to report faithfully the various views then current in Britain; and I made no recommendation on whether or not, on balance, it would be in our interest to join.

I was therefore surprised to find myself chased by reporters from the *Daily Express* – whose anti-Market views were well known – during a visit to Scotland over the Easter weekend in 1962, and to read a piece in that paper on the Tuesday headed 'Sir Donald rocks the Market boat', which began: 'The Government faces a new embarrassment over the Common Market from one of its top "backroom" economic advisers' (a strange description, given NEDO's independent position, even though we were paid out of public funds). It went on, not surprisingly, to select from my article most of the arguments I reported against joining and largely ignored those in favour.

I found out later that Douglas Jay had discovered my article and quoted from it in a Sunday paper; the *Express* had picked it up from there and given it much greater publicity than it would otherwise have had. It was quoted quite widely during 1962, both by pro-Marketeers and by anti's, including Hugh Gaitskell in a speech to the Labour Party Conference. Ted Heath was then the Minister in charge of the negotiating delegation in Brussels and Eric Roll deputy leader at the official level. Eric told me that he and Ted had read my article and regarded it as a very fair assessment of the arguments for and against British entry. In doing our sums in NEDO during 1962 we assumed that Britain would join. President de Gaulle's veto on 14 January 1963 came at a most awkward time just as we were about to send out drafts of the Green and Orange Books to Council members, and we had to work overtime making hurried changes.

It is not generally known that the Council went through a long process of mutual education on the subject of inflation, in the twelve months or so after publication of these Books. Their debates, and final agreement, on the two reports had brought about a good deal of understanding between government, union and management members on the need to keep down inflation, and the increase of money incomes, if the economy was to grow faster. The argument was essentially simple. Faster growth required a faster increase in imports of materials and other things to support it. To pay for these, exports must grow faster. This depended on price and non-price competitiveness. But a necessary condition was that our costs and prices must, at worst, not rise appreciably faster than our competitors'; and that meant, among other things, that pay must rise more slowly than in the past. All three parties ruled out devaluation as an acceptable alternative. Also, the need for adequate profits, and thus the danger of trying to control inflation by reducing profit margins, was recognised by most of the union members. In particular, Harry (later Lord) Douglass, of the Iron and Steel Trades Confederation, used to say, in his down-to-earth way, that he liked his members to work for profitable companies, because this meant good wages and job security.

With these basic propositions accepted, and after one meeting at which members had an opportunity to let off steam, it became possible to talk about pay, prices, profits, productivity and related matters in a calm, objective manner. Month after month I wrote paper after paper for the Council with Fred Jones, who had come to us from a teaching post in Ruskin College, having previously been an assistant to George Woodcock at the TUC. Our papers carried forward the Council's discussion step by step and covered such matters as the different characteristics of profits and wages, the determination of prices, possible forms of control of pay, prices, profits, dividends, what the criteria might be, even the machinery for administering the necessary policies.

The TUC was not prepared to make a deal on these matters with a Conservative administration, though Maudling tried, and I think George Woodcock would have liked one. But the mutual understanding resulting from the discussions was the main reason why, on Labour's return to power in October 1964, George Brown was able to agree so quickly a policy on these matters with the TUC and what was soon to become the CBI. In this he was helped by Fred Jones and myself, who went over to the newly created DEA; and he was amazed at the rapid progress we were able to make, having not really taken on board what had been going on in Neddy. By December he had got an agreed Declaration of Intent on Productivity, Prices and Incomes; by February a White Paper; by March a

National Board for Prices and Incomes under Aubrey Jones; by April a 'norm' for pay increases of 3–3½%.

During my last year or so at Neddy I witnessed what I call the 'Keeler' boom in public spending. In June 1963, Mr Profumo, Secretary of State for War, had resigned after admitting that he had lied to the Commons about his association with Christine Keeler. This delayed the General Election by up to a year; and we watched from NEDO with amazement as the Government made successive announcements of increases in public expenditure plans. These went well above what we thought could be afforded with 4% growth in the economy. This despite the fact that Douglas-Home – who succeeded Macmillan as Prime Minister in October 1963 – assured everyone that the spending proposals had been fully costed, which he pronounced 'causted', being an even more anglicized Scot than myself. So Labour in 1964 inherited a big Conservative public spending programme, just as was to happen in 1974, following what I describe later as the 'Armstrong' public spending boom.

In April 1963, in line with a recommendation in the Orange Book, Maudling appointed a Committee on Turnover Taxation to study, in effect, the implications of substituting a Value Added Tax (VAT) for either Purchase Tax or what was then called Profits Tax. The Chairman was Gordon (later Lord) Richardson, a merchant banker, the other members being Sir Henry (later Lord) Benson, an accountant, and myself. One reason for this study was that France had a VAT and it was thought that this might have something to do with their rapid rate of growth. In fact, when we visited Paris, the officials concerned asked why on earth we were thinking of introducing VAT, when our Purchase Tax was such a very much more efficient way of collecting revenue.

I enjoyed this committee. It took up a good day a week on average over ten months. Meetings were usually in Gordon Richardson's office in Schroder Wagg's in the City. Apart from taking a good deal of evidence, much of the time was taken up by arguments between Benson the accountant and MacDougall the economist with the Chairman saying rather little. We two argued from the point of view of our own disciplines and got closer and closer having started a considerable distance apart. Then in the closing stages Gordon – whom I increasingly admired as a Chairman – did what little further banging of heads together was needed, together with some kindly slave driving, to enable us to produce an unanimous report coming down firmly against VAT as an alternative to either of the existing taxes. On the day of publication we were rewarded by a splendid lunch in No 11.

Before leaving Neddy, I spent a lot of time in late 1963 and early 1964 discussing the sterling exchange rate with Hans Liesner. (I had supervised him at Nuffield and he was then a Don at Cambridge, working part-time in Neddy; he later joined me in the Treasury, and after I left became Chief Economic Adviser to the Departments of Trade and Industry.) I became convinced of the need for a lower pound if we were to get sustained growth and avoid endless balance of payments troubles.

I promised in Chapter 5 to explain more fully how I reconcile this with my strong opposition to a floating of the pound – which would certainly have fallen – during the ROBOT controversy a dozen years earlier. The answer is that the situation was completely different. Our international competitiveness had worsened very markedly since then; for example, our labour costs per unit of output in manufacturing had risen by one-quarter in relation to the average of our competitors'. Also, compared with the situation in 1962, exports were limited much less by supply shortages and much more by demand, and imports to only a very small extent by direct controls; so that a devaluation would have been much more likely to improve the balance of payments by increasing exports and reducing imports. The dollar, moreover, was no longer a scarce currency, and the pound and other major currencies were by now convertible, so there would have been no threat to our exports, as there was in the ROBOT plan, from an accompanying move to convertibility. Finally, we foresaw a large prospective deficit in the balance of payments in 1964 and beyond if we tried to keep growth going at a respectable rate at the current rate of exchange. I shall have a lot more to say about this in the next chapter.

Neddy did not of course persuade – or even ask – the Government to devalue; nor did it stop it embarking on an irresponsible spending spree. But it did notch up a considerable number of successes while I was there. It stimulated quite a few 'supply side' initiatives. It achieved a consensus over a wide range of economic policies, and a large degree of understanding between the three main parties on the Council on what caused inflation and on the relationships between pay, profits and jobs. It also began setting up the 'Little Neddies' which have in general proved their worth. So the NEDC, in those early days, was really quite influential – and, I believe, an influence for the good – and much more so than it later became. It never recaptured its earlier enthusiasm; but it has at least survived for quarter of a century. I have heard a great deal of criticism of it from many people, including its members; but I think most of them feel, at the bottom of their hearts, that if it were abolished, something pretty like it would have to be re-invented to take its place.

8

DEPARTMENT OF ECONOMIC
AFFAIRS: 1964–68

DURING the months leading up to the 1964 General Election I was permitted by Conservative Ministers, and senior officials, to discuss with Opposition leaders possible changes in the organisation of departments. I was also asked whether, if Labour won and they set up some sort of Department of Economic Affairs, I would join it and I said yes. So when Labour did win I went to the newly-formed DEA with the title of Director-General. We were housed at the west end of the 'New Public Offices', where I had worked during the war and in 1951–53. The Treasury remained housed at the east end, and there was an invisible line running north and south between the two departments, which only the cognoscenti could identify with confidence. I was allotted a lovely, large room on the second floor overlooking St James's Park.

Sir Eric (later Lord) Roll became Permanent Under-Secretary. Our respective responsibilities were at first a trifle obscure but soon clarified. I had known Eric since before the war when we were teaching economics not far apart – he at the University College of Hull and I at Leeds University. He stayed in public service after the war but I continued to see him, especially in 1949 in Paris. It was then that I first became aware of the fantastic stamina he continued to display for many years thereafter; following a long day's work he quite often wanted to go off to a night-club.

I took with me to the DEA about half the economic staff from NEDO. I had much heart-searching deciding whom to take and whom to leave behind; nearly all wanted to come. The industrial staff stayed in NEDO although George Brown had wished to take them into the DEA. I persuaded him before the Election to postpone a decision on this; and after the Election he agreed to keep them and the Little Neddies in the Neddy machine. I am sure this was right, because in the DEA they would soon have lost much of their independence, and we should have sacrificed much of the excellent work which many Little Neddies have done in identifying and remedying weaknesses in particular sectors.

In addition to the economists I brought to the DEA from Neddy, I recruited others from various walks of life. I was particularly fortunate to get John Jukes as my Deputy. He had had wide experience in the Cabinet Offices, the Treasury, our Embassy in Washington, the Atomic Energy Authority and elsewhere. He served me and the DEA loyally and with great ability; and, when the Department was wound up, continued a distinguished career in Whitehall. Another recruit was Samuel Brittan. Already well-known as a brilliant young writer on the *Financial Times* and *The Observer*, and as author of *The Treasury under the Tories*, he later became much more famous both as a journalist and as author of many other books. His year or so in the DEA, while no doubt highly educational, may have been something of a disappointment to him in that George Brown used him more for his journalistic talents and less for his powers of economic analysis than he had been led to believe when I introduced them and George more or less gave him the impression that the three of us would run the Department. (During the interview, Sam offered to tell him how he had voted in various General Elections; but George did not want to know.) We have remained close friends, even though our views on economics have diverged considerably from time to time.

There were several secondments of administrators – often good economists as well – from other Departments. These included Douglas Allen (later Lord Croham), whom I first knew in Berlin after the war. He came across from the Treasury at the start and succeeded Eric Roll in 1966 when Eric left to begin a highly successful career in the City. Douglas went back to the Treasury to succeed William (later Lord) Armstrong as Permanent Secretary in 1968, so he was there when I arrived in 1969.

George Brown also recruited some businessmen under Fred (later Sir Frederick) Catherwood as his first Chief Industrial Adviser. Fred, who had been Managing Director of British Aluminium, later became Director-General of NEDC, and later still an MEP. I used to call his large collection of original ideas for improving the efficiency of the economy 'Catherwoodery'; and it says a lot for his sense of humour that he forgave me when I circulated a memorandum where this got mis-typed as 'Cottonwoolery'. While he was at Neddy, he used to phone me for instant reactions to economic events. Once it was about a Public Expenditure White Paper published that day on which he had agreed to comment on TV in the evening. When I said it was a complicated document requiring

My parents

Between my sister Jeannette and brother
Ian

Shrewsbury: with Hartley Ayre in
Sunday wear

BRITAIN
MEANS
BUSINESS

Sir Terence Beckett receives a standing ovation after his 'bare knuckles' speech at the CBI Conference in 1980. I am immediately to the left of Beckett; on the extreme right is Sir Ray Pennock, the President

Greeting Len Murray, General Secretary of the TUC, at my farewell party at the CBI, 1984

Farewell party (left to right): Lord Richardson, former Governor of the Bank of England and Chairman of the VAT Committee 1963–64 of which I was a member; Sir Adrian Cadbury, former Chairman of CBI's Economic and Financial Policy Committee; Sir James Cleminson, President of the CBI 1984–86

Farewell party: Lord Benson (left), the third member of the VAT Committee; Sir Campbell Adamson, former Director-General of the CBI

Farewell party: admiring the £-shaped cake, with Sir Campbell Fraser, the President, and attendants

Glan Williams' cartoon which was signed by guests arriving at my farewell party

careful study, and he said it was his responsibility to the British people to give his views, I could not resist asking whether his responsibility was not to the National Economic Development Council.

The morale of our somewhat motley crew was remarkably high. Especially among those who had come in from outside, there was a Brave New World atmosphere. Despite growing frustration and disillusionment, a camaraderie developed which survived the demise of the Department; there is even a DEA tie (I never acquired one being allergic to such things), and there have been several reunions of old members.

When I joined the DEA I had, sadly, to resign my Nuffield Fellowship – I could hardly have asked the College for more leave – but they very kindly made me an Honorary Fellow a few years later. (I have thus held four types of Fellowship at Nuffield, a record which I do not think has been broken, if indeed equalled: Faculty, Professorial, Official and Honorary.) I now became for the first time an established Civil Servant, having in each of my previous excursions into public service been a 'temporary' on secondment.

While at the DEA I chaired quite often a group of Economic Advisers. We were mostly consulted on macro-economic questions like the latest short-term forecast or medium-term assessment, but sometimes on more specific questions like state pension schemes and even fisheries policy – possibly to keep us too busy to have mischievous thoughts about things like the exchange rate. The group was a strange assortment consisting normally of six people. Three might be termed 'political' advisers. First, there was Robert Neild, who had made a name for himself in government and international service as well as in academic life and research at Cambridge and in the National Institute of Economic and Social Research; he became an Economic Adviser to the Treasury. Then there was Nicky Kaldor, already mentioned, well known not only for his academic works but for his advice to governments throughout the world (the popular belief that this always led to a revolution is exaggerated). He was appointed Special Adviser to the Chancellor on taxation, but did not by any means confine himself to this subject. Finally there was Tommy Balogh, effectively adviser to the Prime Minister. The other three were non-political: Alec Cairncross, John Jukes and myself. Classified in another way there were two Scots (Cairncross and MacDougall); two Englishmen (Neild and Jukes); and two former Hungarians (Balogh and Kaldor). None of us – to put it mildly – was averse to speaking his mind or to disagreeing with his colleagues. So it was a good training in chairmanship.

I could usually cope with those born on this island; and had had experience of Balogh in Oxford. Kaldor could at times be a problem. When we had meetings shortly after lunch, he had a habit of going to sleep while everyone else was talking, and then waking up to make a long speech, sometimes – even more maddening – as if he had heard all that had been said. Years later, in 1976, I had to wake him up on a different occasion. He was currently President of the Royal Economic Society, having succeeded me in that office, and was sitting next to me at a banquet in Glasgow University during a celebration, attended by economists from all over the world, of the two hundredth anniversary of Adam Smith's *Wealth of Nations*. Long before my time came to make the last – I think the fifth – after-dinner speech, Nicky was fast asleep. This was excusable because it was by then well past eleven o'clock; although most of the other guests had been revived before I started by a glass of malt whisky. But I had a joke about him in my speech and thought it only fair to wake him.

'Wake up, Nicky', I said, 'I have a story to tell about you.' He was immediately wide awake. The story was this. Late in 1969, after he had left the Treasury, he went to the Department of Health and Social Security as a Special Adviser to Dick Crossman, then Secretary of State for Social Services. After he had been there a fortnight, a friend asked him how he was getting on. 'Oh', said Nicky, 'it's no good. I got there too late. All the major mistakes had been made already.' He took it very well; in fact he seemed rather pleased.

The first great mistake of the new Government was not to devalue at once. In my view this dominated – and distorted – economic policy for the next four years. There was no detailed discussion of it before the momentous decision was taken. On the Saturday evening after the Election there was a short meeting at 11 Downing Street attended by George Brown, who had been given the splendid title of 'First Secretary of State and Secretary of State for Economic Affairs' (the first part indicating, in is view, that he was effectively Deputy Prime Minister); Jim Callaghan, who had become Chancellor; and three civil servants – William Armstrong, Eric Roll and myself. We went round the room asking whether anyone thought we should devalue. I was the only one who said yes and gave my reasons briefly. The two Ministers then went into No. 10 where, with Harold Wilson, they took the decision which was to stand for three years and cause grave difficulties throughout this period, and indeed for the best part of a further twelve months after we did eventually devalue.

One consequence of our more or less continuous balance of payments troubles – with only occasional respites – was that we became obsessed with the monthly figures of exports and imports, and waited for their appearance rather like an inveterate punter waits for the results of the 2.30. During one of the respites I was at a Buckingham Palace garden party, when the sky overhead was grey and threatening, and ran into Vic Feather, then Assistant General Secretary of the TUC and a friend through our common membership of the (London) Political Economy Club. He had just been talking to the Prime Minister and said to me: 'Donald, I've just seen Harold, and he said what a lovely day it is; the trade deficit last month was only £X million'.

I believe the main reasons why the three senior Ministers were against devaluation in October 1964 were as follows: Wilson because he was aware of the economic and political risks that were undoubtedly involved, but also because Balogh had persuaded him it was unnecessary since 'socialist' policies could surely cure the balance of payment problem in quite a short time; Callaghan, as he told me one evening before the Election, in Nuffield where he was a Visiting Fellow, because he had promised the US Secretary to the Treasury he wouldn't devalue; George Brown because he regarded it as an act against the working class, despite my efforts to explain to him that, though it might reduce real wages somewhat, it would help to maintain employment. In political terms, Ministers cannot have wished to give further credence to the argument often used by the Tories that Labour was the Party of devaluation because of Cripps' devaluation in 1949. This was largely a myth: it was a National Government supported overwhelmingly by Conservatives which went off gold in 1931, let sterling depreciate in 1938, and devalued it in 1939.

The week after the Election was absurdly hectic. Apart from the practical problems of making our rooms habitable (they had just been decorated and the powers that be had, I believe, prolonged the exercise and kept them unfurnished to prevent them being allocated to another Ministry, just in case some sort of a DEA had to be housed after the Election), innumerable decisions were taken at breakneck speed, with a minimum of discussion, in addition to the most important one about sterling.

One question was whether, having failed to devalue, we should impose an import surcharge or import quotas. The former was preferable insofar as it relied on the price mechanism, but illegal under international rules. The latter were legal for a country in balance of payments difficulties, but involved direct controls reminiscent of war-time. Early in the week, I had a lengthy meeting in my room with officials from departments concerned to thrash out the pros and cons. When we had nearly finished I was summoned into George's room next door where he was discussing the question with Douglas Jay, President of the Board of Trade. I was allowed time to give only the briefest analysis of the arguments and then George, after virtually no further discussion, came down in favour of the surcharge. This was confirmed by the Cabinet, despite Jay's opposition.

The speed of decision-taking was greatly to George's liking, and the week was exhilarating to live through. But it really was rushing things much too quickly – and quite unnecessary – to have a Government Statement ready for the printers by Friday 23 October – only a week after the Government took office – for publication on Monday 26 October (my fifty-second birthday) covering such a wide range of complex and controversial subjects as a 15% surcharge on a wide range of imports; an export rebate scheme (designed to repay exporters the estimated indirect taxes entering into the cost of producing their exports, but regarded by many foreigners as a straight export subsidy); Concorde; and many others. And indeed several chickens soon came home to roost. Discussions with the French showed that insufficient homework had been done on the implications of stopping the Concorde project; and the European Free Trade Area (EFTA) countries were furious about the import surcharge, mainly, I think, because of our failure to consult them properly in advance, which could easily have been avoided had not everything been done in such a rush.

Not long after, when George, having rejected my argument that sustained growth was not on without devaluation, insisted that I produce an alternative policy, I said 'OK' and reeled off, out of the top of my head, a long list of impracticable suggestions, including borrowing another few billions from the Americans and doubling the import surcharge. George said 'right', went off to a meeting of EFTA Ministers, and when he came back had to tell me, rather shamefacedly, that he had promised to *reduce* it.

In those early days at the DEA – and for a long time thereafter – the daily movements in our gold and dollar reserves were awaited with concern. One evening William Armstrong asked me along to his office in the Treasury and told me we had lost I don't know how many millions of dollars that day. I felt I should tell George Brown whose immediate reaction – a typical one – was that we must *do* something. I failed to calm him down and he insisted on arranging a meeting for later in the evening with the Chancellor, William and myself. This duly took place in No 11 and quite late at night William and I were dismissed while our political masters stayed on to discuss matters of high policy.

I returned to my flat near Westminster Cathedral, and had just got into my bath when the 'phone rang. It was George telling me to come round at once to his official residence – a flat in Carlton Gardens (between Pall

Mall and the Mall). I dried, got my clothes on and went across. He told me that Callaghan was contemplating the possibility of devaluation. When I said 'Why not? You know my views', he replied that the Government had promised not to. When I reminded him that Stafford Cripps had devalued in 1949 after saying several months earlier that he would not, George really flew off the handle. After all, can you imagine two people more different than the austere Stafford Cripps and George Brown? (Also – something I did not know until later – Cripps had taken such offence at a speech made by George in 1939, when seconding a resolution expelling Cripps from the Labour Party, that he never spoke to George again.)

George instructed me to draft a letter to the Prime Minister threatening to resign if there were a devaluation. I dutifully did this at the expense of getting to bed very late; but when I went into his office the following morning and said 'Here is the letter you asked me to draft for you last night', he had completely forgotten and rather sheepishly put it in his pocket. This was one of many resignation letters drafted for or by George, quite a few of which were delivered. I heard later that they kept a special file for them in No 10 which had grown pretty large by the time his resignation – from the Foreign Office – was finally accepted in 1968, probably to his great surprise and even dismay.

In November 1964 we nearly did depreciate the pound. The reserves were fast running out and one evening I was summoned to No 10 and put in a room to the left of the Cabinet room but opening into it where I found myself with some of the other economic advisers, as well as a Mrs Williams (whom I thought was Shirley but who turned out to be Marcia, later Lady Falkender). Harold Wilson, who was interviewing the Governor of the Bank of England and Cabinet colleagues, kept popping into our room and saying he was thinking of floating the pound and refusing to slash public expenditure. The next day Robert Neild and I – trying to resist interruptions from Balogh and Kaldor who were in a highly excitable state – drafted a paper we had been instructed to prepare on the relative merits of floating and devaluing, how much of the latter might be appropriate and so on. (Tony Crosland – an old Oxford friend whom I had known since he was the Economics Fellow at Trinity after the war, before going into politics, and who was effectively Minister of State at the DEA – spent the day looking at how the opinion polls had behaved after the 1949 devaluation!)

But meanwhile Lord ('Rowley') Cromer, the Governor, succeeded on the telephone in raising $3 billion from his Central Bank colleagues around the world, so the pound was 'saved'. The mood of the meeting that evening in No 10 was one of relief and even celebration, although some of us were sad that the opportunity had not been taken to let the pound drop. Robert Neild described it as a 'Munich'. After the meeting broke up, when I went round the Cabinet table and started talking to Harold Wilson, George shouted from the other side of the room: 'Come here, Donald'. When I obediently did, he reminded me that I was his economic adviser, not the Prime Minister's.

After that, the question of devaluation or depreciation was taboo. I used to sit at my desk doing sums on the subject on odd bits of paper but whenever someone came through the door I hastily put them into my drawer. Tony Crosland and I were once carpeted by George Brown who had discovered we had actually been discussing the forbidden subject, but he had the decency, when we went into his room, to offer us a couple of stiff drinks first, saying: 'You'll need these; I've got some pretty unpleasant things to say to you'. And at a working supper in No 10 just before Christmas 1964 the economists present were severely warned by the Prime Minister against talking or even thinking about the matter.

I think that was the evening when George was angry with the PM about something and deliberately kept the DEA team in his room drinking until well past the time fixed for supper, so that when we arrived at No 10 the others had nearly finished, Harold Wilson was understandably annoyed, and I had to make do with a slice of cold ham eaten off a plate that had already been used. I think it was also the evening when, after supper and we had moved to another room, some abstruse question about the forward exchanges came up. When I agreed with the other economists, George said to me, very sharply: 'Come on now, Donald, don't be so cowardly; pull your chair forward and say what you were telling me this morning' – I had had a working breakfast with him in his flat. I tried to keep calm and said: 'But, First Secretary, we were talking about quite different matters.' He nevertheless kept on bullying me, to such an extent that, after the meeting, Jim Callaghan apologised to me for his colleague's behaviour.

Then, in the summer of 1965, I woke up one morning and decided something really must be done about the exchange rate. I drafted a note which I proposed to give to George Brown and found that Neild, Balogh and Kaldor had – quite independently of me – drafted one of their own. We conflated the two and presented copies simultaneously to Wilson, Callaghan, Brown and their Permanent Secretaries. Shortly afterwards, Eric Roll and I were summoned into George's presence. I went in expecting a really rough ride but to my surprise George started by asking Eric why we should not devalue rather than upbraiding me for having proposed it.

He thereupon arranged a week-end house party at the country seat near Cambridge of his friend Lord Walston, then a Junior Minister in the Foreign Office, to which I was invited together with Tony Crosland (who had by then left the DEA to become Secretary of State for Education and Science with a seat in the Cabinet) and Roy Jenkins (who, as Minister of Aviation, was not yet in the Cabinet but a rising star and influential). Eric decided not to come and none of the other economists who had signed the memorandum were invited. After dinner on Saturday, Brown, Jenkins, Crosland and I retired to a separate room where it became apparent that the other two Ministers could not give George sufficient political support in a campaign to get devaluation; and the next morning I said to George 'I suppose I had better go back to Oxford and get on with this bloody old Plan'; because by then I had reluctantly become very busy preparing the 'National Plan'. This was based on growth in the economy of 25% over the six years 1964 to 1970, an average of 3.8% a year. This was no greater than the growth achieved over the previous six years, but I had convinced George it was not on without devaluation. He actually wanted a higher figure than 3.8% so that he could have a higher pay 'norm', but I successfully resisted this.

I have described how greatly discussions in NEDC under the previous administration helped George to put a prices and incomes policy together in the early months of the DEA, including the setting up of a National Board for Prices and Incomes, under Aubrey Jones, in March 1965. I had got to know Aubrey while at Neddy. He gave me some (very expensive) lunches which I always found enjoyable and stimulating. I was struck by some of his views on economic matters which, coming from a Conservative MP who had held Ministerial posts, seemed to me – to say the least – unorthodox. One day, early in 1965, he invited me to lunch at the Savoy Grill. I had suggested to George that he might be a suitable Chairman of the Board and asked if I should cast a fly over him. George said 'No, I'd like to wait a bit' (though he did invite him not long afterwards). So off I went to the Savoy Grill. But I had hardly started my smoked salmon when the Head Waiter came and said I was wanted on the 'phone. When I picked it up I heard the most extraordinary noises which I eventually deciphered as an apoplectic George apparently demanding my instant return to the DEA; reminding him that I had just started lunch with Aubrey cut no ice. So, after hasty apologies to my somewhat surprised host, I left him – and my delicious but largely untouched smoked salmon – and took a taxi to the DEA.

I soon found out what the trouble was. George had been unexpectedly summoned to see the PM in No 10 at 2.30 and, wishing to be briefed in advance by his officials, had come to the DEA to find his Private Secretaries' Office unmanned. I went into his room to find him berating

Tom Caulcott, his Principal Private Secretary – by no means for the first time – for this unpardonable sin against the First Secretary of State. George certainly had a point, but instead of getting the briefing he wanted, he spent the time 'phoning all the top officials he could get hold of and castigating them as they one by one came back from lunch. So by 2.25, when he had to dash off to No 10, he had got no briefing at all – and we were not even sure what the meeting was about.

George also discovered that some of his chief officials had gone off at lunchtime without saying where they were going. He regarded this as outrageous and issued an edict that we should all leave in our offices, easily accessible, an exact description of where we would be during the following forty-eight hours, to be brought up to date continuously.

The next afternoon I was going to Paris for a meeting of the OECD on the day after. So I dictated a meticulous time-table of when I would be in the car between the DEA and Heathrow; at the airport; in the plane; in the car to my Paris hotel; at dinner with the British Ambassador to the OECD; at the Château de la Muette for the meeting on the following day; and so on. As a matter of principle – or human rights – I refused to say where I would be, or what I would be doing, between 11 pm and 7 am. I considered that this would be an unacceptable intrusion into my private life; although in fact I fully intended to, and did, sleep innocently and alone in my hotel. The new regime quickly fell into desuetude and after a mere day or two was conveniently forgotten by both George and his obedient servants.

The work on the National Plan was sufficiently advanced to be put formally before the NEDC for their meeting on 5 August 1965. I always tried to discover the day before such meetings what line the management team was going to take, and usually had no trouble finding out from Ken Johnson of the FBI, with whom I was on very good terms. (He had in fact just become a staff member of the Confederation of British Industry – CBI – which formally came into being on 30 July with the merger of the FBI, the National Association of British Manufacturers and the British Employers Confederation.) But on this occasion I could not get hold of Ken or indeed anyone else who could help, and when it came to eight o'clock I thought I should tell George, who immediately came over from the House of Commons to the office. He got his secretaries to ring round every management member of the NEDC and their secretaries and wives and anyone else they could think of to find out where they were but could get no information at all until eventually, after hours of trying, one clever secretary – Pat Kelly – tracked down the CBI team at a house near

Sunningdale owned by Courtaulds, of which Frank (later Lord) Kearton – a CBI member on NEDC – was Chairman.

George at once rang them up, reprimanded them for hiding themselves away in such a conspiratorial manner and, when they told him they were not going to endorse the Plan at Neddy in the morning, said that he and I were driving down immediately to talk to them. As we were preparing to leave, George shouted in the corridor – we had both had a few drams – 'where is the bloody Plan and where is bloody Donald?' And on the way down he asked me how long it would take to redraft the Plan if we devalued. I said 'perhaps ten days' – one of my forecasts that was never given a chance of being proved wrong.

When we arrived – it can't have been much before midnight – they had had dinner, and kindly gave us sandwiches, for we had had nothing to eat. We went on arguing and trying to reach a form of words to issue after the Neddy meeting, with Ken and I preparing draft after draft. When things seemed hopeless, George got up, put his Plan under his arm – as it was still in typescript, and several inches thick, it looked huge – and made for the door saying he was going to ask the Prime Minister to call a General Election and blame the CBI. It was like a customer walking away from a carpet dealer during a bargaining session in an Eastern bazaar. To complete the analogy, just before he reached the door, they shouted 'come back, come back', and he did. I was thus spared the embarrassment of deciding whether to follow my master, or wait to see whether he was bluffing – of which he was perfectly capable as an experienced bargainer – and would come back in any case.

Eventually we argreed a draft – effectively endorsing the Plan – and departed in the early hours in George Brown's Austin Princess (a grander and more spacious vehicle than today's sleeker models), giving a lift to Ken Johnson. The car soon afterwards broke down, but conveniently near a public telephone box. The driver got out and, when George was very rude to him about the breakdown, pulled himself up to his full height and said: 'I too am a member of the Transport and General Workers' Union'. He then rang up the Government car pool and came to say that another car was on its way. But George got increasingly impatient and said 'this is impossible; it is now 3 o'clock in the morning and I have to chair this very important meeting at 10.30'. So to calm him down I said I would go to the phone box and try to get a taxi. When I came out, having failed, George had disappeared. He had thumbed a lift in a Mini driven by a man with a red beard, accompanied by a girl in pink trousers, who took him home. Shortly afterwards the reserve Austin Princess arrived and Ken and I drove back to London in much better style. (George left his copy of the

Plan in the Mini, but its driver very correctly returned it as soon as he found it.)

After a few hours' sleep I went over to George's flat before the Neddy meeting and found him elated by his success with the CBI, and by some encouraging advance trade figures for July. We then went to Millbank Tower where the NEDC endorsed the National Plan more or less on the lines agreed with the management team. The statement issued by the Council after the meeting was later published at the beginning of the document, and can be found by the keen researcher immediately after George's Foreword.

Despite George's difficulties with the CBI's Neddy team on that occasion, he generally got on remarkably well with businessmen, at least in the early days of the DEA. When on his best behaviour he could be extremely impressive. One observer said 'he really could charm the birds off the trees'; and during a discussion at Nuffield one weekend, Frank Kearton said: 'I've been a life-long Tory; but I must say I have the very greatest admiration for George Brown'. I reported this to George and it may not be entirely coincidental that Frank became one of the group of businessmen with whom George had regular dinners and discussions in his flat, and that he later appointed him Chairman of the Industrial Reorganisation Corporation, set up in 1966.

But he could also be extremely rude and offensive to some business-men. I believe that Sir Maurice Laing, Chairman of the well-known construction company, and the first President of the CBI, suffered from George Brown nearly as much as I did. When, however, nearly twenty years later, I expressed this view to Beatrice Gilpin, a great repository of knowledge about CBI Presidents, having been Personal Assistant to every one of them, she expressed surprise and told me how George had asked after Maurice in the friendliest possible terms when he was unwell. But that was just like him. He said some pretty nasty things to me too; but when I got ill towards the end of 1965 he could not have been more solicitous.

I mentioned the chauffeur who was a member of the Transport and General Workers' Union. George, in his earlier days, had been a relatively minor official (although he is on record as saying that, had he continued to work in the union instead of going into politics, his chances of rising to the very top would have been quite high). When he got fed up in the DEA he sometimes used to say: 'I can always go back to my union'. Now Frank Cousins *had* risen to the very top and was at the time General Secretary of the 'T and G' – the big white chief – but on secondment as Minister of Technology in the Wilson Government. He was well below

George in the Government pecking order, but when the two were together I sometimes thought I detected a certain deference on George's part; but it may have been just my imagination, for this was hardly a usual posture for him to adopt.

Not long after the August meeting of NEDC, George went for a holiday in the South of France to stay with his friend Harold (later Lord) Lever, whom I got to know when he became a junior Minister in the DEA after George left, and later when he was Financial Secretary to the Treasury; he was a wealthy financial wizard, charming, intelligent and an inveterate talker. While George was on this holiday he (George) repeatedly rang up the DEA to ask how the gold and dollar reserves were doing and was most reluctant to accept that this was not information he could have on an open line.

In fact, despite the good July trade figures, the position of sterling remained precarious; and later in August we were put under pressure from the Americans, who were giving us a lot of financial support, to tighten up our prices and incomes policy. So George came back from his holiday and called the TUC and CBI to the DEA. I was interested that the TUC did not immediately dismiss his proposals as a 'bankers' ramp'. After a preliminary meeting in George's room overlooking St James's Park, the CBI team repaired to my room, just to the south of George's, the TUC stayed in George's room and George, Eric Roll and I went into Eric's room, just to the north of George's. I kept popping into the other rooms to see how they were getting on. The CBI did not have too much difficulty in accepting the proposals but the TUC were far more of a problem.

When the three sides got together again and, after a marathon session, Woodcock and the TUC seemed quite unwilling to accept, George Brown rang up Harold Wilson in the Scilly Isles and said he would have to call an Election and blame George Woodcock. Woodcock paid not the slightest attention but eventually it was agreed that he would 'put' the proposition to the TUC General Council, with George Woodcock understanding 'put' in the sense of explaining, and George Brown in the sense of recommending. Ater that, following hours in which the two had called each other the most terrible names, they were virtually embracing and on the very best of terms – and no doubt talking about religion; for George Woodcock was a Roman Catholic and George Brown an Anglo-Catholic and they indulged in such conversations. (Just before he died George was received into the Roman Church.) The proposals were broadly accepted by the General Council and by the Trades Union Congress at Brighton in September, after a further marathon of negotiations in that watering place between George Brown and the TUC leaders.

I first met Woodcock at the NEDC early in 1962; and I knew and had dealings with him while on the staff of NEDO, in the DEA and at the beginning of my time at the Treasury until he retired. He was in my view a great man, but not easy to get to know. The only time I felt I was really getting on intimate terms was late one evening in Oxford. I had taken him to dinner at Nuffield after we had driven from London together. I doubt whether he really enjoyed the dinner and subsequent chatting very much, but when I took him back to my house where he was staying and we started drinking cocoa – his choice, not mine – in the basement kitchen, he really began to let his hair down and talk about some of the personal things in life – until my then wife shouted from the top of the stairs that it was time for us to go to bed.

Intellectually, he towered over his colleagues on the General Council, having a brilliant mind, and a well-trained one, which few of them had had the opportunity to acquire. He was at Ruskin and New College, where he got a First in PPE and a research scholarship. Then, after a brief spell as a Civil Servant, he joined the TUC, where he remained for thirty-three years. He could sometimes appear arrogant, but was essentially, I believe, modest. He was a man of high principle – and kindly. Unlike some of his predecessors (and his two successors) he definitely did not want a Peerage or even a Knighthood. The only honour bestowed by the Monarch which he coveted was to become a Privy Councillor – which he did; although many academic honours were showered upon him which he accepted.

One felt that he at times despised some of his colleagues for their inferior intellect; but if so he usually managed to conceal his feelings, at least in public. At times too, it seemed that his colleagues felt he was too much of an intellectual and out of touch with the real world. I once listened to a conversation over drinks before lunch, after a Neddy meeting, between Woodcock and other members of the TUC team. They were discussing what the average British working man thought about something or other. The argument got quite heated and one of them asked Woodcock: 'When did you last talk to a British working man, anyway?' He was rather taken aback and paused a little before replying: 'Oh, I think about a fortnight ago.'

It was perhaps a little unfair, because he had an impeccable working-class background, having left school at an early age and worked for over ten years as a cotton weaver before going to Ruskin; but admittedly that was long before; and admittedly his colleagues had more contact with rank and file trade unionists than he did.

Vic Feather succeeded Woodcock in 1969, but had only four years in the job as he reached the retirement age of sixty-five in 1973. During the whole of this time I was in the Treasury although, as mentioned earlier, I had known him as a member of the Political Economy Club before that. He was elected to the Club – founded in 1821 and still going strong – in 1956, a couple of years before his fellow trade unionist, Frank Cousins, in 1958; I was a relatively new boy, not having been elected until January 1963. Vic was a keen member. While we were both members he opened the discussion at least three times – a much better record than mine.

He was a contrast to Woodcock in almost every direction, except that they both spent the greater part of their working lives in the TUC and were both good General Secretaries – but in very different ways and with very different styles. Unlike Woodcock, Feather had no formal education after leaving school at an early age. Also, compared with Woodcock's way of talking, he could, on first hearing, sound almost like a buffoon. But one quickly realised that his particular idiom was in fact an extremely effective form of exposition, and that what he said was based on a lot of thought by a highly intelligent mind and backed by a shrewdness based on long and varied experience; for although he was in the TUC for thirty-six years he did not by any means live in an ivory tower but got around a lot both at home and overseas.

In his *Who's Who* entry he listed as his recreations 'painting, reading, cricket' – George Woodcock gave none – and I was at a dinner at the Bank of England at which Vic Feather and Leslie O'Brien, the Governor, had a most esoteric discussion about many aspects of art which made me feel a real Philistine. When the time came, he saw no reason to decline a Life Peerage. He probably regarded it as rather a lark. Whereas George Woodcock was a serious character who did not smile very much, Vic, though equally serious on important matters, always seemed to be bubbling over with fun. After he retired, he had a very part-time job in NEDO. His room in Millbank Tower was next to Margaret's and she tells me how Vic would often say to her: 'Have you half an hour to spare, luv; come in and have a chat', and then regale her with hilarious stories, with a particular liking for irreverent gossip about the Great and the Good.

One story concerned the 1975 Referendum on whether we should stay in the EEC. It used to annoy him, he said, that people always said trade unionists were against the Common Market, so he decided to speak out in favour, up and down the country. He 'found himself on the platform with some funny people'. One was Ted Heath. (In fact I believe they got on extremely well.) They were billed as the two star speakers in some Town Hall, and a large audience was looking at the platform (where 'the local dignatories were already seated, hidden behind a bank of flowering potted plants') waiting to applaud the speakers whom they expected to come on to the platform from one side or the other. Unfortunately, the organisers had arranged that they should proceed up the gangway in the middle of the hall from the back. After they had advanced several paces in deafening silence – because the audience were looking in the wrong direction – Ted, with great presence of mind, did a right about turn, walked out again and said sharply to the usher: 'when we go in again, start the clapping'. This he did, and on their second entry all heads quickly turned and they were greeted with a crescendo of applause as they walked to the platform. 'Would you believe it?' said Vic to Margaret. 'It was a good laugh.' He was a lovable soul.

When Lionel Murray – often known as Len – succeeded Vic as General Secretary we had already worked closely together for over ten years while he was Head of the TUC's Economic Department and later Assistant General Secretary, and I was at Neddy, the DEA and the Treasury. We saw a great deal of each other, as backroom boys – if I may be modest on behalf of both of us. Given this relationship, I talked to him during that period a good deal more than I ever did to Feather or Woodcock.

Although our bosses, and sometimes Len and I, did not always see eye to eye on quite a lot of matters, I cannot remember a single cross word passing between us. We had many long discussions – often à deux – about whether, for example, the economy could grow at 6% a year, as the TUC were wont to argue in the latter part of the first Wilson Administration, or only at a much lower rate as the Government – and I – believed; and if, when I thought I had convinced Len of our point of view, the TUC later behaved as if our conversation had never taken place, that is only in the nature of backroom boy relationships. Soon after he became General Secretary I moved from the Treasury to the CBI, but continued to see him regularly, mainly at Neddy meetings and informal get-togethers between the CBI and TUC – described in Chapter 11 – and at Nuffield, which made him a Visiting Fellow.

Like Woodcock, Murray had had a good training in economics. He spent most of his working life in the TUC, like his two predecessors. Though a less colourful, less unusual, personality than either of them, this does not mean he was not a good General Secretary. I believe that he was, and did a lot of good by stealth, in his quiet way, in what was a difficult period.

When the Conservatives won a second term in 1983, with a large majority in the Commons, he showed his pragmatism by trying hard, and with considerable success, to persuade the TUC to come to terms with this fact of life and do its best to cooperate with the government in power – something in which he had always believed – despite the brush-off it had had during much of the first Thatcher Administration. But the TUC's 'new realism' was knocked sideways by the Government's decision to ban the civil service unions at its Cheltenham communications headquarters; and it must have been a bitter pill for Len to swallow when the TUC decided – against his advice – to boycott meetings of NEDC, of which he was a strong supporter. I do not know how far it was disillusionment with the Government, with things that were happening in the trade union movement, or concern about the state of his health, that made him decide to retire early, in 1984. But it saddened me greatly, not only because here was an old friend who must be suffering, for whatever reason, but also because I felt the TUC were losing prematurely a man of great common sense, integrity and courage.

Coming back to 1965, the National Plan was published on 16 September and received a lot of press coverage and probably more favourable comment than it deserved. We had a party that evening in my room, to which George Brown was invited. I had prepared in my mind a very short speech starting 'Will you please all stop enjoying yourselves for a moment and listen to me?' Then I intended to say how honoured we were to have the First Secretary with us and ask him to say a few words. Unfortunately, everything was running late – I was long overdue at a dinner to meet my old friend 'Nugget' Coombs, Governor of the Australian Central Bank, who was visiting London – and decided I must truncate my speech still further, with disastrous results. I clapped my hands for silence and said: 'Will you please all stop enjoying yourselves and listen to the First Secretary?' George started his speech by saying he would send me to Oman if he went to the Foreign Office – but did not carry out this particular threat.

That evening George said he wanted me to leave almost immediately for the United States to 'shadow' the Chancellor who was going first to New York, then to the annual meeting of the IMF and World Bank in Washington, taking in en route a meeting of Commonwealth Finance Ministers in Jamaica. My instructions were to see that Callaghan did not make 'deflationary' statements or commitments that might prejudice growth and the National Plan – rather a ludicrous task for someone in my position when you come to think of it – and to present copies of the Plan with George's compliments to some of his pals in the US.

So off I flew to New York, with a pile of newspapers full of the Plan (and containing some photographs of myself which greatly impressed the stewardesses). The Chancellor, his wife Audrey, and his entourage – who were already there – were very kind and understanding. After a day or so in New York, we flew to Jamaica. As soon as the plane landed I was given a message to 'phone George immediately in London. This I did and he gave me, in semi-code on a crackly line, instructions which I could not make head or tail of. I think it was about something he had been discussing with Eric Roll and he assumed, wrongly, that I knew all about it; this happened not infrequently and could be extremely embarrasing. However, I said I would do my best and rang off.

In Washington I spent little time at the formal meetings. Shortly before they began, I was invited to a party by a New York banker – Roy Rierson – for officials, bankers, journalists and economists, both American and non-American. As we sat down to the meal he said he would ask me in a couple of minutes to talk about our National Plan; and before I had time even to finish my grapefruit I had to get to my feet and give a completely off-the-cuff speech. Whether it would have been better if I had had a little time to marshal my thoughts into a brief account of a huge matter on which I had been working for months I do not know. But I had no opportunity during the next week because apart from innumerable parties – a not unimportant part of these occasions – I spent most of the time rushing from place to place to talk about the Plan, about which there was a surprising amount of interest, and approval for many of the things we were trying to do. I talked to the Council of Economic Advisers; White House staff; groups at the Federal Reserve Board, Treasury, State Department, Bureau of the Budget, Department of Commerce, the Brookings Institution, the IMF, the UK Embassy; representatives of the OECD and of several governments, including those of Germany, Sweden and Italy.

After a time, I felt I could have done my spiel on the Plan in my sleep. The only troubles were, first, that in the middle of a speech I sometimes wondered whether I had already made a particular point to that audience, or to one before. Secondly, I almost began to believe that everything – yes everything – I was saying was one hundred per cent true.

When I got home, I first felt fine, then began to get little low fevers which were no more than inconvenient, then pleurisy which turned into pneumonia. I took an unconscionably long time to get fully fit again.

Whether I got up too early, or had picked up some mysterious bug in Jamaica, whether it was the delayed result of overwork, I never discovered, despite numerous medical examinations, during which I found that doctors could disagree almost as much as economists. So I decided that my failure to recover sufficiently to go back to work for several months was due to a disease I christened 'georgebrownitis'.

Not long before I got ill, the Rhodesian crisis came to a head, Ian Smith made a unilateral declaration of independence, and the government imposed economic sanctions. George Brown saw a chance of getting the DEA in on the act and putting the Treasury, whose policies were increasingly threatening his expansionary objectives, in the shade. He summoned his chief officials to his room in the House of Commons, reminded us – and me in particular – of the old Ministry of Economic Warfare of 1939–45, and said we were going to be just that, thereby becoming the most important economic department in Whitehall. After a long harangue elaborating his proposals, which a man from Mars might reasonably have assumed was about warfare against an enemy called Callaghan, he remembered to say: 'Of course the whole object is to bring down this man Smith.'

The General Election of 31 March 1966 gave Labour a majority of nearly a hundred, so the Government no longer had to struggle with the precarious parliamentary situation that had existed since October 1964 when they were returned with a minute majority. This was sometimes adduced as one reason for not devaluing at that time, and some of us hoped that now they would take the plunge. But they did not – no doubt, in part at least, because they had nailed their colours so firmly to the mast of £1 = $2.80.

In the summer of 1966 the idea of a pay freeze, which was being mooted, was rejected out of hand by George Brown as completely unacceptable and unworkable, but he still wanted devaluation. Then one day, after a meeting he had just had with the Prime Minister, he summoned me to his office and told me he had had a great success in getting agreement that Ministers would discuss the exchange rate in a few weeks' time – which meant virtually nothing – and then added, to my amazement: 'by the way, I have agreed to have a pay freeze' – an example of how Harold could twist George round his little finger. But having agreed, he put his heart and soul into getting the freeze accepted by the TUC General Council and through the House of Commons; and it was endorsed at the Trades Union Congress in Blackpool (after George had left the DEA).

At the same time a severe deflationary package was being prepared to complement the pay freeze in defence of the pound. George Brown opposed this unless it was accompanied by devaluation. So did most of his officials and advisers and a good number of his Cabinet colleagues. George put his point of view in a nutshell: 'What is the point of digging a hole in the ground by slashing domestic demand unless you create extra demand from exports and import substitution to fill it up again?'

The fortnight or so before the package was announced on Wednesday 20 July – without a devaluation or depreciation of the pound – was a hectic, confused and sometimes emotional period for those concerned, including myself. There were continuous comings and goings, uninterrupted by the usual weekend breaks. These involved, among others, George Brown, Ministerial colleagues, officials and advisers in the DEA, Treasury and No 10. Apart from lots of telephone calls there were many meetings and huddles – in Government offices, in private homes both in and out of London, in George's flat in Carlton Gardens, in the Reform Club (conveniently located in Pall Mall, little more than a stone's throw from George's flat, and of which a good many of the officials and advisers concerned were members). Perhaps the strangest location of all was where George and I met on the Sunday before the package. I was in the DEA and phoned him at his flat, but the 'scrambler' (supposed to make conversations unintelligible to anyone tapping the line) would not work. So we arranged to meet half-way, on the Duke of York Steps (where we were snapped by a sensation-seeking press photographer), and walked up and down the Mall discussing a new suggestion I wanted to put to him.

On the previous evening George had summoned his chief DEA officials – about half-a-dozen of us – to a meeting at his flat at 8.30. When we arrived at the door we saw Leslie (later Lord) O'Brien – who a few months earlier had succeeded Cromer as Governor of the Bank of England – going in, and were told to come back later. Some ten days earlier the Governor had entertained George Brown and a few of us from the DEA to dinner at the Bank. The Governor had been a perfect host, but George in one of his belligerent moods; we wondered how Leslie would get on in George's flat that Saturday evening. After the Governor, George saw several other important visitors – Wilson had flown to Moscow that day and did not get back till Tuesday; and George regarded himself, as mentioned earlier, as Deputy Prime Minister.

It was not until about 10.30 that we were admitted to George's presence. It was a tense and disagreeable meeting, with extremely tough talking all round. George taunted most of us for letting him down at a critical moment and failing to resign when he was determined to do so if, as seemed likely, we had a deflationary package without devaluation; but he sent us all a written apology a couple of days later. During the next few days, George kept on threatening to resign, resigning, de-resigning. It was not an easy period for him; and he was not helped by being kept – so he told me – in the Commons till the early hours of Tuesday 19 July, and then having his granddaughter jump on his bed at 7 am. Yet, when I had lunch with him in the House that Tuesday and discussed, among other things, what he might do if he resigned, he was perfectly fresh and calm, and very cheerful and friendly with his fellow MPs – and the waitresses.

On 20 July, when the statement on the package which the Prime Minister was to make to the House that afternoon was being completed, some of us from the DEA were in the Cabinet Offices while the bits and pieces of the statement came out of the Cabinet. Sometimes we were not consulted, sometimes we were; and I have the distinct impression – though I cannot prove it – that it depended on whether the latest report was that George had resigned or de-resigned.

That afternoon he was not in the House to hear the PM's statement, so it was generally thought he must have resigned. He was in fact in his room in the DEA, drafting a letter of resignation, having given strict instructions that no-one should be allowed in who might dissuade him. But even then I remember Jimmy Clark – Number 2 to his Principal Private Secretary – a wonderful man who was both unflappable in the turbulent atmosphere of the Private Office and an experienced George-watcher – telling me he reckoned George was still no more than two-thirds of the way to resignation. A letter of resignation did go over to No 10, but Harold Wilson returned it and asked George to think again; and there were letters from many Labour MPs urging him to stay. I went home and watched the World Cup on TV – it was the year England won – and heard on the 11 o'clock news that George was seeing the PM again. It was officially announced at midnight that he had not resigned.

The deflationary package of 20 July – unaccompanied as it was by a devaluation or depreciation of sterling, either simultaneously or a few months later, finally ditched the policy of expansion – and that part of the National Plan which analysed the consequences of sustained growth at $3\frac{1}{2} - 4\%$ a year. But many of the policy recommendations in the Plan – which George just before publication got me to summarise in five pages under the heading 'Check-list of Action Required', showing also who was responsible for each action point – remained valid. For they were largely independent of the figuring, just as many of the policies in the NEDC Orange Book in 1963 had been largely independent of the figuring in the Green Book.

The package of 20 July was the first major U-turn of Harold Wilson's Government. The second was devaluation in 1967. Following the package, unemployment rose from 315,000 in the second quarter of 1966 to 515,000 in the first quarter of 1967. This does not seem high by later standards; the effects are hardly discernible in the statistics of Gross Domestic Product we now have; and they only show up as a temporary 'blip' in the index of industrial production. Nevertheless, the package had a profound psychological effect at the time.

Eventually, in August 1966, George did leave the DEA, but he did not resign. To his delight he was sent by Harold Wilson to the Foreign Office, swopping jobs with Michael (later Lord) Stewart, who came to the DEA. The next year of my life was very different from the previous two. Michael Stewart and George Brown were as unlike as chalk and cheese. George, when I came to work with him, had told me, to my dismay: 'we're not going to bother about facts and figures, like the people at the other end of the corridor (meaning the Treasury); we're going to rely on 'Fingerspitz-gefühl' ' – a rough translation of which might, I suppose, be 'the seat of our pants'. Michael Stewart, by contrast, wanted to know the evidence and read his briefs carefully – again, so it seemed to me, unlike George who seemed to ignore them, although one of his Private Secretaries assures me he read them assiduously. Michael listened politely while officials round his table put their points of view, asked some pertinent questions and then said he would make up his mind, which he did after due consideration. So in many ways he was a model Minister to work for, though he certainly lacked the flair and ebullience of his predecessor. Insofar as it is possible for a senior Minister and Member of Parliament, he tried to work sensible hours and did not share George's frenetic desire for activity, sometimes seemingly for its own sake. I remember George telling his Private Secretaries to arrange him some 'eight-day weeks'; and how he enjoyed driving his Jaguar at great speed to his consituency in Derbyshire whenever he could at weekends.

To do George justice, despite his apparent dislike of facts and figures, and possibly some feeling of inferiority vis-à-vis colleagues who had had much more formal education and in several cases brilliant academic careers, his instinct on major issues was as often as not extremely sound. Some would say that this is an understatement; that his mind, though relatively untrained, was intellectually high class; that the combination of this and his capacity to bully both officials and others – a capacity which he freely admitted and was not ashamed of – made him a formidable Minister; but that sadly, on occasion, his effectiveness declined as the day progressed.

During my period with Michael Stewart I worked a great deal with the Treasury and played a large part in cooking up with their economists (especially Wynne Godley) a proposal for a Regional Employment Premium (REP). This was in effect a subsidy to manufacturing employment in the Development Areas – broadly those with the highest unemployment rates. We argued that, for various reasons, which some found abstruse or even implausible, our particular proposal – unlike most other schemes to help less prosperous areas – need involve no real economic 'costs' to the economy.

Briefly, the argument was that it would not increase inflationary pressure or worsen the balance of payments, the two main things we wished to avoid at the time. The rise in demand in the Development Areas – where there was little danger of 'overheating' – would be accompanied by some shift in demand away from the rest of Britain. Although we calculated that the combined effect would be a small net increase in the national product, there should be some slackening of demand for labour in the South and Midlands – then fairly fully employed – so that the increase in national output could occur without an inflationary chain reaction. Also, the increase in imports resulting from higher demand in the country as a whole would, we reckoned, be offset by the favourable effects of the premium on our international competitiveness, so there should be no worsening in the balance of payments.

The DEA was jointly responsible with the Treasury for putting out the proposal, and Michael Stewart insisted – characteristically – that it should first be published as a discussion document. I had the job of deciding what colour the cover should be, and had discussions with the Stationery Office. It could not be white because that would make it a White Paper and thus official Government policy. It could not be blue because that would make it a Blue Book. It could not be red for obvious political reasons. The only other colour in stock was green so we chose a green cover. This was the origin of the 'Green Paper', now part of our political language when we wish to describe a discussion document.

During the time allowed for public discussion, I was asked by Sir Douglas Haddow, Permanent Secretary at the Scottish Office, to go to Edinburgh one evening to convince businessmen in Scotland that the REP was a good idea. After several Scots had expressed scepticism, an American running a branch of a US company said in effect: 'this could never happen in my country, and I can't understand you fellows; here is a senior Government official offering Scottish industrialists scores of millions – and you are criticising him.'

In August 1967 Peter Shore succeeded Michael Stewart at the DEA.

He favoured devaluation. We got on well and I spent much more time discussing matters with him than I did with either of his predecessors. But I found his mathematical ability rather limited. When some Treasury forecast showed unemployment at 2% in one half of the year and 2½% in the other half, and he said this was intolerable because it meant 4½% for the year as a whole, it took me some time to convince him that one had to divide this figure by two.

I also thought his priorities as a politician rather questionable on occasion (although officials who worked with him in the next Labour Administration spoke highly to me of his abilities as a Minister). One weekend in the spring of 1968, during a foreign exchange crisis, this time about the price of gold, a number of Ministers and economists were duly summoned to Whitehall. Now this was primarily a matter for the United States over which the UK Government had only limited influence (although what happened was important for us), and Peter Shore really no influence whatsoever.

But he got interested in the intellectual complexities and spent much of the weekend trying to master them. Instead, in my view, he should have been working on a very important speech he had to make in the Commons in the following week on prices and incomes policy, and preparing for interruptions and the subsequent debate. As a result, he put up a poor performance; and it is interesting that, not long after, responsibility for the whole of prices and incomes policy was transferred to the Ministry of Labour, rechristened the Department of Employment and Productivity, under Barbara Castle who was moved from the Ministry of Transport.

During the months before devaluation we had to be particularly careful what we said in public about our external financial position. One night I had a dream. I was going in to a cocktail party and met coming out Maurice Allen, my old tutor and then in the Bank of England. 'Be careful, Donald', he said; 'there are a lot of foreign bankers in there and they will ask you about our gold and dollar reserves.' I asked him how I should reply and he told me to say 'Oh, they're declining along'. I woke with a start and wrote 'declining along' on a scrap of paper by my bedside. I had no intention of using the phrase in public, but it seemed a brilliant Maurice-like way of showing a proper mixture of concern and confidence; and I did not want to forget it.

Next day, I was having lunch in the Cabinet Office Mess in Whitehall, where the food was only moderate but the opportunity of getting the latest gossip from senior Civil Servants unrivalled in London. I found myself sitting with Wynne Godley. I told him about my dream, and he said: 'That's funny; I had an interesting dream last night too.' He had been a professional oboist before joining the Economic Section of the Treasury where he built up a great reputation as a forecaster; and his dream was this. He was on a platform in a concert hall before a large audience, oboe at the ready, with his music on the stand in front of him, just about to start his performance, when his accompanyist whispered to him: 'Before you begin, Mr Godley, are you sure your notes are seasonally adjusted?'

On 18 November 1967, we at last had devaluation – at least three years too late in my view. Partly as a result 1968 was a nightmare. Confidence did not recover quickly and the phenomenon known to economists as the 'J-curve' meant that devaluation worsened the balance of payments before improving it. While still in the DEA I did a lot of work with the Treasury on what we should have to do if there were a real run on the pound and foreign governments and international institutions refused to bail us out any further – for we could not really contemplate another devaluation or a floating of the pound at that time. The more we looked at the consequences the more appalling they seemed to be. I began to understand how a country really could go bankrupt and how this could quickly necessitate controls of all kinds reminiscent of war-time, and risk upsetting our whole social fabric if imposed in peace-time. Fortunately the nightmare did not come true. We got through 1968, and by the time I had moved to the Treasury on New Year's Day 1969 things were on the mend, although this was not really apparent until well into the year.

Alec Cairncross had announced his intention some time before to retire early from the Treasury to become Master of St Peter's Hall, Oxford. There was naturally speculation about his successor. Nearly two months before the date of Alec's retirement Peter Jay – who the year before had left the Treasury to take up journalism – announced categorically in *The Times* that I had been appointed. There was no truth whatsoever in this. Roy Jenkins wanted me to go to the Treasury and Harold Wilson was content provided Peter Shore agreed. But Peter did not want to let me go and the matter was not finally decided until shortly before the event. However, Peter Jay's announcement in *The Times* (some other papers reported it simply as a rumour, which was legitimate) led on the next Friday to a rather vicious attack on me in an article in *The Economist*. It went through a list of misdeeds and misjudgements I was alleged to have committed during my career, the first being that I helped Prof to persuade Churchill that mass bombing of German cities would win the war, whereas I knew nothing about that side of Prof's work or the advice being offered until it became public knowledge long after the war.

Happily, I was strongly supported by everyone in Whitehall, including the Prime Minister, who described the article as 'character assassination', and wrote a letter for the following week's *Economist* (16 November 1968). I dealt in turn with the specific criticisms in the article, and concluded: 'I hope, by the way, that if you ever write about me again you will take the trouble to spell my name correctly.' (They had spelt it 'Mc' instead of 'Mac'.) This final remark – which I was urged to include by Margaret Hall – naturally cast doubt on the veracity of everything else they said: and Alastair (later Sir Alastair) Burnet, then Editor of *The Economist*, wrote me an abject letter of apology for this misspelling, but not for anything else in the article.

It also contained disparaging remarks about other economists, including those at the National Institute of Economic and Social Research. David Worswick, the Director, considered writing his own letter. He started looking up the files of *The Economist* to see what they had said at the time about my alleged misjudgements and found that in most cases they had taken the same line as I was alleged to have done.

The DEA continued for nine months after I left, so that its total lifespan was just under five years. After my experience of the ROBOT controversy in 1952, I had naturally been keen on the idea of an 'Opposition' to the Treasury within the government, if only to provide some safeguard against the Treasury pulling a fast one on an important matter of policy without the issues being properly debated. I suppose the events of July 1966, when George Brown helped to ensure that the pros and cons of devaluation were discussed more fully than they might otherwise have been, could be regarded as a rather macabre justification for the DEA in this role. But in general the idea of 'constructive tension' – as it was sometimes called – between a department (the DEA) responsible for growth and the long term and another (the Treasury) controlling policies affecting the short term, did not really work. The long run is a succession of short runs, and, in the event of a clash of interests, the Treasury was bound to win, at least so long as we had severe balance of payments difficulties. Any advantages of having two departments to some extent in rivalry were, I suspect, offset by the delays and conflicts that resulted; although I must say that, while George Brown and Jim Callaghan had some pretty good rows, relations at official level were really very good.

On the other hand, I think there was a need, in the early years of the Wilson Government, for a senior Minister, with a Department like the DEA, to coordinate the many other economic policies, outside the traditional Treasury responsibilities, which a Chancellor could not possibly have had time to cope with adequately, especially as he had recurring external crises on his hands. For the new government had a very ambitious economic programme covering many fields: industrial policy, regional policy, prices and incomes policy, the formulation – and quickly – of a National Plan. The first three could in principle have been carried out by the executive departments concerned, but I think it was useful to have a DEA in the early stages to initiate and coordinate the new policies while they were being worked out, and then quite sensible to allow the DEA to die off – it might have been better had this happened sooner – and let the executive departments carry on.

9

THE TREASURY: 1969–73

ON THE first of January 1969 I became Head of the Government Economic Service and Chief Economic Adviser to the Treasury. None of my predecessors had held both jobs, but all my successors have done. I shall say something about the first job later.

Shortly before my move to the Treasury, Audrey Carruthers, who had been my truly wonderful Secretary for nearly eighteen years – at Nuffield, Neddy and the DEA – announced that she was going to marry Keith Skeats, who lived in Oxford. But waiting in the Treasury was Mary Davies, the highly experienced Secretary to my predecessors for many years. I thought it would be helpful if I also had in my outer office a young economist to act both as a high grade research assistant and as an intermediary between myself and others, in the Treasury and elsewhere, when this seemed the most efficient way of conducting business and a knowledge of economics was necessary. This worked extremely well. There was no problem about the division of labour between my Secretary and the young economist. The latter received – I like to think – a valuable training, and my productivity was increased. So I had a succession of bright young men and women while at the Treasury and continued the practice at the CBI, giving it up only as a contribution to cost-saving when the CBI faced a worrying financial outlook.

When I arrived at the Treasury, Roy Jenkins was Chancellor, having succeeded Jim Callaghan a year before. He was very much in control of economic policy, having been proved right on devaluation whereas Harold Wilson had – in my view at least – been proved wrong. By contrast, both Callaghan and Barber were much more under the control of their Prime Ministers. By the summer of 1969 it was clear that the balance of payments problem had really been solved, and I was able to produce a truly convincing brief for Jenkins to use at the IMF meeting in Washington in September. Over the eighteen months or so since devaluation for which figures were available there had been a classic transfer of resources: a fall in public spending, hardly any increase in personal consumption, a large increase in private investment and a very large increase in exports coupled with a much smaller rise in imports. I used the brief a great deal myself during the IMF meeting – with US officials, bankers and others. Most were impressed, but some still sceptical. These included Roy Rierson. At a party similar to the one he gave in 1965, when I talked about the National Plan, I described the remarkable turn-round in our balance of payments – and this time I really meant it all; but a newsletter written by my host a fortnight later told his readers that the pound was still in a fragile state.

(Two years later, at the IMF meeting in September 1971 which I attended with Tony Barber, I found myself in a very different situation. The world's major currencies had been floating since the summer, and we were jockeying for position ahead of what became the Smithsonian Stabilisation Agreement in December. We hoped to negotiate a rate for sterling below that operative before we all floated. So I was free to tell all and sundry that the pound was too high. One British journalist wrote in his column that he had never imagined he would live to see the day when the Treasury's chief economist could be heard talking the pound *down* at a round of parties attended by the top people in the world's Central Banks and Finance Ministries.)

In 1969, turning to the home financial front, we actually had a negative Public Sector Borrowing Requirement (PSBR). I cannot claim credit for this (nor is it necessarily, or even normally, something to be proud of, although I believe it was appropriate in 1969). But I *am* proud that, during Barber's Chancellorship, I nearly halved the forecast PSBR for 1971/72, from just over £2 billion to just over £1 billion, in 48 hours *without any changes in policy*. When I saw the first draft of the relevant table for the 'Red Book' (Financial Statement and Budget Report) I felt instinctively that the figure was too high. So I spent two whole days having in my room in succession the officials who had estimated the various components of revenue and expenditure – about half a dozen groups on each side. On cross-examination they nearly all agreed that they had put in a small margin 'to be on the safe side'. Those estimating blocks of expenditure had raised their best 'central' estimates by perhaps 2% on average, while those on the revenue side had knocked a similar amount off. These quite small errors resulted in a huge percentage error in the PSBR – the difference between total public revenue and expenditure; and as both were of the order of £25 billion, the PSBR was over-estimated by £1 billion. My revised estimate proved very close to the mark; and incidentally, a billion pounds in 1971 is equivalent to nearly five billion in the prices of the mid-1980s.

I enjoyed my eighteen months with Roy Jenkins. He was a highly intelligent person to work for, as were his Ministerial colleagues – Jack (later Lord) Diamond, Dick Taverne, Harold Lever and Bill Rodgers. (Interestingly, all this Treasury team, except Harold Lever, joined the Social Democratic Party; as did a former political master – Lord George-Brown, as he had by then become.) I introduced Roy to a type of analysis I invented for forming a budget judgement which took account both of the uncertainties in forecasting and of the trade-offs between, for example, growth and unemployment on the one hand and the balance of payments on the other. I illustrated this by graphs which took the form of ellipses for different budget options and became known as MacDougall's 'flying saucers'. Roy found these illuminating and took them home at week-ends to his house in Oxfordshire to ponder over them. On some Friday evenings, he got off the train at Didcot while I was on my way to Oxford and on Monday asked for further elaboration.

In his first Budget after I joined the Treasury, in April 1969, Jenkins stressed the uncertainty surrounding economic forecasts. Then in his 1970 Budget Speech he reminded the House that, a year earlier, he had 'suggested that the outcome of such forecasts could not, except by accident, be wholly accurate'. He went on to say: 'In 1969, however, we nearly had an accident.' The estimate in the 'Red Book', published on Budget Day, for the percentage growth of national output between the second halves of 1968 and 1969 was precisely the same as the forecast in the 'Red Book' a year earlier, which was given to one decimal point.

By contrast, the forecast prepared for the 1970 Budget was far too optimistic about growth – and Jenkins settled for a mildly reflationary budget whereas we should have had a more expansionary one. However, this went down well with the voters because a General Election was expected soon and it was a pleasant change for a Chancellor at such a time to introduce what people regarded as a responsible Budget instead of the usual pre-election give-aways. A few weeks later, on my way back from an OECD meeting, I saw at the Paris airport a poster for a British newspaper saying, in huge letters, 'Labour Ahead'; and discovered that an opinion poll had suddenly shown Labour ahead of the Conservatives for the first time since 1967. When I saw Roy a year later in Leeds, when he was in opposition and we were getting honorary degrees, he agreed that the 1970 budget judgment had been a bad one economically but good politically.

Despite this the Conservatives beat Labour in the June 1970 General Election. One reason was the arrival of two jumbo jets from the US in one month (out of three scheduled for the year as a whole); this inflated the import figure for May, announced shortly before polling day, and cast doubt on Labour's claim that the balance of payments problem had been solved. Another reason was that inflation was an important issue, and Brian Reading had put out a Conservative Press Release two days before the Election explaining how it could be reduced 'at a stroke'. I did not find his analysis convincing, but have to say that Brian was my pupil at Oxford. I taught him first as an undergraduate at Wadham. He was one of the few who had benefited from studying economics at school, one reason – if I may be immodest – being that he was taught by an earlier pupil of mine. After getting a First in PPE he was elected to a Studentship at Nuffield where I supervised him, and after a spell in the Bank of England worked with me at the DEA. One evening he came to my room and said – to my surprise, for I had no idea he had party-political leanings – that he had accepted a job in the Conservative Central Office, but would not be taking it up for a few months. I said 'I suppose I had better tell George Brown.' So I sent him a minute and said that, as Brian would not be leaving for some time, we should have to decide what we were going to do with him (meaning how far his access to confidential papers should be limited, and so on). The minute came back within the hour with a marginal comment in George's handwriting: 'Shoot him!'

After the Election, Treasury senior officials gave a dinner for Roy Jenkins and his junior ministers. I do not know whether the incoming Chancellor knew, but he would certainly have had no objection. Another illustration of what relations between politicians of different parties can be like was an incident at a reception for Commonwealth Finance Ministers towards the end of the first Wilson Administration. I listened with a tiny Finance Minister from one of the smaller Commonwealth members to a conversation between Jim Callaghan, who had ceased to be Chancellor and become Home Secretary, and Reggie Maudling, then in opposition. It went something like this. Callaghan: 'When you get back, Reggie, you really ought to try the Home Office. It's much more fun than the Treasury.' To which Maudling – whom Callaghan had succeeded as Chancellor after Labour won the 1964 Election – replied: 'Well, I'll see, Jim. I certainly did leave rather a mess for you at the Treasury, didn't I?' The tiny Finance Minister was, to put it mildly, puzzled.

One advantage of being Home Secretary was that you had a personal bodyguard; although Roy Jenkins told me that when he held that Office and asked the bodyguard if he could stop him being assassinated he replied: 'I doubt it, but being so close to you I could write a much better report'.

Both Jenkins and Callaghan, who succeeded him at the Home Office, were men of courage and something that happened when Jim was Home Secretary convinced me that, whatever I may have thought of his economic policies, I could have every confidence in his ability to deal with people in a tricky situation. I spent most weekends in Oxford at the time, and went into Nuffield one Saturday morning in the spring of 1968 for a discussion on some matter of current interest with the other Fellows, including Callaghan who had been elected an Honorary Fellow when his stint as Visiting Fellow came to an end. When I arrived shortly before the meeting was due to begin, I found the quadrangle full of noisy students from various colleges, some carrying banners showing their disapproval of the Home Secretary's policy on the immigration of Kenyan Asians. I was told not to go into a small room on the ground floor where Jim was receiving a deputation of the protesters. So I went upstairs to the Common Room where the meeting soon began.

Jim came in a few minutes later, but the noise in the quad got louder and louder and it became difficult to carry on the meeting. Jim slipped quietly out; gradually the noise subsided and eventually ceased; and after ten to fifteen minutes he returned to the Common Room and took part in the discussion. It appeared that he had stood up in front of the indignant mob – a tall, imposing figure – suggested that it was discourteous to be interrupting the meeting upstairs which had nothing to do with Kenyan Asians, and invited them to come out of the quad, through the lodge, into the street, where they could continue their discussion without disturbing the other. This the students obediently did, following him like the Pied Piper of Hamelin; and then gradually dispersed.

During the Election campaign in June 1970 I felt able to fulfil a longstanding engagement to give a public lecture in the Festival Hall on 'the short-term regulation of the national economy.' I naturally took care what I said and in answering questions. But it was uncontroversial, and the only press comment was a friendly one headed 'Sir Donald Faces The Music': apparently those with good ears in the audience could hear faintly a concert going on in a neighbouring auditorium. It is hardly conceivable that ten years later a non-party civil servant could have given a lecture at such a time on this subject, by then a matter of acute political controversy.

When I learned that Iain Macleod was to be the new Chancellor in June 1970 I was delighted. I had heard about his intelligence, courage and wit. I had attended a lunch when he was guest speaker and his party in opposition. Talking about the Labour Government's record on economic growth, which had sunk to around zero after the July 1966 measures, he likened it to that of Scotland's rugby team when they once played the Springboks (when sport with South Africa was still respectable) at Murrayfield in Edinburgh. After the match someone asked a disconsolate Scottish supporter emerging from the ground 'how did you get on?' 'Och,' he replied, 'it was terrible, they beat us forty-two–nil; and we were lucky to get nil.' This sounded very funny, because we had never had *negative* growth since the war, in the sense of a significant fall in national output, apart from short periods when we had severe weather or long strikes. 'Recessions' had meant either a temporary cessation of growth or sometimes just a slowing down in the rate of growth. A dozen years later the story would not have seemed so humorous because we suffered a substantial *absolute* fall in output both in the mid-1970s under Labour and in the early 1980s under the Tories; nil growth then would have been quite an achievement.

Senior Treasury officials expected to be summoned to see Macleod for a long briefing during the weekend after the Election but were told he was unwell and would see us on Monday morning. So several of us fulfilled a longstanding engagement at a Ditchley Park weekend conference with a group of Americans.

Going down in the train one of them said to me: 'I hear Heath is going to abolish SST' – American for supersonic transport. I said 'splendid' because I had always thought Concorde a waste of public money. (This is one of the few economic matters on which I have disagreed with Margaret. She thinks it was well worth it, partly because she evaluates the 'spin-off' differently, but also because it is so beautiful; and it certainly is – we often see one flying over our roof garden in Pimlico on its way to Heathrow.) But my American friend had misheard when someone had told him the Conservatives were going to abolish *SET* (the Selective Employment Tax). This was common knowledge and I had always disliked the tax, being unable to accept the economic reasoning underlying its discrimination against services and in favour of manufacturing. But I would have been even happier had its abolition been combined with stopping the Concorde project. During the Jenkins period I had a running battle about SET with Nicky Kaldor, who had largely invented the tax when Callaghan was Chancellor. We sent successive minutes to Jenkins challenging each other's statistics and arguments, until Roy said this correspondence must now cease.

A little later, when Value Added Tax (VAT) was going to be introduced by the Conservative Government, partly because it was required of members of the EEC, but also because something had to replace the revenue lost by abolishing SET, I sent a minute to the Chancellor and other Treasury Ministers. They all knew I was glad to see the end of SET, but had been on the Richardson Committee which reported against VAT. So I put at the top of my minute (without apologies to Richard Lovelace) the following couplet:

> I could not love thee, VAT, so much,
> Hated I SET not more.

This prompted Maurice Macmillan (son of the great Harold), then Chief Secretary, to compose a Gilbertian poem about me, in the style of a well-known song in *The Pirates of Penzance*. This was one of the highly confidential papers I clearly could not take with me when I left the Treasury. I was about to write to Maurice to ask whether he had a copy when, sadly, he died; but I remember at least one line:

> He is the very model of adviser economical.

The Conference I attended at Ditchley Park in June 1970 was one of numerous weekends I have been privileged to spend in that delightful house, in superb grounds, a dozen miles north of Oxford. My only complaint is that one has had to work, when it would have been so nice simply to have lazed away the weekend, in pleasant company, eating, drinking, sleeping, playing croquet and walking round the lake.

In 1968 there was a Conference on 'Taxation and Economic Growth'. As is the usual practice, we split up, following a plenary session on Friday evening, into groups which discussed various aspects during Saturday and on Sunday morning, and presented their reports to plenary sessions on Sunday afternoon and evening. Not surprisingly, given such a controversial subject, the groups had to report a wide variety of opinions – particularly the one of which Kaldor was a member. Going back to London by train on Monday morning we made up parodies of the group reports, one on the following lines: 'The group was asked to consider whether the earth was round or flat. Some took the view that it was round, others that it was flat. Some thought there was insufficient evidence to support either view, others that it was round in one sense and flat in another. There were also a few who thought it a damned silly question.'

Another Ditchley Conference started on Friday 8 February 1974, the very day after Heath had announced that there would be a General Election three weeks later. Several MP's had been due to come but all pulled out hurriedly – save one. This was Enoch Powell, who had decided not to stand – after twenty-four years as a Tory Member of Parliament –

and became an Ulster Unionist MP in the October General Election that year.

I was Chairman of this Conference and one of my duties was to go round each of the groups and take part in their discussions. I particularly enjoyed my visit to the group of which Powell was a member. It was discussing, when I came in, monetary policy. Powell was better known then for his monetarist views (as well as his views on racial problems) than for his thoughts on Northern Ireland; and I took a mischievous pleasure taking him through one by one – rather like a tutor – the various steps in a speech he made purporting to prove that the rate of inflation was determined by the money supply, and – to my satisfaction at least – showing that nearly every step contained a *non sequitur*. I also remember watching Sir Michael Stewart, Director of the Ditchley Foundation, taking Mr and Mrs Powell for a gentle stroll to show them the garden. Every now and again Enoch would walk smartly ahead for twenty yards or so, then wait for the others to catch up, then walk smartly ahead again – a performance he repeated several times. I could not make head or tail of what he was up to. But I was told later that, at another Ditchley Conference, he had walked fifteen miles between lunch and tea. So I presume he was simply irritated by the leisurely progress of his companions.

We sadly had Iain Macleod in the Treasury for little more than a fortnight before he went into hospital and died a fortnight later. During this short period I formed the highest regard for him, partly because the two major things I advised him to do he did. One was as follows. As part of his desire to cut public expenditure he proposed to abolish investment grants to industry – but to put nothing in their place. Now under Jenkins I had got worried about the downward trend of profitability after allowing for inflation; and had a lot of work done on it. We reckoned that the real rate of profitability had fallen during the previous ten years by two-fifths; and I was afraid – as it turned out correctly – that this downward trend would continue. When I showed a couple of the charts we had prepared to Iain Macleod he quickly took the point and agreed that the abolition of grants must be offset by some kind of reduced taxation on companies; and this was in fact done by his successor, Tony Barber.

I had reason to be grateful to Iain Macleod several years after he died. While Margaret and I were on a fishing holiday in North West Scotland, we saw a beautiful basket of trout in a hotel porch and longed to fish on the loch from which they had come. So we called on John Macdonald at Inverpolly who, we were told, might give us permission. He was polite but somewhat dour, saying how difficult it was to arrange fishing on the lochs he looked after. Then, when he discovered I had worked for Macleod, a broad smile came over his face – he had for years been a gamekeeper for the Macleods in the Outer Hebrides. 'Well, well now', he said, 'so you worked for Iain Macleod. Och, of course you can fish on any of the lochs whenever you like'.

I found it very sad that both Iain Macleod and Hugh Gaitskell died so young and have a feeling that political developments in this country might have been a good deal better had they both survived much longer.

During the fortnight while Macleod was away before he died, Ted Heath took a great interest in economic policy. One day, Douglas Allen and I spent many hours discussing it with him in the garden at Chequers. I got horribly sunburned and suffered for many days afterwards. One of Ted's ideas was to keep out of industry's hair, which included not interfering in pay negotiations. And during the day, when the Department of Employment rang up from time to time about a negotiation which looked like leading to too high a settlement, Ted got increasingly irritated.

Another aspect of his desire – in the earlier part of his Administration – to 'disengage' the State was the abolition of what might be regarded as unnecessary Councils and the like, wholly or partly financed by the taxpayer. One evening when I was leaving Chequers for Oxford, after a talk with Ted, he asked, while seeing me off on the doorsteps, whether I was dining in one of my Colleges. I said no, I was dining in another College with Betty (Dame Elizabeth) Ackroyd, who was, I think, speaking at a Business Summer School there. Betty had been a fellow graduate student at Oxford and subsequently had a distinguished career in public service. Ted asked me what she was doing and I told him she was Director of the Consumer Council. He said 'Oh, I don't know whether we really need that', turned to his Private Secretary and said: 'make a note of that'. Not so very long after, the Council was abolished. If my conversation with Ted was the reason I am sorry to have been the cause of an old friend losing her job; but she had little difficulty in finding other ways of exercising her many talents.

Although we overlapped at Balliol during the academic year 1935/36, Ted Heath was a freshman and I was a research student living in digs and did not get to know him then. Nor did I get to know at Balliol the rest of the remarkable political galaxy, spanning the political spectrum, who were at the College in the 1930s. In addition to Heath there was Grimond, later Lord Grimond and Leader of the Liberal Party, Healey, later Deputy Leader of the Labour Party, and Jenkins, first Leader of the Social Democratic Party; the last two came up shortly after I had gone down, but I was to see a good deal of both later.

I first got to know Ted Heath in the summer of 1951, when I went to New York to do a UN job. I had been told by Maurice Allen, who had taught Ted as well as myself at Balliol, that Heath – who had become an MP the year before – was going there as an employee of Brown Shipleys, the London merchant bankers, to see how their corresponding outfit in New York operated; and that we might find it interesting to meet. I was earning an enormous tax-free sum in dollars and had a flat in Manhattan while Ted's supply of dollars was, I believe, less plentiful. He not infrequently came to supper and we got to know each other rather well. During the rest of the 'fifties he quite often came to Oxford and we went for long walks round the University parks discussing economics.

Then, when in October 1963 he succeeded Freddie (later Lord) Erroll as President of the Board of Trade (and so joined the Ministerial team on NEDC) he wished, very courageously – for it was a political hot potato – to abolish Resale Price Maintenance (RPM). He asked me – I was then in the Neddy Office – if I could write a quick paper on it for him. I recommended instead Margaret Hall, who knew the arguments backwards; as mentioned earlier, we tried unsuccessfully to get a recommendation to abolish RPM into the Orange Book. So she prepared the paper that Ted needed and thus played a part in bringing about a change which was accepted by Parliament, despite hostility from MPs who feared the effects on small shopkeepers, and revolutionised developments in an important part of the economy for years thereafter – with, I believe, beneficial consequences for the consumer and the country generally. Later on, working as a civil servant under a Labour Government in the DEA and then the Treasury, I ran into Ted Heath, who seemed to regard me with some suspicion. One evening at Nuffield, where he was a Visiting Fellow, I said to him 'if you win the next Election, etc etc'. He said, rather roughly, 'you must say "*when* you win the next Election" . . .' However, when he became Prime Minister we got on very well. Unlike his successor as Leader of the Conservative Party, Ted could be a very good listener. I knew this long before he became PM; and after he did there were several occasions when, at very small meetings – sometimes à deux – he listened attentively and without interrupting while I talked for ten to fifteen minutes about the economic scene and then waited, sometimes in an almost embarrassing silence, for a minute or two, before he began to ask questions – which were always pertinent.

I listened in a different kind of embarrassed silence when he was discussing music, or the latest stereo he had installed in No 10 or Chequers, with his Principal Private Secretary, Robert – later Sir Robert – Armstrong. For I am an ignoramus on music while Ted was an organ scholar at Balliol and continued music-making at a near-professional level; and Robert (son of Sir Thomas – 'Tommy' – Armstrong, well known as the Organist at Christ Church when I was an undergraduate) was already himself Secretary to the Board of Directors of the Royal Opera House, Covent Garden. When, during one of their discussions, Ted asked me what kind of stereo I had, and I said 'none', he was nonplussed. (Robert Armstrong – not to be confused with William – was to become a great Pooh-Bah and power in the land during the Thatcher Administrations – and was much in the public eye in 1986 when he spent many embarrassing days in the witness box of a Court in Sydney trying to defend the British Government's attempt to stop publication in Australia of a book about the British Secret Service by Peter Wright, a former member of that Service.)

On Macleod's death Tony (later Lord) Barber became Chancellor. He had a distinguished war record, including the remarkable achievement of taking a Law Degree with First Class Honours while a prisoner of war, and also of escaping. I got on very well with him – as I had with Roy Jenkins. Although highly intelligent he did not perhaps possess the exceptional intelligence of Jenkins; but was in some ways a warmer character.

Before describing the fascinating developments in economic policies generally during the next few years, I should say something about a matter that occupied me greatly in late 1970 and early 1971 and was not unimportant in the national context.

On 15 December 1970, an overtime ban and work-to-rule in support of a pay demand by electricity supply workers, which led to severe power cuts, were ended after the unions and the Secretary of State for Employment agreed terms for the setting up of a Court of Inquiry. This was established on 29 December. The Chairman was Lord Wilberforce (a Law Lord). The other members were Raymond Brookes (later Sir Raymond and then Lord Brookes), Chairman of Guest, Keen & Nettlefolds (GKN); and James Mortimer, a former Trade Union official and later General Secretary of the Labour Party. (He was the father of one of the series of young economists who worked in my Private Office.)

The Court asked the Treasury to give evidence 'on the significance of the dispute under consideration to the interests of the national economy' and Douglas Allen and I were the victims chosen for the assignment. For a considerable time we worked on virtually nothing else except the written evidence – presented to Parliament by the Chancellor on 11 January 1971, so that there was little time for Christmas or New Year jollifications – and then on our oral statements, and answers to the many difficult questions that might be put to us. Although most of our evidence was about the danger to the economy of excessive pay settlements generally, we had to master as much as we could of the dispute in question; and I understood for the first time how complicated pay negotiations could be.

The day for giving our oral evidence finally arrived. It was a Saturday – 23 January – and took place in Church House (not far from Westminster Abbey), and in public, with the press well represented. It went on during the morning and afternoon; we had beer and sandwiches in a pub during the lunchtime break.

We knew before that our job was not going to be easy. The employers (the Electricity Council) did not seem to have their hearts in keeping the settlement down, being more interested in industrial peace. The employer member of the Court, Raymond Brookes, appointed because of his reputation as a tough guy, had, we suspected, formed the opinion that craftsmen in the electricity industry were getting substantially less than his in GKN, making him not unsympathetic to the unions' claim. What we had not foreseen was how the Chairman would conduct the Inquiry, allowing us to be cross-examined by the union side in a pretty rough manner. He did not, for example, rule out of order, or even limit in duration, a long cross-examination of Douglas Allen about his own salary by Frank (later Lord) Chapple, of the Electricians' Union.

However, we had done our homework carefully, and managed to deal with most of the questions fluently and with authority. We were also able to go on the offensive because some of the evidence submitted by the unions' witnesses made such blatant misuse of statistics. But however well we may have acquitted ourselves as representatives of the public weal, we failed to prevent the Court from recommending what we regarded as an excessive package of pay increases and benefits. I think it fair to say that as a result Lord Wilberforce became regarded as a soft touch; he was appointed Chairman of another Court of Inquiry about a year later which helped to end a six-weeks' miners' strike with a recommendation for a very large pay increase.

Tony Barber became Chancellor on 25 July 1970 and during the rest of the year pursued a broadly neutral fiscal policy, with planned public spending cuts roughly offset by a proposal in October 1970 to take sixpence off income tax from April 1971. Then early in 1971, when he was giving lunch at No 11 to a few of his senior officials, I – and I think most of my colleagues – got the distinct impression that he would not worry unduly if unemployment rose to significantly over a million early in the Government's term of office provided it could be brought down later.

The aim of this would be to help reduce inflation. Now in those days it was generally thought that unemployment above a million would be politically dangerous (and I was doubtful about its effect on inflation both in the short and in the longer run). However, Barber's view – which is the kind of judgement that a Minister is there to make – coloured policy decisions.

The March 1971 Budget, though somewhat expansionary, consisted mainly of rather slow-acting measures. The Treasury forecast of unemployment showed a very steep rise during 1971 but it was not published, although any reputable economist who looked at the modest growth of output during 1971 forecast in the 'Red Book', and allowed for the lagged effects on unemployment of the relatively slow growth during the previous couple of years, could have deduced that this was the case.

At that time one of my jobs was to produce a brief monthly report on the economic situation and outlook for the Chancellor and the Prime Minister which went to hardly anyone else and certainly not to any Minister outside the Treasury. In nearly every report in 1971, I estimated that the 'headline' total of unemployment in the UK as it was then measured was likely to approach, or quite possibly top, the million mark in the winter of 1971/72; but neither Barber nor Heath seemed worried. After a time, as unemployment rose rapidly, other Ministers began to complain in public that the Treasury economists had greatly under-estimated the rise. This was irksome, because our unpublished forecasts were only a little below what actually happened – an example of what Civil Servants have to put up with.

Then there was a sudden change in November 1971. Tony Barber, Douglas Allen and I had been invited one weekend to what we expected to be a routine meeting at Chequers with the Prime Minister. Shortly before, we were told that both the meeting and the scope of the discussion were to be enlarged; and that William Armstrong, who had moved from the Treasury about three years before to be Permanent Secretary of the Civil Service Department, and (Lord) Victor Rothschild, Head of the 'Think Tank' (Central Policy Review Staff) set up by Heath, were also going. When we arrived, Ted started by asking William – who was obviously delighted to be back in the economic policy game again – what he thought. He said that, coming down in the car, he had been brooding over the situation and thought we should think big, and try to build up our industry onto the Japanese scale. This would mean more public spending. We should ask companies what they needed in the way of financial and other help, and give it to them. To my surprise Ted warmed to this and said 'fine, and of course we must give it only to the good firms, not the bad ones'. I had to pinch myself to make sure I was not dreaming because I had heard an almost identical remark from Harold Wilson in the same room in Chequers several years earlier. This was the occasion when Heath was converted – or at least first announced his conversion in my hearing – from a 'hands off industry' policy to one of selective intervention; and also to a major reflationary policy.

On the first point, Ted had got increasingly disillusioned during talks with industrialists, and dissatisfied with their investment performance; and judging by his and other Prime Ministers' behaviour I have almost come to believe that it is an occupational hazard of the job that after a time you begin to think you can run the whole of British industry by yourself in one afternoon a week.

William Armstrong was asked, in effect, to go away and organise some increased spending, particularly to encourage investment. Also, it now looked very probable that – despite some relatively modest expansionary measures in the summer – unemployment would top the million mark as I had repeatedly warned (in fact it did so in January); so Ted instructed me to prepare a plan for reducing it by 400,000 during the following twelve months.

During the next week I wrote a minute explaining why, although I was all in favour of an expansionary policy, I thought an attempt to reduce unemployment so quickly would be dangerous because it would lead to inflationary shortages and bottlenecks. But Ted dismissed my arguments. In the event, among the main reflationary measures that were then taken, I was less worried about the income tax reductions in the 1972 Budget than I was about the increase in public spending plans, which I argued would mostly become effective considerably later at the top of the boom, just when we least wanted such a boost to demand. This is what happened and, as with what I called the 'Keeler' spending boom of 1963/4, a Labour Government inherited, in 1974, what I sometimes naughtily call the 'Armstrong' spending boom – although this is perhaps unfair to William as he cannot be held responsible for by any means all the increase.

The explosion of the money supply – which many people are often thinking about when they talk about the 'Heath/Barber boom' – was, in my view, not an intentional part of the November 1971 shift to an expansionary policy. At the root of it was the Bank of England's consultative document 'Competition and Credit Control', published in May, which reflected a rethinking by the authorities over a period of years, and the new regime it proposed came into force before November.

I was much less involved in this aspect of policy than I was with others; but as I saw it, my interpretation of what happened – deliberately over-simplified – would go something like this. First, the Bank produced an inherently inflationary scheme (even after the Treasury had done all it could to improve it). Secondly, Treasury Ministers were warned that, if they wanted to get rid of the quantitative ceilings on bank advances then in force – a major object of the scheme – they would have to let interest rates go up and down – and that might well mean up – if they wanted to control the money supply. They said 'that's fine; we believe in the price mechanism.' Thirdly, the large increase in bank advances and the money supply – which, as we had expected, followed the introduction of the scheme before long – was tolerated for a time as not inconsistent with the new expansionary policy. Fourthly, at the first sign of interest rates going up Ted Heath, who thought – with some justification – that he knew a good deal about finance having worked in a merchant bank, blew up. How far his resistance delayed, or reduced the extent of, the very substantial increases in interest rates that took place I cannot say; but in so far as it did, this contributed to the continued rapid increase in the money supply.

The result of the reduction in taxation, the increase in public spending, and the monetary expansion was a boom. Barber got the rapid growth predicted in his 1972 Budget; but after the first few months of 1973 output levelled off because of the growing shortage of labour, materials and capacity which I had feared, and which were shown clearly in the CBI's Trends Surveys. Unemployment came tumbling down, though it took about two years for it to fall by the 400,000 that Ted had asked me to plan for over a period of one year.

Price inflation had come down from 10% to 6% between the summers of 1971 and 1972, helped by the CBI's remarkable initiative in getting pledges from members not to raise prices by more than 5% in return for the expansionary government measures mentioned earlier. But after that, both prices and wages began to rise more rapidly. There were long talks between the Government, the TUC and the CBI in an attempt to get voluntary restraint. They broke down and a statutory policy was introduced in November 1972. Early in 1973 a Pay Board was set up under the Chairmanship of Sir Frank Figgures (with whom I had worked in Paris in 1948–49 and during the convertibility dispute in 1952) and a Prices Commission under Sir Arthur (later Lord) Cockfield.

I had crossed swords with Cockfield over Resale Price Maintenance in the early days of Neddy and worked with him later in the Treasury when he was brought in as Adviser on Taxation Policy to Tony Barber. He was a great expert on this, having been for years in the Inland Revenue before going into business. He worked hard on a scheme to reform the tax and social security systems which was described in a Green Paper 'Proposals for a Tax-Credit System'.

But this was a scheme that would take years to get working; and my experience as a tax payer did not convince me that Arthur had had much success in the shorter term objective of simplifying income tax and making it more intelligible to the public. One weekend, when I went back to Oxford, I found an envelope from the Inland Revenue containing a leaflet similar, I suppose, to one put through the letter boxes of millions of fellow sufferers that week. It began something like this: 'your earned income tax allowance has been abolished' – hardly calculated to encourage the taxpayer, although it was in fact part of a sensible reform of the old system and did not mean that the tax man was going to take more of one's salary. The leaflet went on to 'explain' the new system in incomprehensible Revenue jargon and then, I suppose, told me my PAYE code or something of the sort.

On Monday morning I stormed into Arthur's office, flung the offending piece of paper on his desk and said: 'I thought you were supposed to have been simplifying the tax system, and look at this'. He agreed it was awful; the Chancellor had asked him to get it simplified and made less discouraging; but the Chairman of the Inland Revenue had virtually threatened to resign if a single comma was altered. Subsequent experience has confirmed my view that there is a long way to go to make the tax system more intelligible; I believe this might do more to improve incentives, and reduce dissatisfaction with the level of taxation, than reductions in the actual burden of tax costing billions of pounds.

When Cockfield became Chairman of the Prices Commission I imagine he must have agreed to do so reluctantly, out of a sense of public duty; but once he had accepted he typically threw himself heart and soul into the job. But it was bound to be a bed of nails. He was bound to leave himself open to comments such as one I made to him after I had gone to the CBI, when profitability was abysmally low, and the Commission had issued a report containing a diagram showing – with apparent pride – how price control had held back what could have been an upturn in profit margins. Arthur invited some of us from the CBI to lunch at the Prices Commission and I said – only half jokingly: 'I suppose you know Arthur – as an old friend – that you are destroying British industry'. He was not too pleased, and defended himself; and perhaps I was being unfair because he was, after all, carrying out the job he had been appointed to do.

I promised at the beginning of this Chapter to say something about my job as Head of the Government Economic Service (GES). Before I joined the DEA, in October 1964, there were around 20 in the GES (excluding NEDO), mainly in the Treasury (where the numbers had increased considerably while I was at Neddy, possibly – in part – to cope with competition from that quarter). By the time I moved to the Treasury at the beginning of 1969 there were something like 180. During my period of nearly five years as Head of the Service the expansion continued, but at a more modest pace – around a hundred were added.

During the earlier period the great bulk of the expansion was in departments other than the Treasury. First, there was the creation of the DEA. Secondly, there was a substantial increase in departments connected with trade and industry as economists took over more of the work traditionally done by statisticians. Thirdly, Barbara Castle liked to have economists around, and wherever she went recruited them in large numbers – at the Ministry of Overseas Development, the Ministry of Transport, the Department of Employment. Fourthly, there was a widespread building up of small economic staffs throughout Whitehall, often in departments previously employing none.

When I got to the Treasury, I soon realised that the GES, which had grown like Topsy during the past four years, needed a lot of tidying up. But I was busy enough as Chief Economic Adviser to the Treasury – and trying to fulfil my administrative responsibilities as head of the Treasury economists. For a time I was helped, very efficiently, by my Deputy, Fred Atkinson (later Sir Fred and a holder of my post). But he was busy with economics as well, and in any case went to another department before very long. I appealed to William Armstrong, as Head of the Civil Service Department (CSD), for an Assistant Secretary to help me run the GES. This seemed a reasonable request, for my job covered the whole government machine, but it was turned down. So I appointed one of our own Senior Economic Advisers (equivalent in rank to Assistant Secretary) who was willing – and indeed keen – to do the job. This was Peter Davies.

I could not have made a happier choice. He had been in the Treasury since 1955, apart from a brief sortie outside, and had experience of many aspects of its work; this had brought him into contact with numerous other departments and with economists and administrators at all levels. He was an excellent administrator and a master of English prose. Before joining the Treasury he was on the *News Chronicle* and *The Times*. On top of all this, he had a charming, sympathetic manner. I do not know how many economists he must have helped – privately and informally – in his quiet way by listening to their problems and offering friendly advice.

Possibly this was as important as the formal changes we made, with the help of others, in the management of the Service. Some recruitment during the period of rapid expansion had been pretty slap-dash – sometimes resting on no firmer basis than a half-hour interview – and some departments had not been setting sufficiently high standards. So we pressed ahead with more rigorous, and uniform, selection procedures – with, for example, the same full day of written and oral testing of those coming straight from university, whichever department, or selection of departments, they expressed a preference to work in.

Also, with more economists wanting to make a career in the Service, and the need to provide for mobility between departments (and especially out of those employing only a few) we felt it necessary to set up boards to discuss with members of the GES their career development – their ambitions, their preferences, their fears – and to assess their potential for promotion, on a Service-wide rather than departmental basis. When we started these boards we always asked, at the end of the discussion, what those interviewed thought of this new experiment. The response was almost universally favourable; and one man thought it was absolutely marvellous. He had been employed, he said, for nearly twenty years as the sole economist in an out-station of a department which shall be nameless, and no one had ever before discussed his career with him. I think we got him a transfer fairly soon afterwards.

As Head of the GES I sat on a Committee under William Armstrong with the task of implementing a Report on the Civil Service by a Committee set up by Harold Wilson to consider how it might be improved. It had been chaired by Lord (John) Fulton, who had tried, not very successfully – my fault not his – to teach me political philosophy at Balliol. The Report contained some good ideas, but a lot of it was, in my view, rather general and even woolly; and I was obliged to read, and sit through discussions of, long papers by the CSD which I thought were sometimes like sermons. First there was the text – a paragraph from Fulton; then ten pages discussing what it might mean; then another ten considering what might be done about it; and a final section quite often saying why nothing was possible or, worse still, with no conclusion at all.

But some of the Fulton recommendations were accepted. One was that intermediate grades and salaries should, so far as possible, be eliminated. This concerned me personally. When I joined the DEA as Director-General in 1964, the question of my salary arose. After some bargaining with Laurence (later Lord) Helsby, then Head of the Home Civil Service, we agreed on a salary higher, in relation to Administration Class salaries, than any – or almost any – economist employed as such had received in the past. But it did not correspond to any grade in the Administrative Class. During my early years in the Treasury it was £100 below that of a 'Second Permanent Secretary' (a grade which existed only in the Treasury and a very few other Departments where there were 'Super-Permanent-

Secretaries' who got paid more than Permanent Secretaries elsewhere). This token gap was intended, I suppose, to preserve the notion that economists should be 'on tap' rather than 'on top'.

But after the Fulton recommendation I have mentioned had been accepted, along with the principle of an 'Open Structure' at the top of the Civil Service for administrators and others alike, this gap could not continue. My salary would either have to move up £100, or move down much more to that of the rank below – Deputy Secretary. The answer was obvious, but I had to waste a couple of hours being interviewed about my job by three people sent along by the CSD, including a management consultant, before it was decided that my salary, and status, should be that of Second Permanent Secretary. My successors have mostly continued to enjoy this position; so my bargaining with Helsby, and my endurance of the two hour interview, struck a not unimportant blow in raising the standing of economists in government.

I felt strongly that it would have been better had the CSD spent less time writing long, metaphysical papers for the Armstrong Committee and conducting pointless job evaluation interviews, and more on such mundane matters as pensions. During my last couple of years as Head of the Service I had a lengthy correspondence with William Armstrong about the unsatisfactory pension provisions for Government economists who had spent much of their working life – as I had – either in University work or on temporary secondment to Government jobs. William sent polite replies to all my letters. They were always long and often contained largely incomprehensible jargon. I once said to him: 'I bet you didn't read that one before you signed it'; to which he replied: 'No, I read it but I admit I couldn't understand it'. I did however make some progress, but it was not until about eighteen months after I had left the Treasury that a scheme very much on the lines I had advocated was introduced. I was delighted, on behalf of economists then in the Service, but just a little put out that the new arrangements were not adopted earlier; for my own pension from University and Civil Service work combined would have been twice as much.

One little thing happened while I was at the Treasury which might be regarded as symbolic of some aspects of economic policy. The Chancellor's room had for long been on the second floor overlooking Parliament Square. But Tony Barber found the noise from the traffic distracting. So he decided to move 180° round the great circle in the Treasury building to a room overlooking King Charles Street, which was much quieter. This meant that all his senior officials also had to move their rooms 180° to maintain the same position – geographically speaking – relative to the

Chancellor. We all, in other words, did a U-turn. Those who know the inside of the 'New Public Offices' will understand how difficult it can be to know just where one is in that great circle, with no windows looking onto the outside world – in particular which way is East and which West; and after the 180° movement of my office I quite often came out of my door and made my way to what I thought was Whitehall only to find I was coming out opposite St James's Park – or vice versa; although I had worked in this building for many years, I had completely lost my sense of direction.

The location of the Chancellor's room has not, so far as I know, changed again, but it would be optimistic to conclude that the disturbing and bewildering changes of policy of the last twenty years or so, with each major party on returning to power wanting to reverse the policies of its predecessor – almost, it often seemed, for the hell of it – and then doing a U-turn itself in mid-term, have come to an end.

10

TOKYO AND BRUSSELS

BETWEEN 1970 and 1977 I spent some time in Tokyo and Brussels. As these visits spanned my time at the Treasury and the CBI, and do not fit easily into my chapters on either, I describe them together in this separate chapter.

I first visited Japan in 1970 for a Conference on 'Economic Planning and Macro-Economic Policy' organised by the Japanese Economic Research Centre. I arrived some days before the Conference, partly to have time for calls on Japanese officials and the mandatory visit to Kyoto. But more important was that Sir John Pilcher, our Ambassador, had invited me to stay at the Embassy. It seemed to me that, insofar as it is possible for a Westerner, he really knew his Japan. He had served there in the Diplomatic Service before the war, and studied Japanese in Kyoto for two years. He later served in China, and when I arrived in Japan had been our Ambassador there for several years. So I got from him at least as many insights into the mystery that is Japan as I did during the rest of my stay.

Of the Conference participants, roughly ten were from the West, and twenty Japanese – half civil servants, half academics. Their mastery of English was enormously improved since I used to have excruciatingly embarrassing visits in Nuffield ten to fifteen years earlier from Japanese who hardly knew a word, and we seldom got much beyond the inevitable smiling, bowing and handing over of gifts. I had agreed to come on the understanding that I need not prepare a paper, but found myself talking a lot. It was familiar stuff: monetary policy, incomes policy, regional policy, public expenditure, economic planning, forecasting – the lot. The standard of discussion was high – and there was quite a lot of open disagreement between the Japanese. I was later told that this was unusual. Some 'Young Turks' kept on complaining that projections of public expenditure in their national plans were repeatedly under-fulfilled and those of private investment over-fulfilled. (I explained that in our country the problem had usually been the reverse.) The result was, to some extent, a combination of 'private affluence and public squalor'.

I was particularly interested in a paper by a Japanese official which attempted to measure standards of living, not by conventional national accounts statistics, but by 'social indicators' such as those relating to housing conditions, sanitation, leisure, nutrition. When these were averaged to make composite indicators so that seven industrialised countries could be compared, Japan came well at the bottom of the list. The UK came very near the top – a much better showing than conventional measures indicated. I asked the author for details of his findings, which his paper gave only in outline. He promised to send them, but they never came. I saw him regularly during the next few years at OECD meetings in Paris and he always had a plausible excuse; but I suspect the real reason was that his government found his results embarrassing.

On the third day the Conference moved from Tokyo to Nihondaira, near Mount Fuji – a three-hour bus ride. One evening we had a traditional Japanese-style dinner in the annexe of our hotel at which many Japanese wives were present and we were served and entertained by Geisha girls. The presence of wives was unusual and it was the first time many had seen Geishas. It was a delightful occasion, apart from the agony of sitting cross-legged on the floor; and I was touched when Hisao Kanamori, an old Oxford pupil working in the Economic Planning Agency, came to sit opposite me and talk to me as his 'master'; and we ceremoniously poured out sake for each other. I then was taken down to the basement under where we had been eating by two Japanese colleagues, accompanied by John Meyer, President of the National Bureau of Economic Research in New York. The contrast was shattering. From the quiet Japanese elegance above we were suddenly transported into the vulgar din, immediately below, of a mob of people playing American fruit-machines, and bowls in numerous alleys; and they were drinking coca-cola rather than sake. I wondered how the Japanese could combine the two cultures without contracting schizophrenia.

In 1975 Margaret was invited to a Conference in Tokyo to take part in a session on 'Problems and Countermeasures in Small Business Management'. This did not convey very clearly the intended content of the session. But she wanted to see Japan, wrote a paper – she had worked for the Bolton Committee on Small Firms – and flew off to Tokyo, giving a couple of lectures in New Delhi on the way. Although, as a foreign woman, she was fêted, interviewed by the media, and in effect treated as an 'honorary man', she was amazed at the treatment of Japanese women and felt it was a time-bomb ticking away under the structure of Japanese society. She had a woman Professor friend who would have had to resign her job had she got married. She also had a young female interpreter and one day, before a television interview on the distributive trades, she was checking with her terms like 'one-stop-shopping' to make sure there were Japanese equivalents and, just for fun, asked if anyone would understand the phrase 'Women's Lib'. The interpreter replied, rather sharply: 'I am one'.

Then in 1976 I was invited to a Conference in Tokyo to commemorate the hundredth anniversary of the *Nihon Keizai Shimbun* (Japan Economic Journal) which – believe it or not – was founded in 1876, not long after Japan was opened to the outside world. It is a daily paper rather like the *Financial Times*, but has a huge circulation – 1.8 million when I was there – and an evening edition. My letter of invitation said that the organisers would pay for a first-class return air fare, but added: 'If you take your wife or secretary with you, economy-class return fares will be paid for two'; also the living allowance would be 50% greater. I thought this very considerate; and also most convenient because I was not sure whether my divorce would come through in time for me to marry Margaret before going to Tokyo. In the event she came as my fiancée but, though neither wife nor secretary, we got the two economy-class air tickets and the higher living allowance – *and* were invited to lunch by the Ambassador, by then Sir Michael Wilford.

This time I had to write a paper – on 'Economic Growth and Social Welfare'. But it was not a chore. It was closely connected with problems we were then grappling with in the CBI. It also proved to be a multi-purpose paper (like the piece I wrote just after the war on 'Britain's Foreign Trade Problem'). I gave it later, suitably adapted, as a lecture at Leeds University; then in Glasgow at the University of Strathclyde (who had kindly given me an Honorary Doctorate); and it was published in the *Scottish Journal of Political Economy*.

In a paper with such a title I naturally talked about the ratio of public expenditure to Gross Domestic Product (GDP), and could not resist a friendly swipe – tinged with admiration – at my former Treasury colleagues; for in less than a year – if not quite 'at a stroke' – they had recently reduced this politically sensitive ratio by 12–13 percentage points without cutting a penny off public expenditure. They had performed this feat of magic, first, by revising the definition of such expenditure (the numerator in the ratio) to exclude a lot of capital spending by nationalised industries – which made sense – and in other more debatable ways; these together took 7% of GDP off the ratio. Secondly, they had increased GDP – the denominator – by measuring it at 'market prices' (which include net indirect taxes) rather than 'factor cost' (which excludes them). This brought us into line with international practice – and conveniently knocked a further 5–6 points off the ratio.

Before leaving Tokyo we called on the Keidanren, the CBI's counter-part in Japan. Most of their senior people happened to be touring Europe – and visiting the CBI. We were received by a friendly elderly gentleman from whom we learned a great deal, including the gist of a science fiction novel about how the Japanese islands sank slowly under the sea and the inhabitants had problems getting accepted as refugees elsewhere. The moral was that Japan should make greater efforts to tell the world about Japan and the Japanese, even at the expense of spending less effort studying other countries. This made me recall my journey home from the 1970 Conference when I found on the plane a large party of Japanese embarking on a tour of Europe to study in detail how VAT worked. I did not begin to offer my views; I wanted to get some sleep.

I first visited Brussels on business while in the Treasury. Although Britain was not an EEC member until 1973, we were invited to some meetings in 1972 as a member-elect. Once, when some crisis arose, I went over for a day or two with Tony Barber. We were allowed to attend certain meetings of the Six and not others, and there was nothing we could do about the crisis anyway. So it was a waste of taxpayers' money; but we had fun – Tony was an agreeable companion – and got an inkling of how chaotic meetings of EEC Ministers could be.

I also went to meetings of Government officials, especially after we became full members, along with Denmark and Ireland. I recall my first meeting when an Irishman was present. For an hour or so it was deadly boring as the Chairman went round the table and everyone (including myself) made long, pretty meaningless, but polite speeches, based on rather indifferent papers by the Secretariat – until we got to the Irish delegate, whose turn to speak came nearly at the end. He was magnificent. 'This is disgraceful', he said, 'I only got the papers – and not very good ones at that – a few hours before I left Dublin; and now I find in front of me a pile of addenda and corrigenda which I have naturally had no time to read. How can we carry on a useful discussion on this basis?' The second time round the table we let our hair down in no uncertain manner; but very little came out of the discussion.

When I went to the CBI and started attending meetings of UNICE (Union des Industries de la Communauté Européene) – broadly the CBIs of Europe, including some not in the EEC – I found them equally unproductive. In 1976 I was persuaded to be Chairman of a newly formed Economic Policy Steering Group, but after a couple of meetings could not stand it any longer, pleaded pressure of other work – I was chairing another group in Brussels, described below – and resigned. Some, however, of UNICE's non-economic committees did useful work; and at least one economic committee – the Groupe Conjoncture – produced very useful information on the economic situation and prospects in Europe; but this was hardly surprising since it was chaired by Doug McWilliams, a very able Deputy-Director of Economics at the CBI.

Now to be more positive about my visits to Brussels. In 1973, shortly before I joined the CBI, I was invited to be a member of an EEC 'Study Group on Economic and Monetary Union 1980'. I was reluctant to agree, knowing how busy I expected to be at the CBI. But they were keen that I should accept because the CBI wanted to become more involved in Europe, and the Chairman was to be my old friend of Paris days, Robert Marjolin; so I agreed. The Group comprised fifteen economists, lawyers, sociologists and others. There was another British member, Andrew (later Sir Andrew) Shonfield, and one of the things I enjoyed most was coming back on the evening plane from Brussels with him after our meetings. We were usually pretty exhausted and, whenever we could, bought a half bottle of duty free whisky (much cheaper than the equivalent in miniatures). But with or without this stimulant, I could be sure of a fascinating, amusing, talk with this gifted, lovable, character – even though some of the broad-brush, imaginative ideas he tossed around were not always comprehensible to my 'tiny little Chinese mind'- but perhaps that was only when I had had too much Scotch. He was then Director of Chatham House, and in 1978 became Professor of Economics at the European University Institute in Florence, a post he held until his untimely death in 1981.

He published many thought-provoking books, including his seminal *Modern Capitalism* in 1965. At the time of his death he was writing a major sequel. He left numerous drafts and notes, and in the last weeks of his life wrote an outline of the final chapter for the book which he knew he could not complete. Then his talented widow performed a prodigious labour of love and edited this material into two books 'by Andrew Shonfield, edited by Zuzanna Shonfield'. Margaret and I attended both of the parties to celebrate their publication, given by Zuzanna in their Chelsea home. They were joyous occasions – as Andrew would have wished. (The only thing I hold against him dates back many years. He interviewed me on the radio when it was the civilised convention to agree the questions in advance. We duly did this over dinner in the Reform Club, then went off to the BBC where he asked me completely different ones.)

At its first meeting the Marjolin Group had no difficulty in agreeing that monetary union, meaning either a common currency or irrevocably fixed exchange rates between national currencies, was a long way off; the target date of 1980 proposed some years previously was wildly unrealistic. For the second meeting I submitted a paper giving some idea of the enormous changes required to achieve and maintain a monetary union in Europe – far, far greater than was implied by people who said, in effect: 'How nice a symbol of European unity it would be if we had only a single European currency; and surely this would involve only minor technical problems'.

I showed how wrong this was by describing, and quantifying, the extremely powerful 'equilibrating mechanisms', as I called them, which enabled – but only just – a nation like the UK to sustain a common currency (equivalent to irrevocably fixed exchange rates between different parts of the country) without intolerable *regional* disparities developing in levels of unemployment, living standards and rates of economic growth. (The Scottish and Welsh national movements then quite powerful reflected in part dissatisfaction with such disparities as remained.) These 'equilibrating mechanisms' were numerous, but many stemmed from our large national budget and social security system. This meant that, when a part of the country tended to get depressed, the effects were cushioned to a very considerable extent by lower payments of taxes and insurance contributions to the centre and higher receipts of unemployment and other benefits. There might be a further cushioning as a result of arrangements between the central and local governments which helped less prosperous areas to maintain public services despite a fall in local revenues; and deliberate regional policies to help such areas through subsidies, tax reliefs and public investment. My analysis was broadly accepted by the Group and one of its conclusions was that monetary union could be achieved only when there was a much larger Community budget; it was then around ½% of the Community's GDP, compared with an average of around 45% in member states.

A second conclusion was that, while there had been much discussion of *customs union* and *monetary union*, there had been very little of *economic union* – there was a deathly silence when I asked the Group what it meant – and hardly any analysis of one major aspect of it, namely *public finance* – public expenditure and taxation (including social security arrangements).

In the light of these conclusions of the Marjolin Committee, the Commission decided to set up a group of seven economists – a much better number than fifteen – to study the role of public finance in

European economic integration; and I was asked to be Chairman. It was
an almost embarrassingly English-speaking set-up. Of the seven members, one was Scottish (myself), one English (my friend Arthur Brown
from Leeds, who had done much relevant work on regional economics),
one Irish; and those from Belgium, Italy and Germany spoke excellent
English. The odd man out was the Frenchman, whose knowledge of
English was limited. He was, however, very nice about it, especially when
he agreed that we could excuse the interpreters from coming in one
Saturday and carry on the discussion entirely in English. Also, our two
main consultants, knowledgeable in the field of 'fiscal federalism' (a
fascinating branch of economics I first discovered on this job) were from
the US and Australia – in both of which countries, few would deny, the
main language is a form of English. Finally, one of the brightest members
of the Secretariat was an Englishman, Michael Emerson – a contemporary of my son while reading PPE at Balliol. When it was announced that
Roy Jenkins was to be President of the Commission I recommended
Michael to him as the economics member of his Cabinet, and Roy
appointed him to that post.

The Commission did us proud in providing a first class Secretariat; and
these words are sincerely meant, unlike some conventional expressions of
gratitude in prefaces to Committee reports. To a considerable extent our
Group was a Steering Committee of highly qualified Commission staff,
who did an enormous amount of original, detailed, statistical and other
research, although each member of the Group (except the Chairman – I
try to justify this later), and our two consultants, also contributed papers.

We had fourteen meetings between April 1975 and March 1977.
These usually took up the whole of a Friday and sometimes spilled over
into Saturday. It was quite an effort – for I was hardly idle in the CBI – but
well worth it. We started by studying eight *existing* economic and monetary
unions: five federations (West Germany, USA, Canada, Australia,
Switzerland) and three unitary states (France, Italy and the UK). While
recognising that the Community could not be anything like so fully
integrated for many years, we believed that our analysis threw light on how
its public finance activities might be expanded and improved during the
next decade or so. We established many interesting orders of magnitude
and other facts: for example, that inequalities in income levels between
member states in the Community were at least as great as regional
inequalities within the existing unions, even *before* allowing for the
re-distributive effects of public finance; and much greater *after* allowing
for these effects, which were negligible in the Community but very
important in the eight countries. We also found that public finance in the

existing unions played a major role in cushioning short-term fluctuations, thus confirming one of the Marjolin Group's conclusions.

We discussed the implications of these findings, and many others, for the future of the Community's finances, distinguishing three scenarios. First, it was possible to conceive at some distant date a Federation in Europe with federal (as distinct from state and local) public expenditure of around 20–25% of GDP, as in the existing federations. An earlier stage could be a Federation with a federal expenditure of 7½–10% of GDP, which we judged might just be sufficient to support a monetary union, provided it concentrated much more than in existing federations on reducing geographical disparities in productivity and living standards and the cushioning of temporary fluctuations.

But we concentrated mainly on a third scenario, of more immediate relevance, with Community expenditure building up to 2–2½% of GDP. This figure was not plucked out of the air, but justified in detail. We recognised that most governments were reluctant to see any significant increase in total public expenditure at all levels – Community, national, state and local. So we looked at possible transfers of expenditure from national to Community level; for savings in existing Community expenditure (eg on agriculture); for the most cost-effective methods of achieving the objectives (we learned much from the experience of existing federations); and the avoidance of regulations, harmonisation, etc, which were not worth while, given the bureaucratic and other costs involved. We estimated that our suggestions should not increase public expenditure at all levels (net) by more than 1% of Community GDP; and that this could well be offset – or more than offset – by the efforts being made by governments to restrain their national expenditures.

We argued that extra Community expenditure was mainly needed to help weaker members improve their performance rather than to increase by mere subsidies their private and public consumption. We felt it important that the benefits of closer integration be seen to accrue to all, and that there should be growing convergence – or at least not increasing divergence – in the economic performance and fortunes of member states. We also discussed methods of financing extra Community expenditure.

We finished up with a General Report of some 70 pages and another document of over 500 pages containing 17 original papers by members of the Group, our consultants and the Secretariat. The General Report contains an 8 page 'Introduction and Summary' of which I am rather proud (and which perhaps makes amends for my failure to contribute to the 500-page document). I thought something much shorter than the semi-final draft of the General Report was required, both for readers wanting a quick idea of what we were saying, and to clarify our own thinking about the logical sequence of our argument and the really essential things we wanted to get across.

So on the Thursday before the day-and-a-half meeting at which we were determined to finalise our Report, I sat down in my hotel bedroom in Brussels after dinner and went on until 3 am drafting a summary. This was typed in the morning while we were going through part of the main draft and checked by me over lunch. I gave a corrected draft to the Group at our afternoon session and it was agreed with very few changes on Saturday morning. It is true that some members had to leave before the end of the meeting and one could not attend at all. I was tempted to take advantage of this, but better judgment prevailed; everyone was given ample opportunity to comment by post or telephone, and I was able to give the Chairman's 'green light' to go ahead with the physical production of an unanimous Report two-and-a-half weeks later, on 30 March 1977.

Considering the need for translation into five languages, it was good going that it was possible on 16 May to publish the Report, present it formally to Jenkins (who was very complimentary) and hold a press conference. The PR geniuses in the Commission had arranged this for 12.30 pm, so not surprisingly rather few journalists turned up; and they had not sent copies to newspapers in London. Partly for these reasons the initial press coverage, though friendly, was limited. But I had not expected the Report to catch many headlines, though it did get a few. We regarded it as much more something that would, we hoped, be read, digested, debated and referred to over a considerable period ahead; that it would be useful not only by virtue of our suggested changes in the Community's finances but as a lasting treasure house of information and analysis; and that it would prove valuable, not just as a picture of what might happen in the dim and distant future, but in clarifying thought about problems likely to arise in any case during the next ten years.

I had a stream of requests for copies from academics, research institutions, politicians, businessmen and others. I was asked to talk about it by a House of Lords Select Committee, the Federal Trust, Chatham House, the Economic and Monetary Affairs Committee of the European Parliament. It was discussed a lot in Brussels and to a lesser extent in Whitehall. It was called in aid – sometimes, I fear, incorrectly – in the discussion that followed Roy Jenkins' speeches later in 1977 calling for more rapid European integration; in discussions about the European Monetary System; and in the controversies about the UK contribution to the Community and methods of increasing its total revenue.

The Report became quite well-known among those interested in European affairs. It came to be called the 'MacDougall Report' – the first, and only, time a report has been called after me. I am proud of this, even though it does less than justice to the many others who did most of the work, because I think it was a good report. I cannot help feeling a little sad about the rather meagre progress that has been made so far in the integration of the Community along the modest lines we suggested; but was pleased to be asked in 1986 to chair a conference on 'The Future of European Community Finance', based on a report recently completed by an international group in Brussels, which drew quite a lot on the report we had published nearly a decade before, and regarded many of our recommendations as still valid.

11

A FRESH VIEWPOINT –
THE CBI: FROM 1973

WELL before I reached the normal retiring age for civil servants of 60, Douglas Allen and William Armstrong asked me to stay on at the Treasury until I was 61, which great age I attained on 26 October 1973. I wanted another full-time job and started looking round early that year. One day I lunched with Campbell (later Sir Campbell) Adamson, Director-General of the CBI, whom I had got to know when he was Co-ordinator of Industrial Advisers at the DEA, on secondment from Richard, Thomas and Baldwins, the steel concern; he was also a Visiting Fellow of Nuffield. He asked if I would come to the CBI. My first reaction was that it was out of the question. I had made a point of being non-political throughout my working life, and this would look like coming off the fence. But on reflection I decided this was rubbish, since the CBI was not affiliated to any political party. I also felt that, although the CBI's job is to further the interests of its members, its actions to that end are nearly always of benefit to the nation as a whole. To call it 'the bosses' union' – as the popular press often does – gives a highly misleading impression.

So I accepted the job of 'Chief Economic Adviser'. I declined Campbell's suggested addition 'and Deputy Director-General', although I had that status. I could claim literally to be old enough to be the father of the next most senior economist, because Dermot Glynn, the Economics Director, was my son's contemporary at Balliol.

After leaving the Treasury I took a few weeks off. I wanted to finish, so far as possible, two volumes of collected articles and lectures, which I called *Studies in Political Economy*, and to start preparing my Presidential Address to the Royal Economic Society (RES), which I entitled 'In Praise of Economics', because similar Addresses here and abroad had in recent years been so critical of the subject. I had to spend some time on

RES matters during my first year or so at the CBI, both while President, and also afterwards when clashes developed between officers of the Society, and uncertainties about its finances; as immediate past President I could hardly refuse to join a committee to sort things out.

Another 'extramural' activity while at the CBI (and after) was Chairmanship of the Executive Committee of the National Institute of Economic and Social Research. I soon discovered that it was relying far too much on Government finance – both directly, and indirectly through the Social Science Research Council (SSRC) – and getting far too little from the Foundations and business, which fifteen years earlier had provided virtually all its income. So we started a campaign to get more business support. This was quite successful, which was just as well, for we were soon to have threats to other sources of finance.

Professor Ralf Dahrendorf, Director of the LSE, was prominent in a campaign to found a 'British Brookings', based on the famous Institution in Washington, DC. Given the relative sizes of the US and UK, the scale of such an organisation made it impracticable; it would have absorbed a large part of the total funds and brain power available for the purposes envisaged. So we opposed it strongly in conjunction with related bodies – Chatham House, PEP, and the Centre for Studies in Social Policy (the last two later merged to become the Policy Studies Institute). We argued that it would be better to build on existing institutions; and when the more grandiose proposal foundered, were able, through forging closer links between ourselves, to replicate at least some of the US Brookings' activities.

Later, there were great uncertainties about the funding of our activities by the Treasury and the SSRC; and even a threat to the SSRC itself when Sir Keith Joseph, Secretary of State for Education and Science, asked Lord (Victor) Rothschild to report on it. I submitted evidence to him, as did David Worswick (who did a marvellous job as the Institute's Director for seventeen years, being succeeded in 1982 by Andrew Britton from the Treasury, where he had been an outstanding younger member of my staff). Rothschild came out strongly in favour of SSRC continuing (it is now called the Economic and Social Research Council – ESRC), with a most enlightened defence of the use of public money to support social science research.

When 'monetarism' became increasingly fashionable, the Institute was vulnerable as a supposed bastion of 'Keynesianism'; but, despite occasional sniping from MPs and others, I do not think this affected our income from any quarter. Also, I kept reminding people that the Editor of the *National Institute Economic Review* was for over a year an arch-monetarist, Patrick Minford, who had worked with me in the Treasury and later became a Professor in Liverpool.

I arrived at the CBI – then at 21, Tothill Street, a few hundred yards from my old haunts in the Treasury and DEA – in mid-November 1973. At only my second meeting of the CBI Council, just before Christmas, I had to make a statement on the economic situation. We were in the middle of a huge oil price hike by Arab producers, who were also restricting their output; and the miners were operating an overtime ban in support of a huge pay claim. It was a depressing state of affairs, with oil prices rocketing, oil short, coal short, steel short, electricity short, transport difficult, a three-day week due to start in the New Year; and Tony Barber had introduced a restrictive mini-Budget. I argued that it would be a wrong response to the oil producers' action if the UK and other industrial countries took further deflationary measures; these would do little to reduce their enormous external deficits on current account resulting from the jump in oil prices and would largely result in a pointless, beggar-my-neighbour cutting of imports from each other. I got some criticism from a few members, but was told by old hands that I had done all right.

The CBI Council, the governing body of the organisation, meets nearly every month, with some 125–150 members present – sometimes more. Before attending it, I thought it must be impossibly unwieldy, but it works remarkably effectively, due partly to the convention of very brief speeches from the floor. Votes are rare, and much depends on the skill of the President, as Chairman, in summing up the mood of the meeting.

I now started attending NEDC meetings in yet another capacity. The first had been as a Neddy staff member with Conservative Ministers at the table; the second as a DEA official under a Labour Government; the next as a Treasury official under a Labour, then a Conservative, Government; and now as a CBI official, with Conservatives, then Labour, then Conservatives again, in power. Two things that happened during my early days at the CBI may be worth recording.

Early in 1974 the TUC suddenly offered at an NEDC meeting to put a ring fence round the miners should they get a pay increase far above that allowed by the pay policy, so that other settlements would be unaffected. They had not warned the other parties in advance and Tony Barber, in the Chair, felt obliged to reject the olive branch. Dermot Glynn, sitting next to me behind the CBI team, asked in a whisper whether we shouldn't suggest that they take up the offer but I thought there was no point. It is just possible that a chance was missed of changing the course of history. But I doubt it. For when Heath heard what had happened, he immediately had meetings with the TUC – and the CBI – and these continued until shortly before he announced a General Election. I believe the TUC's 'offer' was not well thought through and would not have worked in practice.

The second story concerns Sir Michael Clapham, Deputy Chairman of ICI, and then President of the CBI, Hugh (later Lord) Scanlon, President of the Amalgamated Union of Engineering Workers and myself. Michael was a man of great literary erudition; every year he and his wife spent hours in their library choosing an apt quotation for their Christmas card. He also had a habit of getting up very early to write a speech, always brilliantly phrased, often for delivery the same day. The opportunity of checking by CBI staff was thus minimal, and this worried me, having just come from the Treasury where most speeches by Chancellors were checked carefully by numerous officials. However, Michael's speeches nearly always turned out to be just right. He liked to make them colourful and during the three-day week, when describing the effects on sewage works should they run out of power, talked about the danger of people being 'drowned in their own sewage'.

One Tuesday I recorded a TV interview about the three-day week – for broadcasting on Thursday – and used this phrase. The BBC would obviously put out only part of what I said because I unwisely talked for quite a time. On Wednesday, at an NEDC meeting, Scanlon said he wished people would stop talking about things like people drowning in their own sewage. After the meeting I explained to him what I had done, that I would not have used the phrase had I known how strongly he felt, and hoped this was not part of the recording that the BBC would select. But – surprise, surprise – they concentrated on it. Hugh was very understanding. We got on well together. We had the same birthday, though he was a year younger. After he had seen our names in the same birthday list in *The Times*, he always greeted me with: 'hello, young fellow'.

How differently the BBC used to behave. In 1950, while an Oxford Don, I did a broadcast in London on the economics of re-armament during the Korean War. One sentence of my script put the 'guns versus butter' choice we talked about in the 1930s in a contemporary setting: 'if the bombs begin to fall', it read in effect, 'would you rather have a washing machine or an air raid shelter?' The BBC deleted this as too sensational. But when I got back to Oxford I discovered that the local paper had seized on the offending sentence, with the headline 'Oxford Don says . . .', not having checked the handout of the speech against what was transmitted over the radio.

On 7 February 1974 a General Election was called for Thursday, 28

February. The issues were essentially the miners' strike and 'who governs Britain?' although others emerged during the campaign. Heath lost his overall majority and resigned on Monday. By that evening Harold Wilson was once more Prime Minister.

One factor thought by some to have influenced the result concerned Campbell Adamson. On the Tuesday before the Election he fulfilled a long-standing engagement to talk to a meeting of the Industrial Society. Naturally he took great care to make his prepared speech non-party-political. But after the speech he agreed to answer questions. Representatives of the media were present and his clear intention was that his answers should be off the record, but it is difficult to determine whether he made it sufficiently clear that this applied to all his answers or only to those which he prefaced with this proviso.

In one answer he said that the Heath Government's Industrial Relations Act had 'soured the industrial climate' and should be the subject of discussion with the Trade Unions after the Election if the Conservatives won; he hoped that agreed amendments could be made, but if this was not possible, the Act would have to remain on the Statute Book. This happened to be the personal view of most industrial relations experts working on CBI Committees at the time, but it was not official CBI policy; and its utterance just before a General Election by a Director-General of the CBI would certainly, if it became public knowledge (and inevitably reported without all the qualifications surrounding it), be political dynamite.

The BBC man at the meeting was, unknown to Campbell, taping his remarks and, no doubt in good faith believing that this was not one of the answers off the record, went straight off after the meeting to play back his recording on the six o'clock news. This caused a tremendous sensation, banner headlines in some, but by no means all, of Wednesday morning's papers, and all hell broke loose in Tothill Street. On Thursday – polling day – Campbell motored to the Gloucester constituency where he was registered to record his vote. He also immediately offered his resignation to the President and this was reported in the press and on television.

On Friday morning, when it had become clear that Heath had lost his majority in the Commons, the President, Michael Clapham, summoned the senior officials of the CBI – about a dozen of us in all – to a meeting. He told us he had accepted Campbell's resignation. Then Campbell came in, ashen-faced, said little more than 'Sorry, chaps', and left. Then, one after another, those present insisted that this could not be the end of the story; and when Michael saw that we were, according to my recollection, unanimous in this view, he agreed to think again. An early meeting was arranged of around fifty important members of the CBI, at which it was agreed that Campbell should stay; and this was endorsed not long after by the CBI Council. I had dinner with him, during which he seemed remarkably relaxed, the night before this Council meeting at which he made a very dignified statement. The only jarring note was a hostile speech by Sir Raymond Brookes – whom I had encountered during the Wilberforce Inquiry into the electricity workers' dispute in 1971 – at the end of which he announced the resignation of Guest, Keen and Nettle-folds from the CBI, and stalked out of the Council Chamber. I am glad to say that GKN were back in the fold before too long.

Campbell stayed on as DG until 1976, when he had completed roughly seven years in the job. He had told me when I came that this was about the time he intended to stay, so I do not think he left earlier than he would have liked because of the mud that continued to be slung at him as a result of what was regarded as his 'gaffe' in 1974. Indeed, for long after he left, newspaper references to him continued to hark back on this, largely or entirely ignoring the good job that he did throughout his time at the CBI.

A few months after Heath had lost the Election but while still Leader of his Party, he asked me to his room in the Commons to discuss the economic lessons to be learned from what had occurred during his administration. I expected a cosy chat with Ted, but found instead a large table on one side of which were Professor (later Sir Alan) Walters (then at the LSE and later Personal Adviser to Mrs Thatcher) and Professor Jim (later Sir James) Ball, then Principal of the London Business School, who had to leave after half an hour. I was asked to sit beside them. On the other side of the table, and round the room, were not just Ted but Keith Joseph and – so it seemed to me – most of the Shadow Ministers concerned with economic affairs. We had a long discussion, much of it between Heath and myself on the one hand and Joseph and Walters – then his economic guru – on the other. In the course of this, two memorable exchanges took place.

First, I said to Keith Joseph, who was arguing for a purely monetary approach to the inflation problem, that, if we relied on this alone, it would in my view mean unemployment rising far above a million. He said this was rubbish. I asked why. He said Professor Walters had worked out that nothing like that would be necessary. Alas, how wrong he turned out to be. Later in the meeting I asked Keith whether, if money supply had been strictly controlled, this would have prevented the miners getting a large pay increase. He said no, but other pay increases would have had to be less to bring the average down to the percentage increase in money supply. When I pointed out that there was the question of how fast the

money went round – what economists called the 'velocity of circulation' –
he said this did not change much. I said that in fact it could change a great
deal and perhaps he might get a tutorial from Professor Walters on the
subject. After the meeting, in the Private Secretary's room, Keith tapped
me on the shoulder and said: 'Tell me about this velocity of circulation.
It's only gone up by a few per cent during the last few years, hasn't it?' I
replied 'in fact it's gone *down* – by about *25 per cent*; and I'll send you the
reference to a chart in *Economic Trends* (published by the Central
Statistical Office) which shows this.'

On 26 March 1974, three weeks to the day after becoming Chancellor,
Denis Healey introduced his first Budget – thus allowing far too short a
time for the preparation of such a long and complicated set of proposals.
He was also in my view badly advised by the Cambridge economists he
employed, though I confess to a certain bias. They convinced him, first,
that the balance of payments current account deficit was the mirror image
of the budget deficit (in economic jargon, the 'public sector financial
deficit') – which was empirically just wrong – and that the latter had to be
cut to a certain figure to deal with the balance of payments problem.

After adding up all the things he wanted to do he was a few hundred
million pounds short, so he put extra taxes on profits in various ways –
quite apart from other measures injurious to business, including tighter
price control. He also said in his speech that profits had been doing rather
well. Now this was true on a *historic* cost basis, not allowing for inflation,
but no one seems to have told him that they were doing disastrously badly
on a *replacement* cost basis, after allowing for inflation. Nor do his advisers
appear to have recognised that the outlook for company *liquidity* was very
poor indeed – here too they misinterpreted figures of companies' cash,
bank borrowing, and the like.

Two days after the Budget, a CBI delegation saw the Prime Minister,
the Chancellor and about half the Cabinet at No 10 to protest, only to be
met by a rather truculent response. Healey was particularly scathing,
claiming to be baffled by the CBI's criticisms since, he argued, he had
done so much of what we wanted. He concluded – and I noted his exact
words: 'I might well say: "O generation of vipers, I've done all this to help
you and then you kick me in the teeth".' Despite the detailed knowledge
of the New Testament aquired during my schooldays, about which I
boasted in Chapter 1, I did not immediately – in truth, not till I came to
write these memoirs – realise that he was comparing us with the Pharisees
and Sadducees whom, according to St Matthew's Gospel, John the
Baptist castigated, beginning with the first four words of Denis's 'quotation'.

Following this, we conducted an intensive operation, presenting our case to Government, to MP's and, through speeches, publications and the media, to the general pubic. Between Healey's March and November budgets, there were eleven meetings on the subject with Ministers – at No 10, at the Treasury with the Chancellor, at the Department of Prices and Consumer Protection with Shirley Williams, and at NEDC. The ground for these meetings was prepared by meetings of officials of which we had about a couple of dozen, apart from innumerable contacts with individuals. I was deeply involved and spent much time trying to persuade my old friends and colleagues of the error of their ways. My work in the Treasury on trends in *real* profitability (after adjusting for inflation) under Jenkins, Macleod and Barber came in handy; as did similar work which two CBI economists, Tony Webb and Graham Burgess, had been doing. We also proposed a scheme for not charging tax on stock appreciation – the increase in the value of stocks resulting merely from price increases. This was at the time very large indeed, and threatening to play havoc with many companies' finances, especially if it were taxed as part of profits. I think we had persuaded officials – and probably Healey – by the summer; but with an Election looming, he held his hand. Then, soon after the October Election, he introduced an Autumn Budget, the centerpiece of which was a stock relief scheme very much on the lines we were advocating. This was worth billions of pounds to business, and may well have saved many CBI members – as well as non-members – from financial disaster.

An amusing aspect was that my old friend Wynne Godley, who had been advising Healey but was now back at Cambridge, sent a piece (written by himself and Adrian Wood) to the newspapers, embargoed for publication on Friday 1 November, barely ten days before the Autumn Budget, arguing that it was quite wrong to relieve stock appreciation from tax. I got a full copy from Wynne and took it home at the weekend to study. I discovered two things. First, it contained a fundamental misunderstanding of our proposals. Secondly, it was prefaced with numerous disclaimers, pointing out that the numerical example used in the article to illustrate the argument was based on some highly simplified assumptions that seemed to have little to do with the real world, and warned that: 'Of course, no conclusions about what should now be done can be simply and immediately drawn from this example, which is highly artificial'. Naturally, of course, the newspapers had largely left out these disclaimers.

On Monday, following a lengthy telephone conversation with Wynne in Cambridge, I wrote a letter to *The Times* pointing out both the disclaimers and the misunderstanding, and Wynne (with Adrian Wood) wrote one agreeing with me. This naturally relieved the Chancellor by removing the danger that critics of his Autumn Budget would cite the opposition of one of his recent advisers. My letter appeared on the Wednesday before the Budget, when the NEDC happened to be meeting. As I entered the ante-room before the meeting Denis Healey greeted me cheerily with the words: 'jolly good letter in *The Times* this morning, Donald', thereby in a sense, one might say, giving away a budget secret.

At the CBI, while there was a much smaller staff of economists – though one of high quality – than I could call upon at the Treasury, I had the immense advantage of being able to have discussions with, and get information from, many CBI members in a wide variety of ways – not only in Standing Committees and Regional Councils but on less formal occasions. One morning I got half a dozen Finance Directors round my table to find out their views on just how serious the financial position of companies was. I could thus check ideas based largely on statistics – of which we had most that the Treasury had – against experience at the sharp end of business; and this gave me much greater confidence in forming a judgment than I could have had if still cabined in the Treasury. (I also had regular meetings with Henry Benson, my old colleague on the VAT Committee, who was from 1975 till 1983 Adviser to Gordon Richardson, our Chairman, by then Governor of the Bank of England. One of Henry's main jobs was to see what could be done to keep individual businesses, often fundamentally sound but in temporary difficulties, from going under; and I found it invaluable to check up how he thought company finances in general were going.)

Of course, as my good friend Sid Robin, of Great Universal Stores, once reminded me, one had to be discriminating in the sort of business-men one talked to. At one meeting of the Economic Situation Committee – of which he was a faithful, and sometimes delightfully irreverent, member – he criticised strongly a statement put out the day before by the CBI on some industrial issue. I assured him it had been agreed by a dozen Chairmen of some of the most important companies in the country. He was unrepentant. 'Donald,' he said, 'they are less likely to know what is really going on than almost any other group I can think of.' In fact, most members of this Committee held less exalted positions in the business world, but they covered a broad spectrum of trade, industry and finance. Meeting nearly every month they were an invaluable sounding board, confirming – or otherwise – the Staff's interpretation of official statistics, the effects of government policies and other developments, as well as the CBI's own Industrial Trends Surveys which had been going since 1958.

These proved remarkably accurate and CBI staff became increasingly experienced in interpreting them. Quite often they were convinced that the official index of manufacturing output was giving a false reading; and the latter was then nearly always revised later to bring it much more into line. Government statisticians got worried when their statistics were getting out of kilter and discussed possible reasons with our people. Politicians of the party in power were more inclined to chide us when our Surveys showed industry performing less well than the official statistics, and call them in aid when the opposite was the case.

The Economic Situation Committee was set up about the time I came to the CBI and had three Chairmen while I was there, all of whom, as it happened, later became President: Sir Campbell Fraser, Sir Raymond Pennock and Sir James Cleminson. One of their tasks – a useful training for the Presidency – was taking the Press Conferences (followed by interviews on radio and television) on the Surveys.

In describing the industrial situation at these Conferences they often indulged in metaphors. Campbell Fraser liked to talk about tunnels, and lights at the end of them. Sometimes the light was brighter, sometimes dimmer, sometimes – when things looked particularly threatening – the possibility that it was the light of another train hurtling towards us on the same track. James Cleminson preferred to talk about ladders when describing the stage of recovery we had reached. Sometimes we had a foot on the first rung, sometimes on the second – we may even have got on to the third while he was Chairman. But once, when a journalist asked him what would happen in a certain contingency, he feared we might fall off the ladder, which would then come tumbling back on top of us. Ray Pennock was less given to metaphors at Press Conferences; but while chairing the Committee he once asked, in introducing a discussion of the state of the economy: 'Is there perhaps a touch of a tinge of colour in the old invalid's cheeks?'

In the CBI's campaign to help business finances in the mid-1970s, an important part – in addition to pressure for tax changes – was the attempt to get relaxation of price control. This had started under the Heath Administration. CBI argued hard on the details (abolition was not on the cards) and won some victories. The Minister mainly concerned was Sir Geoffrey Howe. Our Prices Negotiating Team was led by Ronny Utiger (then Managing Director of British Aluminium and later Chairman of Tube Investments) and Ron – later Sir Ronald – Halstead (then a Managing Director and later Chairman of Beechams). Both did a marvellous job; and Ronny Utiger, despite the early disadvantage of having been to my lectures at Oxford, later proved an excellent Chairman of our Economic and Financial Policy Committee, and a superb expositor of its point of view – and that of the CBI – to the Council, to our National

Conferences and to Ministers. And if ever a debate looked like going the wrong way – by which I mean against the party line – you could always rely on Ronny, in a few brilliant, devastating sentences, to snatch victory out of the jaws of defeat. I was delighted when we persuaded him, in 1986, to take on the Presidency of the National Institute of Economic and Social Research, in succession to Eric Roll, who had held the post for nineteen years.

Inevitably Utiger and Halstead became known as 'the two Ronnies' after the comedians Ronnie Barker and Ronnie Corbett. But their job was no laughing matter. The Prices Negotiating Team, backed up by no fewer than four working groups – because, as anyone with experience of price control knows, it quickly develops into a fiendishly complex matter – worked incredibly hard. Tony Webb, one of the CBI economists deeply involved, told me of one crucial meeting with officials which started at 3.30 pm and ended at 1.30 am. 'Fairly exhausting stuff', said Tony, 'but an important argument was on the way to being won.'

After Labour returned to power, arguments at Ministerial level were with Shirley Williams, who was Secretary of State for Prices and Consumer Protection for two-and-a-half years before being succeeded by Roy Hattersley. The CBI won some concessions and, although they were limited, our negotiators developed a considerable respect for Shirley. She was referred to affectionately in Tothill Street at 'Shirls'. Although sometimes a trifle late for meetings, she always listened patiently to the CBI's arguments. I believe that those who described her by the anagram of her name – 'I whirl aimlessly' – were wide of the mark. My wife was her tutor when she read PPE at Somerville. She tells me that during her first year Shirley did far too little academic work and spent far too much time on politics – and on comforting fellow-undergraduates who came to pour out their troubles, for she was a compassionate person. At the end of the year, Margaret had to warn her sternly that she must concentrate much more on her studies if she was to make proper use of her time at Oxford. This she dutifully did and, two years later, got a very respectable degree.

By the autumn of 1974, pay and price inflation were both accelerating rapidly. The miners had in effect broken the pay policy early in the year. The Labour Government kept Heath's Pay Code until July, but after that relied on their so-called 'Social Contract' with the unions. The latter undertook broadly that pay would rise only in line with prices. The Government, in return, did a number of things the unions wanted – and it appeared to many in the CBI, who disliked many of these things, that Jack Jones, General Secretary of the Transport and General Workers' Union, was in effect dictating Government policy through Michael Foot, Secretary of State for Employment, acting as intermediary. Jones' nickname 'The Emperor' reflected his supposed power at the time. On the other hand, the Labour Government did follow CBI advice on some major issues. I have mentioned stock relief in the November 1974 Budget, in which the TUC acquiesced; and in his April 1975 Budget, contrary to the TUC's recommendations, Healey accepted CBI advice not to reflate while pay inflation continued at such a high rate. This time Hugh Scanlon at least was not amused. Commenting on the Budget he said: 'There can be no doubt that the overall position was an almost disdainful ignoring of the proposals of the TUC and an almost absolute compliance with the proposals of the CBI and the City.'

Despite the unions' undertaking under the 'Social Contract' we had a pay explosion, with pay rising well ahead of prices. In November 1974, the CBI's Employment Policy Committee, consisting mainly of practitioners in industrial relations, put a paper to Council proposing a mild policy of pay restraint; but this was firmly thrown out. The breakdown of Heath's pay policy was still vivid in members' minds. Some opposed *any* form of pay policy in principle. Others felt they could not adhere to a CBI policy because union action could bankrupt their companies. Some wanted freedom to pay more to keep or attract skilled labour, still short in many areas.

But things got progressively worse. By early 1975, with inflation accelerating rapidly, there was talk of pay settlements in the 40–50% range. Some commentators were even discussing the possibility of a collapse of the currency. Sterling was in serious danger. The strength of the general concern – and the feeling almost of hopelessness of finding a way out – is illustrated by something that happened to me. I was asked by the Political Economy Club to open the question: 'How do we get out of this Mess?' at its February 1975 meeting. I rashly agreed, but only on the understanding that I did not propose to give any cut and dried solution; the collective wisdom of the Club might find one – though I had my doubts.

The number of members and their guests wishing to dine was large and a room was taken in the National Liberal Club rather than the usual, smaller, room in the Reform Club. This, I am sure, was an indication of the widespread worry about the state of the nation among the academics, civil servants, politicians, bankers, other businessmen, trade unionists and journalists of which the Club is mainly composed, rather than any particular desire to hear my views. I quickly identified the main 'Mess' as accelerating inflation, particularly in the field of pay, and devoted my remarks mostly to considering various proposals then current for dealing with the problem. There was no lack of such proposals, some – to put it charitably – less gimmicky and unrealistic than others.

The discussion that followed was lively but no conclusion was reached. At the next meeting of the Club, at which the main speaker at the previous meeting is expected to take the Chair, I duly presided. It was the night of the April 1975 Budget and, as is the custom, the Club met to discuss it. After dinner, before Sir Paul Chambers opened the Question 'What of the Budget?' the Secretary – Paul Bareau – read the minutes of the previous meeting, which said simply, according to tradition, who had been present, and that the Question 'How do we get out of this Mess?' had been opened by Sir Donald MacDougall and discussed. A member then proposed that before 'discussed' the word 'inconclusively' should be inserted. This was unanimously agreed, thereby breaking a long tradition of the Club.

But meanwhile, back at the CBI, a great deal was happening, following the Council's rejection of pay restraint in November 1974. In addition to much staff work, there were numerous discussions at meetings of members, in Tothill Street and throughout the country. This culminated in a Council meeting on 21 May 1975 when there was almost unanimous acceptance of proposals much more far-reaching, detailed and tough than those rejected six months earlier. This change of attitude reflected, not only the hard work and extensive debate I have mentioned, but also the rapid deterioration in the situation, with inflation accelerating at a really frightening rate. By May 1975 the Retail Price Index was 25% higher than 12 months earlier (and in June 26% higher); the underlying rise over the previous *six* months was at an annual rate of no less than 36% (although admittedly this figure was inflated by increases in indirect taxes in the April Budget). Earnings were up by some 30% on a year earlier. Drastic action was clearly necessary.

The paper approved by Council, in addition to reiterating the need for tight fiscal and monetary policies, called on the Government to sponsor a pay policy in conjunction with both sides of industry. It proposed a three-year programme to reduce price inflation to 5% or under; and that price targets should be fixed each year and corresponding pay limits set. Following Council's approval, we got all guns firing – with Ministers, the Civil Service, the Opposition, the Media. Then, just over three weeks later, we were – to our surprise – asked by the TUC to an early meeting to discuss pay. We had had informal talks with TUC leaders for some time, but only on less controversial subjects and never on pay. The meeting took place at their headquarters in Congress House, Great Russell Street (near Centre Point, to which the CBI moved later) on Wednesday, 18 June, with seven or eight on each side.

At our preparatory briefing in Tothill Street, the President, now Sir Ralph Bateman, suggested that we begin by telling the TUC they must accept a 5% reduction in real wages. I argued with respect that our emphasis should be different: we should say instead that the best way of safeguarding the standard of living and jobs of union members was for them to accept *money* pay increases far below the increase in the cost of living over the previous twelve months – quite a different proposition. The lower pay increases would before long be followed by lower price increases; firms would be better able to compete in export markets and against imports, to invest in machines, factories and working capital, and to maintain production and employment generally (all of which were being seriously jeopardised by the rapid inflation). Perhaps most important, the Chancellor would be better able to avoid massive deflationary measures, leading to soaring unemployment and thus reducing severely the standard of living of many working people. If, indeed, inflation could be brought down to much lower figures, the Chancellor would then be able to allow – and if necessary encourage – an expansion in demand which led to more jobs.

Soon after our meeting began, Hugh Scanlon – sure enough – said he could not possibly accept pay increases less than the rise in prices over the previous twelve months, because this would reduce the standard of living of his members. I was then put in to bat and gave my little lecture on why this was precisely what he should do in his members' interests.

To my surprise, while I was talking, I saw several heads nodding – apparently in agreement rather than drowsiness – on the TUC side of the table; and at the end of the meeting it was decided that the two staffs should try to produce an agreed analysis for a further meeting on the following Tuesday. This was done on Thursday and Friday by David Lea, the TUC's chief economist, and myself sitting at a table in my office, arguing and drafting what I think was rather an historic document. In effect it accepted my analysis almost in its entirety and talked about the need for a pay limit of 10–15% if we were to make a decent start in getting inflation down over the following twelve months. Our draft was agreed with very few changes by Campbell Adamson and Len Murray over the weekend and on Monday, in time for the meeting on Tuesday. (On the Wednesday, the front page of *Workers Press*, which described itself as the 'Daily Organ of the Central Committee of the Workers Revolutionary Party', carried an excellent picture of Campbell and myself going into 'the TUC headquarters yesterday for a second round of talks on wage-cutting'. I was smoking a pipe; it must have been just before I gave it up.)

One reason I found it relatively easy to reach agreement with David Lea was that I had started, earlier in the year, informal discussions with him and one or two other TUC and CBI economists; and one evening much progress was made on these matters – the relationships between pay, productivity, prices, investment, exports, imports, jobs – in a long session in my room in Tothill Street over a bottle of whisky; I think its cost to the CBI was a good investment.

At the meeting on Tuesday (24 June) the analysis in our paper was quickly accepted. There was no talk of a pay limit anywhere near the 25% increase in prices over the past year. The argument was between 10% and 15%, and about whether a flat rate increase of £X a week or a percentage would be better – a point to which I return shortly. I should not claim too much for my economic eloquence in bringing this about. At least as important must have been that Denis Healey had scared the daylights out of the TUC leaders a few days before by saying that unless they quickly proposed a very severe form of pay restraint he would have to clobber the economy very hard, to safeguard the pound. Shortly afterwards, however, Healey complimented a few of us privately on our help in bringing about a change of heart in the TUC; and we in turn complimented him on the part he had played. But whatever the reason, an important psychological barrier had been broken; for it had been thought inconceivable a few months earlier that the unions could accept a pay limit significantly if at all below the increase in prices over the previous year, let alone one only half as great.

I found it interesting that the TUC leaders were prepared to restrain pay severely when we had a floating exchange rate. In the summers of 1965 and 1966, when George Brown had summoned them to the DEA, told them the pound was in danger, and that they must tighten up pay restraint, they had in each case done so and got it through their annual Congress. But those were days when the TUC accepted the need to defend the then parity of sterling (wrongly in my opinion). I wondered whether they would now argue that, with a floating pound, we need not worry about an extra few per cent on wages because this could easily be offset by a corresponding depreciation of sterling. This is not what happened in June 1975.

In these talks with the TUC, the CBI agreed that price control would have to continue which ensured that lower cost increases were reflected in lower price increases. But it was also agreed that profit margins must be adequate to maintain and increase investment and employment. So we seemed well on the way to achieving the 'impossibility' of very tough pay restraint without a significant tightening of price control. Thus by late June the TUC had agreed the essential features of the CBI policy. And on 1 July Healey made a statement to the Commons which accepted these essentials.

There were, however, many details to be settled, which meant a hectic July for those concerned – consulting with CBI members and innumerable meetings with Ministers and officials. We gained some points, we lost some; but in the end got a counter-inflation policy which bore a striking resemblance to that worked out by CBI earlier in the year; and one which gave the country, only just in time, a chance to avoid the horrors of galloping inflation. We had found a way, at last temporarily, out of the 'Mess' which the Political Economy Club had been so despondent about getting out of only a few months earlier.

When, at our meeting with the TUC on 24 June, the discussion turned to the nature of the pay limit, I listened with fascination to a debate between two great professionals in the pay bargaining game – Jack Jones, who wanted £X a week, and Ron Owen, one of the CBI team and Industrial Relations Adviser to Unilever, who argued for a percentage. Jack Jones won and we got a £6 a week limit for everyone, except those earning over £8,500 a year who got nothing, for 'Year 1' of the policy – between the summers of 1975 and 1976. This, together with the formula for 'Year 2' which further squeezed differentials, helped to create serious anomalies and tensions that led to an upsurge of inflation later; and had we had a simple percentage the anomalies would have been considerably less serious. On the other hand, Jack Jones' appreciation of the situation may have been right in that only a simple figure like £6, which could also be represented as helping the lower paid, would be accepted and observed – as indeed it was.

In any case, both pay inflation and consequently – as I had predicted – price inflation came tumbling down and between the summers of 1975 and 1976 earnings rose by 14%, compared with some 30% over the previous twelve months, and prices by 13% (compared with 26%) – so there was actually a small rise in real earnings (compared with the reduction which Bateman had wanted to tell the TUC they must accept). It is true that during the following twelve months real earnings fell substantially, mainly because of a temporary reacceleration of price inflation following an excessive depreciation of sterling (described later). But price inflation soon resumed its rapid fall, and over the whole three years between mid-1975 and mid-1978, when the underlying rate of price inflation fell from 36% to 8½% (having fallen to 7% in the spring of 1978), real take-home pay actually rose. It is also true that unemployment rose substantially, but I believe it would have risen even more had we not broken the inflationary spiral.

Some would say that the reduction in inflation would have happened in any case, without a pay policy, because of the tight monetary policy the Government pursued – in line with CBI advice – and rising unemployment. My reply – and I think that of most skilled pay negotiators on the employers' side at the time – would be that these were necessary, but not sufficient, conditions; and that a pay policy was essential as well to stop, and then reverse so dramatically, the inflationary explosion.

After the meeting at six o'clock on 24 June 1975 in Congress House, the TUC entertained us to dinner. We returned the compliment in the autumn, inviting them to a meeting in Tothill Street at six followed by dinner at eight; and for the next five years or so we continued the practice, taking it in turn to be host, the main difference being that, in my opinion, they provided a better dinner than we did. We met on average about three times a year. There were usually around six or seven aside, and I was at virtually all the meetings. They were entirely unpublicised and we had useful, frank discussions covering a wide range of subjects. They came to an end, sadly, in 1981. The last one was, I think, in January of that year, and in the summer the TUC felt obliged to say that, in effect, there seemed little point in further informal discussions with the CBI in view of the latter's attitude to, and failure to consult adequately with them on, such matters as industrial relations legislation. They were also resentful – with some justification – when our Council turned down a document which they considered had been agreed – word by word – as a joint statement during one of our informal meetings.

But personal relations remained good. CBI officials, from the DG downwards, continued to be uninhibited about phoning their opposite numbers in Congress House at any time. Football and cricket matches between TUC and CBI staffs carried on unaffected. We continued to have discussions in Neddy, until in 1984 the TUC pulled out of Council meetings (but not out of the little Neddies) in protest against the Government's action at GCHQ in Cheltenham. I was sad that the last meeting of the NEDC I attended, on 7 March 1984 – strangely enough *exactly* twenty-two years after the first meeting on 7 March 1962 – was the first the TUC had boycotted (on one other occasion they had not attended a meeting but that was because they would not cross a picket line at Millbank Tower of Civil Servants in dispute about something or other).

But even this did not affect our personal relations and I was delighted when Len Murray, and his senior economists, David Lea and Bill Callaghan, came to my farewell party at the CBI in March 1984. I was further pleased to read in October of that year that the TUC were to start attending Council meetings again, following a favourable vote at Congress and agreement with the CBI on a 20-point programme to 're-invigorate' NEDC; and would you believe it, one of these points was a sharper focus on promoting 'conditions favourable to faster economic growth', almost exactly the title of Neddy's 1963 'Orange Book'.

The tensions created in Years 1 and 2 of the pay policy, and the temporary re-acceleration of price inflation in Year 2, led to strong opposition to a third year of pay restraint in 1977–8; the guidance to negotiators by the TUC and Government was unambitious; and the increase in earnings, which had fallen to around 8% in Year 2, rose to nearly 15% in Year 3. Then, in the summer of 1978, the Government decided to go for a much tougher Year 4. We had a meeting with the Prime Minister, Jim Callaghan, when he gave his personal view that the pay norm should really be zero; but that, to be realistic, the limit for settlements should certainly not be more than 5% (which might lead, with 'drift', to a rise in earnings of around 7%). Five per cent was the figure proposed for settlements in the White Paper published two days later.

The CBI team had warned that this was dangerously over-ambitious, as it certainly turned out to be. Earnings continued to rise by nearly 15%; there was the notorious 'winter of discontent'; and early in 1979, in a bid to avoid a series of crippling strikes in the public services, the Government set up a 'Standing Commission on Pay Comparability' which in effect wrote out large post-dated cheques for pay increases in those services, which were cashed in 1979–80.

For several years previously – roughly once every twelve months from 1974 till the spring of 1979 – I had organised small, informal, strictly private half-day seminars (including a working lunch) in Tothill Street on inflation, especially pay inflation. To these were invited interested CBI members and also academics, including both general economists – with a sprinkling of monetarists – and industrial relations specialists, a few of whom may have been regarded as rather 'unsound' by some in the CBI, like my Nuffield colleague Bill (Lord) McCarthy, who was ennobled on the recommendation of Harold Wilson. These seminars had, on one or two occasions, quite an important influence on CBI thinking and policies.

Our Employment Policy Committee had also for several years been working on fundamental questions concerning pay determination and, following widespread consultation with the membership, the CBI published in February 1979 *Pay: The Choice Ahead*. Besides making proposals for restructuring pay bargaining and changing the balance of power between unions and employers, it proposed a 'national economic forum' to produce a broadly agreed analysis of the economic situation and prospects, including the consequences of alternative developments in the field of pay. When it was clear that Year 4 of the pay policy was not working, we decided to produce an 'economic review' by the early summer of 1979 which would in effect be a mock-up of the sort of evidence we might submit to such a body.

In the event the concept of a forum fell by the wayside, but we used much of the material we had got together in preparing for two private conferences of members on pay in July, attended by well over a hundred top executives and personnel managers. These began with a presentation, by myself, with slides, on the economic backcloth to the 1979–80 pay round, about to begin. I stressed how much our international competitiveness had worsened during the previous couple of years, how sharply profitability had fallen, how nothing further could be squeezed out of profits to pay higher wages – on the contrary, higher profitability was needed – and the importance of keeping pay settlements well below the rise in prices over the previous twelve months if we were to avoid continuing high inflation and rising unemployment. I was followed by Richard Dixon, our Director of Social Affairs, on more specific industrial relations aspects. There was then a long discussion during which members spoke pretty frankly about both the general pay situation and that in their own businesses.

Following these conferences, intensive efforts were made to get the message across to member firms. We prepared leaflets and booklets, which we tried to make more and more simple. Many thousands were asked for and supplied free. (One leaflet, intended to help employers communicate with their employees, listed ten 'do's' and ten 'don'ts' of which the tenth was, I am afraid, 'Don't try to explain too much at a time. Six facts at a time are enough.' The CBI economists were not responsible for this particular leaflet.) We sold slide kits, with speakers' notes, for in-company use (a few years later we offered videos, enabling many to hear my dulcet tones).

I found it extraordinary how ignorant many businessmen were about some simple facts of economic life (there *are* a few, despite the hideous complexity and controversial nature of the subject); and their keenness to learn how to communicate these to their senior and middle management and, ultimately, to their workforces was made evident when the CBI held a Conference on this to which 100 were expected and over 600 wanted to come. I was also encouraged by the ability of many companies to complement our facts, figures and arguments about the economy as a whole with information about their own firms.

CBI staff gave the presentations, followed by a usually lively discussion, to meetings of members up and down the country, from Cornwall to Inverness; to trade associations and employers' organisations; to individual firms; and in later years to Civil Servants, Ministers, Local Authority employers, even the Bank of England.

The slide presentation was a nightmare. Apart from such hazards as the equipment breaking down or the slides being out of order, there was the simple question of geometry, which I found it difficult to make my colleagues take seriously – namely working out whether the relative positions of the projector, the screen and the audience would enable everyone (or nearly everyone) to see all (or nearly all) of what was projected, given that most of those present had others sitting between them and the screen. Once I gave a presentation in an Essex hotel at a meeting chaired by my friend and fellow-Scot, Stanley Thomson, Finance Director of Fords. When I arrived I found to my dismay a large number of members sitting down to lunch in a room with a very low ceiling, with the projector and screen so placed that not more than ten per cent could have seen the presentation I was to give while they were having coffee. I somehow managed, with the aid of a pile of telephone directories and various Heath Robinson devices, to change things so that I hope most members saw most of what I was showing – but at the cost of missing my lunch. After that I always inspected the arrangements at least a couple of hours before every meeting; it was extraordinary how often changes had to be made.

Fords themselves prepared excellent films to explain the company's finances to their employees. One started with Sir Terence Beckett, then Chairman, getting out of a Cortina and saying that the firm had had a good year and made so many millions of profits. He then handed over to Stanley Thomson who explained – brilliantly – how, when you allowed for replacing machines at much more than their original cost, for interest, taxation and so on, there was precious little left over for dividends. Later, when Terry came to the CBI as DG and I reminded him about this film, he agreed it was fine – except that, as soon as Stanley came on the screen, his admirable exposition, in a rich Scottish accent, was drowned by roars of laughter because he sported the most extravagant side-whiskers.

Our pay campaigns became an annual event and I spent a good deal of time on them. It would be hard to argue that they had an early effect. In my first presentation in July 1979 I described three scenarios on different assumptions about the increase in earnings over the next twelve months: 14%, roughly the Treasury's working assumption at the time; 6%, which would be necessary to bring inflation down to the average of our competitors'; and 20%, which I said would be disastrous. In fact earnings rose by more than 20%, and at the Conferences a year later I had the dubious satisfaction of saying 'I told you so', because we could see before our very eyes soaring inflation, rising unemployment, slumping orders and output, real profits falling almost to vanishing point – although I freely admitted that all of these could not be blamed on excessive pay settlements alone. Equally there was, to say the least, no clear evidence that our efforts in 1979 to encourage moderate settlements had had much, if any, effect.

But I think our efforts gradually bore fruit. Though it certainly does not prove it – for there were many other factors at work – we were able at the Conferences in 1981 to report a dramatic halving of settlements during the past year; and in 1982 that our labour costs per unit of output had risen considerably less than our competitors'.

I believe we helped managements to get across to their workforces some of the points we were trying to drive home; and that in this we were working with the trade union leadership, not against it. Terry Beckett gave a presentation on 'competitiveness' to the NEDC in 1982 and another a year later, much on the lines of our pay presentations to members; and the TUC team were in broad agreement. They accepted the great importance of labour costs in total costs; also the importance of profits so that managements could have the wherewithal to become more competitive by investment in up-to-date equipment, marketing, R&D, design and the like. I think too that our Conferences, and smaller meetings we had at the start of each pay round with a few managements involved in early key settlements, helped to lower the level of expectations.

Now I knew from personal experience how difficult it is to operate an employers' 'cartel' to prevent excessive pay increases. When I was Domestic Bursar of Wadham shortly after the war, it was very hard to recruit and keep College servants. I attended regular meetings of my counterparts in other Colleges and we would all swear, hand on heart, not to pay our people a penny more – and soon after give them an extra five shillings a week. We quickly forgot any thoughts of collective loyalty or enlightened self-interest when faced with immediate domestic crises.

But I think we managed, in CBI pay campaigns, to get across, to some extent, the idea that 'no company is an island' (a phrase we coined for our presentations one year): that if a company made an excessively high settlement, this could have knock-on effects on its customers and suppliers that could come back and hit it later. I do not frankly know how far the CBI's pay and productivity campaigns contributed to the sharp deceleration in labour costs per unit of output after 1980, and how far it would have happened in any case as a result of the harsh economic climate, but I think we had at least a marginal effect; and would like to hope it was more than that.

12

REACHING OUT

COMING back to my earlier days in the CBI, in 1976 there were important changes in the leadership. Campbell Adamson and Ralph Bateman were succeeded as Director-General and President by John (later Sir John) Methven and Harold (Lord) Watkinson. I was very sorry to see Campbell go. We had got on well and shared a similar sense of humour and fun. I believe, too, that we were an effective combination as part of a team; and some of the CBI's most important achievements during my time were while Campbell was DG. I was also sorry when Bateman's term of office came to an end. I had enjoyed his cheerful, crisp manner; and though I did not always agree with him, he was ready to listen and change his mind if convinced. I admired the fancy waistcoats he sported on social occasions, and was struck by how often his company's Rolls was out of service; but this was hardly surprising because, to combine the jobs of CBI President and Chairman of Turner and Newall, he must have spent a lot of time driving between London and Manchester at 100 mph.

But while regretting the departure of Campbell and Ralph, I was delighted to start working with their successors. John Methven, after five years as Solicitor in the Birmingham town clerk's office, and over a dozen in ICI, had been the first Director-General of the Office of Fair Trading – a post in which he could so easily have ruffled the feathers of businessmen. While there he had assiduously built up contacts with Civil Servants and the press. These stood him in good stead at the CBI and he made a point of developing them.

He was soon on close terms with Ken (later Sir Kenneth) Stowe, Principal Private Secretary to the PM (Jim Callaghan) and could ring him up at any time to discuss how something or other might best be played, or any other matter. (John was, incidentally, proud that it was Callaghan who proposed him for a Knighthood, despite his harsh criticism of the Labour Government which endeared him to many CBI members.) His cultivation of the press undoubtedly helped the CBI to get good coverage for its publications, utterances and Conferences; and he dampened criticisms by papers such as *The Sunday Telegraph* through making friends with journalists like Patrick Hutber, the economist, who was their City Editor and wrote some pretty nasty things about us.

I personally got on well with Methven. He appreciated my work and I his. We had a bond in having both fairly recently separated from our wives and, just as I was waiting impatiently for my divorce to come through so that I could marry Margaret Hall, he was waiting for his so that he could marry Karen Caldwell (then an executive in ICI). We had a race to get remarried first; I won by a short head, and they both came to our wedding party. Some of my staff colleagues, however, found it difficult to put up with his sometimes pretty rough way of handling matters, which contrasted with the easy-going, often jokey, manner of his predecessor. He could be abrasive and even rude (though this was usually, I believe, the result of a laudable desire to get to the point quickly); and his sense of humour did not always come to his aid when dealing with a difficult situation.

He had immense energy and never let up, in work or in play. His passions outside work were music and sailing. He had been converted to the latter by Karen – as I converted Margaret to fishing – and spent a lot of time raising money for *Lionheart*, the British contender for the America's Cup in 1980; he did not live to see the yacht's disappointing performance.

Harold Watkinson, the new President, had been a Conservative MP from 1950 till 1964 and in the Cabinet for five years. He was one of seven who left it on the 'night of the long knives' in July 1962 when Macmillan made sweeping changes; but this in no way implies that he did not share many of the general views of Macmillan, author of *The Middle Way* in 1938, which he thought fit to re-issue in 1966, and the philosophy of which was reflected in his maiden speech in the House of Lords, at the age of 90, after being created Earl of Stockton in 1984. Much of Watkinson's life as an active politician was in the Butskellite era. Although a loyal Tory supporter, this continued to colour his political outlook when he came to the CBI after a long intervening spell at Schweppes and then as Chairman of Cadbury-Schweppes.

While in the latter post he pioneered a scheme for greater involvement of employees in company decision-making, in which he passionately believed. The success of this experiment, described in *Blueprint for Industrial Survival*, a book he published in 1976, helped CBI to argue that such schemes were practicable and, through comparison with successful arrangements made by other companies, that they had to be tailored to individual firms, and could fail if imposed in a rigid form by Westminster or Brussels.

(Watkinson was succeeded as Chairman of Cadbury-Schweppes by Adrian – later Sir Adrian – Cadbury. He was a charming and wonderful man, who did invaluable work for the CBI, especially as Chairman from 1974 till 1980 of the Economic Policy, and then of the Economic and Financial Policy, Committees. Despite the early disadvantage of learning economics at Cambridge, he achieved a mastery of the subject and shamed me by reading more economics articles than I did; his briefcase was usually full of newspaper cuttings on economic matters. He rowed in the 1952 Boat Race which, I am glad to say, Oxford won, though only by a canvas, the closest finish since the dead heat in 1877; also for Britain in the Olympic Games. Despite the common fate of so many rowing men, and his prodigious consumption of chocolate, he retained an immaculately slim figure.

When he became Chancellor of the University of Aston in Birmingham, I was flattered to be included in his first batch of Honorary Graduates as a Doctor of Science – although my scientific knowledge is nil. I was dismayed when in 1981 the University Grants Committee (UGC) imposed on Aston the second largest proportionate cut in student numbers in the country although it had a better record than any other University for producing graduates whom people wanted to employ; and I wrote to the UGC Chairman.)

Watkinson was a shrewd operator; and was still, when he became President, a politician to his finger-tips – in the sense, not of holding dogmatic political views, but of enjoying the fun of public controversy (he usually had a twinkle in his eye); of getting publicity; of dealing with politicians. He kept on saying he could at any time, if we thought it useful, talk to a Labour Minister on a Privy Councillor basis. (I told him I sometimes suspected this was merely an excuse for a cosy chat with Shirley Williams.) Then, when we had our first National Conference, he wanted an emergency resolution – a favourite ploy at party conferences – to get media interest.

In many ways, therefore, Methven and Watkinson were an ideal pair for the task of raising the CBI's public profile. As the last Chapter showed, we had not done at all badly during the previous couple of years mainly, though by no means wholly, working behind the scenes – with Ministers, officials and the TUC. But both men believed we must now, in addition, reach out further. I am sure this was necessary: to find more ways of putting pressure on governments; to educate business men in the things *they* had to do, without seeming to be teaching grandmothers to suck eggs (our pay campaigns, just described, are an example); to get the CBI message across more to the general public; to keep up our membership – and their subscriptions on which the CBI's work so largely depends (which became extremely important during the recession of the early 1980s).

By the time Watkinson became President he had few other burdensome positions, and so had ample time for the job. Opinion among DG's and their staff varies on whether this is in general a good thing, but in Harold's case I am sure it was, although he modestly told me years later that he feared he might have spent too much time in Tothill Street. He certainly started to hold meetings with us there even before he was President (although, as Vice-President, his subsequent election was a formality). He proposed that we should prepare by the autumn of 1976 a comprehensive statement of CBI policies, covering a much wider field than our annual Budget Representations. His political antennae told him that now might be a good time to issue such a document which he suggested might be called 'A Plan for National Recovery based on the Principles of Enlightened Free Enterprise' – quite a mouthful.

The 1975 Referendum on whether we should stay in the EEC had shown indirectly a large majority against extreme left wing policies (even though some leading Tories had campaigned in favour of pulling out). Growing evidence that people believed in free enterprise was confirmed by an opinion poll of employees commissioned by the CBI in 1976. Only 8% thought profits 'a dirty word' and 7% that they were 'immoral' (which pleased me as I had recently argued they were not in an hour-long discussion on 'The Morality of Profit' on the BBC's Third Programme). 86% thought it 'important for them to live in a free enterprise society' (83% among Labour supporters), 89% that it was 'fair for a company to pay dividends to shareholders', and 98% that it was necessary to 'keep some profit to plough back into the company'. But the survey also showed that employees thought profits were far greater than they actually were; so much education was needed.

The Government, following a much publicised meeting of NEDC at Chequers in November 1975, had published a White Paper, *An Approach to Industrial Strategy*, parts of which expressed unexceptionable sentiments about the need for a vigorous and profitable industry. It also proposed, it is true, the setting up of a lot of Sector Working Parties under NEDC to complement the existing Economic Development Committees, which seemed to smack of selective government intervention in industry. But Watkinson supported the proposal. This was partly because he had in effect subscribed to the idea in his *Blueprint for Industrial Survival*. But it was also a ploy – of a type he revelled in – to side-track the Government's proposals for compulsory planning agreements between individual companies, Government and the unions concerned, which most CBI members regarded as anathema, and get instead *voluntary* tripartite planning on a *sectoral* basis.

Finally, Watkinson felt that a plan for 'recovery' would not be laughed out of court, because a world recovery had started and at worst we would get caught along in the upswing. So he concluded that the time was ripe for a counter-attack against extreme left-wing policies, in the context of a programme for economic recovery, which everyone wanted; and in effect a return to something more like Butskellism.

The document finally published in October 1976 contained this sentence: 'The prime groundrule must be the continuity and consistency of government policy towards trade and industry, whatever party may be in power – a bi-partisan policy'; also: 'we recognise fully the highly significant role to be played in our mixed economy by the nationalised industries alongside the private sector'. No call for privatisation here; and not just because nationalised industry members were contributing to CBI income and we hoped for more! But the report strongly opposed any extension of nationalisation, as was being proposed in some Labour party quarters.

Harold's proposals were enthusiastically endorsed in June 1976 by Council. We toiled hard – the staff, the relevant Committees and others – during the summer to produce a document eventually called *The Road to Recovery*. This much shorter title was chosen after prolonged discussion. But it never occurred to me until long afterwards what a risk we were taking that the document might be compared, facetiously and possibly unfavourably, with Bob Hope's famous 'Road' films: *The Road to Morocco*, *The Road to Rio*, even with one called *The Road to Utopia*. What fun the press could have had with that one; but they did not. This was partly because it was a well-researched, well-presented document and partly because before publication – as a discussion paper – Watkinson and Methven personally hawked it round the offices of virtually every Editor in Fleet Street; and it got an excellent reception from the media. A summary was circulated to all MPs and many others; and it was presented to a score of meetings of members around the country, mainly by Watkinson and Methven. Over 2000 businessmen took part in these consultations and it was also discussed with Ministers, Civil Servants, the Opposition parties, the TUC, academics, Old Uncle Tom Cobbleigh and all.

This attempt to reach out to a wider audience was followed by a succession of comprehensive documents of which *The Road to Recovery* was a proto-type: *Britain Means Business 1977*, *Britain Means Business 1978*, *The Will to Win*, 1981; our first National Conference in 1977, repeated annually thereafter; greater cultivation of MPs of all parties, in Westminster and each Parliamentary constituency, and of Local Authority Councillors; improving contacts with the media; getting out more into the regions, both to inform and to consult.

The full process of reaching out was not completed while Watkinson was President or even while Methven was alive. It had also started before 1976, but I believe the major impetus came in that year. This is no reflection on Methven's and Watkinson's predecessors. On the contrary, I doubt whether we had the capability, in terms of expertise in public relations and an established reputation in other fields, to start raising the CBI's public profile in these ways before 1976, with a reasonable chance of being listened to with respect; and previous Directors-General and Presidents, with their staffs, deserve credit for having built up that capability.

Around the end of 1976 a Parliamentary Office was set up. Its first head was Ted Rayner who came to us from the BBC where he had had much experience of parliamentary matters, party conferences and the like; he had also been Parliamentary Press Officer to the Conservative Party when Heath was Leader and before he became Prime Minister. This new dimension in the organisation proved most useful. It was invaluable to have people around who knew, or could find out easily, about individual MPs and the mysterious workings of Parliament – including such mundane details as on which day of the week and at what time a certain party's back-bench Committee on some subject met, so as to know when not to try to get together a group of MPs interested in it.

One evening in 1978 some Labour back-benchers came to Tothill Street to discuss our Budget Representations. They were most interested but had to leave early to vote. When I asked what about, they said it was on whether servants of a Welsh Assembly in Cardiff, if that were set up following a referendum in 1979 (which in fact rejected it), should be required to know Welsh. When I asked how they would vote, no one knew. The Whips would tell them when they got to the House. A good example of lobby-fodder, I thought.

When Labour lost its overall majority and every vote counted, we wooed the smallest parties. By no means the smallest was the Scottish National Party, with eleven Members, and we gave them a working dinner in Tothill Street. We carefully avoided discussing Scottish devolution to which the CBI, especially in Scotland, was strongly opposed, though this was about the only thing uniting them – their views on other issues covered a very wide spectrum. They were a convivial lot and we had a hilarious evening without too much talk about industry and commerce. But they were subsequently helpful on several occasions by casting their votes in the way we wanted.

Intensive lobbying at this time could pay off. In 1978 the Government wished to increase the National Insurance Surcharge (a tax we opposed because it raised labour costs) from 2% to 4½%. The Opposition parties forced them to lower the new figure to 3½%; and to reduce Income Tax below what had been proposed. The Government was also defeated by two votes on retaining powers to use sanctions against firms breaching the pay policy – about which CBI had been fighting a year-long battle.

Coming back to the preparation of *The Road to Recovery* in 1976, at the end of June, Watkinson commented that too much in the draft so far was 'high in diagnosis, low in solutions', and that we needed 'a framework of practical policy initiatives'. I was on holiday, but soon after I got back, at meetings with Methven on Friday 9 July, we agreed with the President's criticisms and also that we were getting bogged down with a shapeless plan without any clear or logical sequence. So I rashly offered to have a shot at a draft introduction, summary and table of contents over the weekend – in *Mirror, Mail, Guardian, Times*, or any other, style. *Daily Mail* was chosen.

Somehow, despite a dinner engagement on the Saturday and a lunch in the country on Sunday (it was a glorious day), I managed to produce something about ten pages long by Monday, although it rather petered out towards the end. It was later circulated, with very few changes, except the filling out of the last few pages, to the Committees concerned and formed the main basis of their first discussion of what the report should look like. Some doubts were expressed about the *Mail* style, but the final report resembled rather closely my hurriedly written piece – greatly expanded of course.

Preparing the '*Road*' involved in part pulling together existing work and CBI policies. But much new work was necessary to make it add up to a comprehensive, coherent strategy; as well as a sharpening up of existing policies, which stimulated some heated discussion between members: should we, for example, go for a top rate of tax on earned income of 60% or 50% (compared with the existing 83% which, with the investment income surcharge, meant a top rate of 98% on investment income)? It was decided to go for 60% to be phased in by 1979/80.

The '*Road*' covered a wide range of topics. Not surprisingly, it gave prominence to two discussed at length in the previous Chapter: the need to reduce inflation and to increase profitability. It also quantified the reduction we thought necessary in the Government's spending plans, and how this might be achieved. I showed a fairly advanced draft of the relevant chapter to my former Treasury colleague Leo (later Sir Leo) Pliatzky who, for his sins, spent years of his life trying to control public spending. He did not like the draft at all, so I went over to his room in the Treasury and, for the best part of a morning, listened to him letting his hair down (which included a fascinating account of his early life) and making some very useful, shrewd and practical points and suggestions. I then went back to the CBI and redrafted the chapter completely. When the revised version was published, Leo went round saying what a splendid chapter it was. How very different from his behaviour in 1981 when, after he had retired from the Civil Service, we persuaded him to join a CBI Working Party on the subject and he objected violently to the attitude of the business members who, he thought, greatly exaggerated the extent to which waste could be cut out in the public sector by reference to their experience in private business.

In the '*Road*' we displayed some 'economic arithmetic' which showed how, if public spending were restrained, a programme of tax cutting could be achieved while still reducing the Public Sector Borrowing Requirement (PSBR) substantially as a proportion of national income if we had a reasonable rate of economic growth. This we took at $3\frac{1}{2}\%$ a year up to 1979, a figure the Government had recently used as an extrapolation of 'past trends'. (Even so we thought it optimistic unless CBI policies were all adopted, which they were not; and in the event we achieved rather more than $2\frac{1}{2}\%$.) I am told that Mrs Thatcher – then Leader of the Opposition – was impressed with our 'economic arithmetic'.

But, while it showed a substantial fall in public borrowing, our judgment about the appropriate level of Government spending was not based on any target for the PSBR, which later played an important role in the Thatcher governments' Medium Term Financial Strategy. Our approach was rather to work out how much would be left over for public spending after allowing for the resources required to improve the balance of payments, increase investment, and provide for a reasonable increase in personal consumption which we thought essential to get sustained pay restraint, and continue to reduce inflation. We also took account of the related need to reduce taxation, and the practical difficulties of reducing public spending. Striking a balance between these sometimes conflicting considerations we then made our judgment.

For me this sort of figuring was hardly new. For the CBI it was the first in a series of medium term projections published while I was there – in 1976, 1977, 1978, 1981 and 1984. The fact that the growth objectives, or assumptions, were not achieved – at least up to those made in 1978 – does not mean that the sums were not worth doing; because they were intended, not as predictions, but as showing what could happen if only government and business pursued the right policies; and, incidentally, the growth objective – up to 1985 – in *The Will to Win* (1981) was achieved, although this did not result in the fall in unemployment we had expected.

During the drafting of the '*Road*' I had insisted on being cagey about the number of extra jobs our proposals might create. But shortly before the document went to press I agreed the following passage: 'Our view, then, is that we must all – Government, unions, management and workforce alike – make a concerted effort to create by efficient industrial and commercial expansion not less than one million new jobs – in trade and industry – and that this can only be done by pursuing the policies set out in this document. It will in any case require quite exceptional efforts from us all if the target is to be achieved.'

This was not the same as saying that our policies would create a million jobs (though it was often interpreted in this way, for it made a good headline), but I felt it presented me with a personal challenge to show that a million extra jobs (net) in a period of three to four years was not unrealistic pie-in-the-sky. In fact, although our proposals were by no means all adopted, employment increased by some 600,000 between mid-1976 and mid-1979, but of course we did not know this at the time.

However, while preparing *Britain Means Business 1977*, published in November as background for our first National Conference, I discovered that there had in fact been four periods of three to four years during the previous quarter of a century when employment increased by getting on for a million. When I told Watkinson his eyes sparkled with excitement. He said it could be 'political dynamite'. When I asked why, he said the periods were mainly during Tory rule. But although the analysis of the four periods figured prominently in *Britain Means Business 1977*, I cannot remember it arousing any political interest whatsoever.

In working out the details of what had happened during these periods I was greatly helped by the young economist I was currently employing as my personal assistant – Charlie Burton, son of Sir George ('Bunny') Burton, then Chairman of Fisons. Charlie later did a marvellous job as Head of the Economic Trends Department. This included setting up, with the *Financial Times*, a regular Distributive Trades Trends Survey, to complement our Industrial Trends Survey which covered only manufacturing.

This particularly pleased me because I had for years believed that 'services' were as important as 'goods', with no clear distinction between them; and the distributive trades were an important part of the 'service' sector. In this I was well tutored by Margaret. In 1965 she, with Ursula (Lady) Hicks, became the first women members of the Oxford University Political Economy Club; and in 1967, at a meeting of the Club I hosted in Wadham, she gave a brilliant analysis – later published in the *Westminster Bank Review* for August 1968 – of the question: 'Are goods and services different?' This ridiculed the distinction in a devastating manner. Then, when John Methven became DG, he talked repeatedly in his early months – as did others in manufacturing – about 'productive' and 'unproductive' sectors of the economy – implying that all true wealth was produced in manufacturing, or at least in the wider industrial production sector including mining, construction, etc; and that 'services' were more or less parasitic.

I eventually convinced Methven that this was nonsense – and the matter far more complicated – by drawing up a list of occupations and inviting him to tick off which were 'productive' and which 'unproductive'. I cannot find the list, but a few of the questions – and his reactions – went something like this.

Shop floor operative in ICI	Obviously productive.
Telephone operator in ICI	After a slightly worried pause, probably productive.
Telephone operator in Marks and Spencer	After a more worried pause, unproductive, I suppose.
Buyer of materials for ICI	Productive, because employed in manufacturing.
Buyer for Marks and Spencer	I suppose unproductive because in a 'service' sector, though can help to develop efficient manufacturing.
Bingo hall worker	Clearly unproductive.
Manufacturer of bingo machines	Oh dear, this is getting very difficult.
Patrick Hutber	I suppose productive because he's in a manufacturing industry, but . . .
Donald MacDougall	I give up and give in.

Soon after, John sent an instruction round the office that no future CBI document was to refer to 'productive' industry or contain the word 'industry' by itself (except when referring to industrial production specifically). Instead we must talk about 'industry and commerce', 'trade and industry', or just 'business'. I like to think this was the result of my questionnaire and not just because we were seeking to increase CBI membership in 'service' sectors such as distribution and banking.

Years later, when helping Terry Beckett to prepare the 1982 Stamp Memorial Lecture on 'Industry and Employment in Britain in the Next Decade', he needed no persuasion to begin by saying that by 'industry' he meant the whole market economy and not just manufacturing; nor was he trying to distinguish between goods and services or 'productive' and 'unproductive' activities. But by 1982 it was also necessary to emphasise the importance of manufacturing, which had shrunk severely in recent years, partly because of a high exchange rate resulting from – among other things – North Sea oil. It was crucial to preserve an adequate manufacturing base against the time when the oil ran down.

Josiah Stamp, in whose memory the lectures were founded, was one of my pre-war heroes – though I disagreed with his war-time economics, as explained in Chapter 2. He was a distinguished economist, statistician and administrator and his many jobs included that of Chairman of the London, Midland and Scottish Railway for which he received a salary of £25,000 a year. We had fun working out, and putting in the Lecture, that to get the same real income after tax in 1982 the salary would have to be £600,000; and to point out to Sir Peter Parker, then Chairman of British Rail, who was taking the Chair at Terry's lecture, that Stamp had been in charge of only one of his regions.

Britain Means Business 1977 developed the themes in *The Road to Recovery* and was overwhelmingly endorsed by the National Conference in Brighton in November, although on some points of detail opposing views had widespread support; these were later discussed by the Council and in some cases led to changes in CBI policy, but there was never – then or later – any question of the Conference displacing Council as the sovereign policy-making body of the CBI. The National Conference was an innovation which I very much doubt would have taken place had it not been for Watkinson and Methven. We had previously discussed the possibility in-house on several occasions and always rejected it because it was so difficult and dangerous. It was certainly both of these – and involved an enormous amount of work – but the effort paid off and the doubters were confounded.

We slipped on very few banana skins, although only a handful of the staff had much, if any, experience of Conferences on this scale, such as those of the main political parties and the TUC (and of their broadcasting);

and much credit is due to this devoted handful. The sheer scale of our first Conference immediately put it in the big league. There were more delegates than at the TUC Conference, to say nothing of numerous observers from the political parties, government departments, trade unions, foreign embassies, academic institutions and countless other organisations. From the media there were well over 150 newspaper, radio and TV reporters and they did not come just for the booze – of which there was plenty. The publicity far exceeded anything previously achieved by the CBI: 50 radio and TV programmes, with much of the Conference brokdcast live and 3,000 column inches of newspaper space devoted to it. (This is how press officers measure it. I prefer to call it 83 yards, meaning that the columns laid end to end would have covered most of the touch-line of a football pitch.)

The speeches may have lacked the panache of those at TUC and Party Conferences – though there were exceptions as when Alf Gooding (then Chairman of a family business in Wales) illustrated the penal nature of taxation by taking off his jacket during his speech and saying he had had to make £10,000 profit to buy his suit. But letters from many who had seen the Conference on TV said how refreshing it was to hear people talking seriously about important matters rather than ranting and raving as politicians (and trade unionists) often do.

Margaret and I arrived in Brighton on the evening of Saturday 12 November, and by the time we got home on Tuesday evening were thoroughly exhausted. Sunday was fully taken up by briefing meetings with the Platform Committee and others; a press conference; a radio interview with Brian Redhead; a visit to the Conference Centre to see how everything would work – or not work – and to make sure that our reference works had come down from London; helping intending speakers. Then in the evening there were receptions and parties given by the Mayor, member companies, Regional Councils and others; and even more on the Monday night.

(The liberality of the hospitality – when I had been writing and talking so much about the desperate financial straits of business – reminded me of my undergraduate days, in the Great Depression of the 1930s, when, during a tour of industry organised by an enterprising don for a few economic students, we had lunch with the Directors at a Sheffield steelworks. After telling us how they were working at only a fraction of capacity and making huge losses, one of them said to me: 'Have another glass of champagne; have a cigar.')

Then there were the sessions – long ones – on the Monday morning and afternoon and the Tuesday morning, at which I had to sit virtually all the time on the platform under hot and dazzling arc lights – seeing, moreover, only the backs of the speakers and sometimes not hearing very clearly what they were saying. But it was all worth while and enormous fun.

The whole thing was sufficiently successful for the CBI Council to give the go-ahead for a second Conference in 1978; and after a poll of members we went again to Brighton. Once again we toiled during the summer producing another comprehensive document, *Britain Means Business 1978*. This time there were 1,200 representatives from member companies and trade associations, 200 observers and no less than 360 journalists, broadcasters and technicians.

John (later Sir John) Greenborough, who had succeeded Watkinson as President, presided. Both his opening address and his handling of the Conference showed that fine balance of the serious and the humorous which characterised his Presidency – and indeed his whole personality. I confess to having stolen more after-dinner stories from him than from anyone else I can think of. He had spent most of his working life in Shell, much of it in Latin America, and told me how, as a result, he had earned early retirement on full pension through bearing the white man's burden in the air-conditioned buildings of Rio and Buenos Aires; and he had had a Latin American friend who made a point of never being late twice on the same day – so when he arrived late in the office in the morning he left early in the afternoon. Many of John's serious remarks were equally memorable. In his speech, when deploring the adversarial nature of British industrial relations, he asked whether anyone in Parliament, in a debate on defence, ever talked about both sides of the Army or of the Navy.

At the 1978 Conference I managed to spend less time on the platform and discovered that, if you sat in areas outside the main hall where you could get a cup of coffee, or something stronger, there were screens which showed the speakers close up – and their faces rather than the backs of their heads – and you could hear clearly what they were saying. Unfortunately, more and more delegates discovered how agreeable it was to follow the proceedings in this way; so in later Conferences we cut down drastically on these screens to keep the hall as full as possible.

Having been to Brighton twice running, we plumped in 1979 for Birmingham. This time, thank goodness, we decided not to produce another major document, but only much shorter background papers. The theme of the Conference was 'The Challenge to Business'. The Tories had won the Election in May and done many of the things the CBI had been asking for, including a slashing of the top rate of income tax and the abolition of price, dividend and exchange controls; and their return to power had removed threats of a wealth tax, compulsory company planning agreements and nationalisation. All this had made it easier – or should have done – for managers to get on with the job of managing. Members thus felt it was now up to them to 'deliver the goods', as John Greenborough put it in his opening address.

But I think many had an uneasy feeling that this would not be at all simple. There had been a second hike in the oil price. Sterling was becoming uncomfortably high, being increasingly regarded as a 'petro-currency' (although our high interest rates were at least as important a cause). The world economic outlook was unpromising. Our latest Trends Survey showed manufacturers in a pessimistic mood. Price inflation had doubled over the previous year; while much of the inflationary situation could be attributed to the failure of 'Year 4' of Labour's pay policy, it had hardly been helped by the new Chancellor, Geoffrey Howe (contrary to our strong advice) increasing VAT to 15% – which, with other Budget changes, was officially estimated to add 4% to the Retail Price Index. I was in Sutherland on Budget day and listened to the speech on the radio while fishing on a loch from a boat. When I got back, John Methven asked if I had fallen out of the boat when I heard about VAT. I said 'no, I hooked a fish.'

This, alas, was John's last Conference. He died in the following spring. In his closing speech he said that Britain was 'drinking in Last Chance Saloon'. I think this summed up the strange mood of the Conference, although I am not sure, to this day, precisely what he meant, having never before heard of this Saloon. He talked about the nation being 'poised between remorseless decline and real success, between poverty and prosperity, betwen disintegration and moral recovery'. But I think this was partly a coded warning to the businessmen present that, unless they pulled their fingers out under this government, they had only themselves to blame if the next was headed by Tony Benn.

Birmingham did not prove so popular a venue as might have been expected of what – at least until recently – was regarded as the heartland of British industry. So in 1980 we returned to dear old Brighton where Terry (Sir Terence) Beckett, who had succeeded John Methven as DG, delivered his famous 'bare knuckles' speech, described in the next chapter.

In 1981 we went to Eastbourne. When Margaret and I arrived on Saturday the hotel receptionist told us he had unfortunately put another couple into the room reserved for us. He suggested another room, which the porter told us was the worst in the hotel. So we protested. Eventually, we were told we could have a better room for the Saturday night, because someone called Edwardes had cancelled, but that he was coming on Sunday when we would have to move. We said this was most inconvenient but reluctantly agreed. It turned out to be a sumptuous suite booked for Sir Michael Edwardes, then Chairman of BL. But Sir Arthur Knight, who had not long before given up the Chairmanship of the National Enterprise Board and had been helping the CBI prepare for the Conference during the temporary absence of Terry Beckett who was unwell, did not realise that Michael was not there. Wishing to talk to him, he knocked on our door. I was at a meeting and Margaret in the bath, so she put a towel round most of her, shouted 'coming darling' and opened the door, to Arthur's surprise and considerable embarrassment.

Then, after dinner, we found in our room a bottle of champagne in an ice bucket with the Manager's apologies for the inconvenience we had been caused. This we consumed happily although Margaret is allergic to wine. To crown it all, Michael did not turn up at all. So we had this splendid accommodation for the whole Conference, far better than had been booked for us, at no extra cost to the CBI, with a bottle of champagne thrown in. It made a good story for Ray Pennock, now President, to tell – typically improved by him – at the 'thank you' lunch for CBI staff when the Conference was over.

Part of CBI policy at the time was that the Government should give a modest boost to demand, of around £1½ billion, although several members thought it should be larger. Norman Record, of Clarks the shoe company, and a member of our Economic Situation Committee, was one of those and told me he proposed to make a speech suggesting £3 billion. I said, jokingly: 'Why not make it £5 billion?' – which to my surprise he did. James Cleminson, then Chairman of the Committee, immediately disagreed and expounded the official view most eloquently. This enlivened the discussion – and, I believe, helped to get the motion being debated passed by a large majority. This said that, while business had a vital role to play in getting the economy moving again, 'the Government should help by cutting business costs (*even if this means temporarily increasing the PSBR*) thus giving a modest net boost to demand without refuelling inflation'. This was a more expansionary fiscal stance than any previous Conference had adopted. We reported it to Geoffrey Howe; the Economic and Financial Policy Committee – by now chaired by Ronny Utiger – asked the staff to prepare two drafts of our Budget Representations, with boosts of £1½ and £3 billion respectively; and the recommendations eventually sent to the Chancellor were more expansionary than they would otherwise have been.

Eastbourne proved remarkably popular so the Conference was held there again in 1982. I got flu so could not go, but watched it on the box. I was annoyed when unfortunate timing made it necessary to go over to a children's programme just before an interesting vote on the exchange rate. When I later heard the result it seemed to reverse a vote at the 1980 Conference arguing that the pound was too high. Discussion at a later closed session showed that members had voted simply against urging on Government an active policy to lower the exchange rate, and were happy to call for a further fall in interest rates, even if this brought the pound down. Many of us felt that the pound, even though it had fallen significantly over the past couple of years, was still too high, but the vote made us more careful about what we said on the subject.

Then, in 1983, to my delight, we went to Glasgow for my last Conference as a CBI staff member. I had been rooting for Scotland for years, in vain. But now we had a Scottish President, Campbell Fraser, and he overruled the doubters who said we would never get enough members to go so far north to fill the hall, or cover the costs of the Conference. In fact the attendance was the biggest for years and I was proud of the way my native city helped to make the Conference such a rip-roaring success. The hospitality was magnificent, and on the Sunday evening delegates were fêted at the Theatre Royal with the cream of Scottish music, opera and comedy. The welcome given to this remarkable performance confounded those spoilsports who had argued that delegates would consider it too frivolous a way of spending the evening, when they should instead have been exchanging views on the serious problems to be discussed during the next two days.

The only thing that marred the Glasgow Conference – and it was a very big blot indeed – was the death of my sister, Jeannette Wallace, a few days earlier, following a road accident. She had lived in a lovely old house near Glasgow ever since she married 47 years earlier, and was the centre of a closely knit family and much loved by all. We went to her funeral on the last day of the Conference.

Looking back on those seven National Conferences I would say that they steadily improved. I remember, just before the first began, John Methven looking at the hall filling up with members, many bracing themselves to speak for the first time at a large Conference, under arc lights and with TV cameras seemingly pointing at them from all directions, turning to me and saying he had never seen so many terrified businessmen in his life. But in successive Conferences they gained more and more confidence. Speakers learned more and more to use notes, or even talk without them, rather than read out set speeches. The discussions were less stage managed, with the leadership, rightly cautious at first, allowing controversial motions to be debated, even at the risk of the house line being defeated. More spontaneity, and cut and thrust in debate, were made possible by using microphones in the body of the hall – something I had repeatedly advocated, always to be told it was impracticable. But the difficulties were overcome and in later Conferences these were used by any delegate wishing to interrupt, jump the queue waiting to speak from the rostrum for three minutes, and talk for a maximum of one.

And there always seemed to be someone prepared to put on a show. I mentioned Alf Gooding's £10,000 suit at the first Conference. At Glasgow, we had Richard Pettit, of Vaux Breweries, who put on a cloth cap to register his breakthrough as the first singing speaker at a CBI Conference; to the tune of 'Blaydon Races' he explained how, as a result of his particular brand of employee involvement, his company in Sunderland had been strike-free since 1966.

In general, I believe the Conferences were successful in putting CBI views across to a mass audience as well as developing into a valuable part of the CBI's policy-forming machinery.

13

CBI – WET AND DRY: TO 1984

WHILE the CBI reached out increasingly to a wider audience from 1976 onwards, we continued to have as close relations as ever with Ministers and officials; and much of this chapter is about our relations – including disputes, both private and public – with successive governments. I continued to see a great deal of civil servants. They were interested in how we saw the economy; and it was useful to discuss policy and ensure that, when the CBI made representations to Ministers, we agreed on the facts, figures and underlying relationships or, when we disagreed, understood why.

On the Ministerial level, while Labour remained in power, I saw a good deal of Denis Healey, the Chancellor. On average, during 1976, 1977 and 1978, he met a CBI team – almost invariably including myself – nearly once every six weeks. I also saw him at NEDC meetings and the drinks and lunch that followed. At one stage, many of our discussions were over working dinners, in No. 11 and Tothill Street. Sometimes Healey had just a few officials with him but, as he was the senior Minister – under the PM – in charge of economic policy generally, we did not discuss only strictly Treasury matters. So he often brought along one or more of his colleagues in charge of other Departments, especially Industry, Employment, Prices and Consumer Protection, and Trade. During most of this time these were Eric Varley, Albert Booth, Roy Hattersley and Edmund Dell; but Healey did most of the talking on the Government side whatever we were discussing.

I got on well with him. I had not seen him much when he was Secretary of State for Defence in 1964–70. But whenever we were at the same meetings he was always friendly. After one of these I was walking up Whitehall and he was chatting with colleagues outside the Cabinet Offices. When he saw me he smiled broadly, sprang smartly to attention and saluted me in the immaculate fashion to be expected of one who had risen, during war service, to be a Major in the Royal Engineers (after a brilliant academic career at Balliol – not in engineering, but in *Literae Humaniores*, thus showing that there is something in the view that anyone with a First in 'Greats' can do anything).

I mentioned his scathing remarks about the CBI in No. 10 after his March 1974 Budget. He could be hectoring at times and even rude. I remember particularly a meeting on 9 May 1978. In our Budget Representations we had pressed for lower income tax both at the bottom of the scale – to alleviate the poverty trap – and higher up, for middle and senior managers (and many skilled manual workers). We argued that these had been badly hit by rapid inflation, high marginal tax rates and pay policies discriminating against them; and that they were the people on whom we must rely greatly for improved economic performance. In our view the Chancellor had not done nearly enough on these matters in his Budget and a letter to this effect was sent to him by the President. The meeting on Tuesday 9 May was arranged to put our views orally.

Healey was due to have come to the CBI the day before for one of our working dinners, but postponed the engagement. This was not surprising. There had been a debate in the House that evening on the Finance Bill and an amendment carried against the Government much in line with our representations. Healey must have known that this was partly the result of our intensive lobbying of MPs. He also knew that the next day two further such amendments would be debated (one was carried against the Government by two votes). So it was hardly astonishing that he was in a somewhat tetchy mood.

Our team was a small one – John Greenborough, Ray Pennock, John Methven, Edwin Plowden (now a leading industrialist and pillar of the CBI), and myself. Healey was flanked by a horde of officials. He started off, not on Income Tax, but by criticising us for presenting our latest Trends Survey in too gloomy a manner, and indeed our respondents for not being more optimistic when the economy was obviously, in his view, picking up. We tossed backwards and forwards across the table figures about profitability, international competitiveness (which he insisted should be called 'competivity'), and the like. I took part in these exchanges and was supported by one of his officials until Denis told him not to speak unless he was asked to. It was not an agreeable meeting.

But while it is easy to remember the few occasions when he was aggressive – though never a patch on George Brown – and when he seemed keener to taunt us and score debating points than to thrash out a problem, these were far out-numbered by the meetings when we had many hours of cool, rational discussion. He soon got over his irritable moods (he was happy to dine with us not long after the dinner that was postponed). He was keen to find out what was going on in industry and commerce; immensely knowledgeable, highly intelligent, fond of a good argument but prepared to be convinced; and a most entertaining conversationalist with a great sense of humour and fun.

Years later I heard him in a radio series 'It Makes Me Laugh', giving examples of what made him – to use his own words – not just 'smile or snigger', but emit a 'real good belly laugh', which he was fond of doing; his tastes, which were catholic, were not all that different from mine – save that he included nothing from Belloc, Thurber or Wodehouse.

When Geoffrey Howe succeeded Healey after the 1979 Election, the frequency of CBI meetings with the Chancellor – and other Ministers – was roughly the same; there was rather less gastronomy, though I remember some excellent meals in No. 11. Following the change of Government my contacts with civil servants continued to be extremely close, friendly and frank – I remember one Treasury official saying to me 'I wish the PSBR had never been invented' – and these contacts proved at least as useful as before. The appointment of Terry (later Sir Terence) Burns as Chief Economic Adviser to the Treasury in 1980 – at an unusually early age – did not affect matters. He was an old friend and, although his 'monetarist' views were very different from mine, we could discuss economic questions in a calm, civilised manner as two professionals.

Meetings with Howe were very different from those with Healey. Geoffrey was the very opposite of rumbustious: he never emitted – at least in my hearing – a 'real good belly laugh'. He was always friendly and courteous, and never lost his cool; but I – and many of my CBI colleagues – often found discussions with him frustrating. Putting an argument to him was sometimes like poking one's finger into a sponge and then, when you took it out again, finding the sponge exactly the same shape as before. He used to say that he fully understood our problems and would do what he could to help – but how difficult it all was. There were so many things over which his control was so limited, like interest rates and the exchange rate (at least when it was going up, though he quickly found a way, by raising interest rates, to stop it falling more than he thought it should). He would say he had got the message on what we wanted, and recognised that we must make noises about it in public, but that if these were too loud it might simply delay action.

A public example of how he talked to us in private was his Budget speech in March 1981. It started with an impeccable analysis of the problems facing business, sounding almost as if it had been taken verbatim from our Budget Representations. Listening on the radio we were naturally elated and waiting with bated breath for all the 'goodies' we had asked for when, to our amazement and dismay, we heard that he had sat down without announcing any of significance – except a 2% cut in interest rates which was reversed within six months – and that he had done many of the things we had asked him not to. But of this Budget more anon.

The different styles of our meetings with Healey and Howe reflected in part their different personalities. But they also took place against very different political and economic backgrounds. Whereas when Labour was in power CBI leaders had no inhibitions about criticising the Government, with Tories in office it was another matter. While the CBI as an organisation is not associated with any political party, many members are Conservative supporters and get uneasy about criticisms of a Tory Administration. It is ironic that CBI leaders can find their job more difficult under a Conservative than under a Labour Government; and this was particularly true under at least the first Thatcher Administration because the recession in the early 1980s was more severe than that of the mid-1970s when Labour was in power, and many businesses suffered more damage. So the potentialities for conflicts of interest, frustration and vacillation were considerable; and all occurred.

At first, there was no great problem. There was euphoria over the return of a Conservative Government; and a (relatively short) period before things got really bad for business. But as more and more companies ran into difficulties, loyalties became strained. The less sophisticated may or may not have approved, or even understood, the tight 'monetarist' policies that were depressing the economy and forcing up interest rates and the exchange rate. They may not have known how much of their troubles to attribute to world recession. But they could see their businesses in danger of falling apart, and became more and more concerned about mere survival, to say nothing of their failure to make adequate provision for the future through investment, R and D, training and the like.

The more sophisticated members also began to question whether the Government was not making a grave mistake, and causing irreparable damage to the economy, by relying so much on trying to control a particular monetary aggregate (Sterling M_3). Though this was rising faster than the Government's target, there were no signs in the real world of the sort of things supposed to result from an excessive money supply:

rising property prices, a consumer boom, a weakening exchange rate, accelerating inflation, falling unemployment, supply shortages. At least by the autumn of 1980 – little more than a year after the Government took office – these indicators were all pointing in the opposite direction, not at overheating, but an exceedingly contractionary situation; with property markets stagnant, consumers' expenditure falling, the exchange rate unrealistically high, price inflation – though still high – beginning to decelerate, unemployment soaring, the CBI Trends Survey reporting virtually no shortages of materials, components, skilled labour or plant capacity.

In the circumstances, asked these worried but friendly critics, might it not be sensible for the Government, not to do a U-turn, but to be more flexible in its policies and, while continuing to pay attention to the money supply and public borrowing, also take account of what was happening in the real world. This would have meant a relaxation of what was in fact a highly restrictionary policy.

Such arguments were put to the Government, first in private then in public, but as time went on and scant attention was paid, there was growing frustration and irritation. Towards the end of 1981, at one of our meetings with Howe, the team had to report that people in the CBI were saying we were having all these cosy little chats with him but they appeared to be having little, if any, effect.

How far this inflexibility reflected pressure from Mrs Thatcher it is hard to say. In the autumn of 1980 she did tell some CBI leaders that she was concerned about the high level of interest rates and the exchange rate, but that there were great difficulties in getting them down; and I describe below how interest rates were reduced later in the year partly, we believe, because of CBI representations to her. Also, when Alan Walters – who, as mentioned earlier, had some years before been Keith Joseph's economic guru – was appointed her Personal Economic Adviser, and came to see us at the CBI early in 1981, he told us – somewhat to my surprise – that he thought both interest rates and the pound were too high. But while the trend of *nominal* interest rates was downwards over the next few years, *real* interest rates (adjusted for inflation) remained high, and fiscal policy was also restrictive, so that the stance of economic policy generally remained very tight.

I saw very little personally of Mrs Thatcher while she was Prime Minister. I recall only once being in a CBI team – of seven or eight – which went to see her not long after the 1979 Election. She normally preferred to see just one or two CBI representatives at No. 10. Apart from that I saw her on the relatively few occasions when she chaired a meeting of the NEDC; and after one of these, when Council members and their advisers were having drinks before lunch, had quite a heated argument with her about the PSBR. This quickly attracted an audience to watch the fun. And then, just after she had left the room to go to lunch somewhere else, she came back, sought me out and said: 'And there's another point . . .' I cannot remember what it was, but in any case had no chance to reply.

I saw her several times *before* she became PM. Not long after I went to the CBI, when she was in opposition but not yet Leader of her Party, she came to Tothill Street to discuss taxation. I was supposed to be chairing the meeting, but within minutes she had assumed control. My goodness, she knew her tax law – her speciality when practising as a Barrister – and before long was, in her own words, 'jumping down the throat' of our tax expert, Frank Harvey, for which – I must say – she apologised handsomely.

When she was Leader of the Opposition, I went one day with some CBI colleagues to see her in the House of Commons. A question arose about a recent debate and she asked her Private Secretary to get the relevant *Hansard*, sidelined the passage concerned and passed it over the table for me to read. Now anyone who has used *Hansard* knows how difficult it is to keep it open at a particular page. I tried by smoothing it down with my hand, which irritated her. So she reached across, snatched it from me and slammed it upside down on the table, clearly regarding this as the correct way of keeping *Hansard* open at the place you want; and I honestly felt that, had I been a little boy, she would have smacked the back of my wrist – but perhaps that flight of the imagination is a little unkind and impolite.

Then there was that dinner in a private room at Lockets, a restaurant near enough the Houses of Parliament to have a division bell which gives MPs eating there just enough time to race back and cast their votes. We had invited Mrs Thatcher and a few of her Shadow Cabinet to put across some points about which the CBI felt strongly. But she was uninterested and talked at length about her own views, so that when the bell rang and she had to go, we had hardly got a word in edgeways. Some of her colleagues stayed behind for a few minutes, running the risk of missing the vote, to apologise and say how sorry they were we had had so little opportunity to have our say.

Incidentally, an interesting quartet of Honorary Fellows of Somerville College is: Indira Gandhi, Margaret Thatcher, Shirley Williams and Margaret MacDougall. What formidable, and diverse, women that College produces.

*

I have described the restrictive monetary and fiscal policies of the Thatcher Government. This does not mean that the previous Adminis- tration had paid no attention to monetary and fiscal numbers. On the contrary, they had been paying increasing attention to them, but their policies and targets were in general, in my opinion, not unduly restrictive in the circumstances (although I believe they allowed the pound to rise too much during their last eighteen months, as described later). Their growing concern with monetary developments reflected in part pressure from the IMF from which we had borrowed heavily. But it was also essential to have regard to the financial markets, and these were becoming more and more influenced by what to many people were mysterious concepts like Sterling M3 and the PSBR.

So, early in 1979, I was asked to prepare, for internal use by the President and CBI staff, an 'elementary background paper on money and related matters'. This was largely a straightforward child's guide. But it also cast doubt on many simplistic 'monetarist' theories rapidly becoming fashionable; and the funny thing is that hardly any of my non-economic colleagues realised – until I told them – how iconoclastic I was being. I showed that, while the numerous measures of money supply might move reasonably in line over long periods, their year to year changes were often very different. One solution would be to follow the recommendations of the Radcliffe Committee on the Working of the Monetary System twenty years earlier and look at what they called 'the state of liquidity in the whole economy'; and policy under the Thatcher Administration did move to a considerable extent in that direction. Another would be to go for money supply targets looking several years ahead. I thought this greatly overesti- mated the state of the economic art, and would be a dangerous hostage to fortune; but it was adopted in the Conservative Government's 'Medium Term Financial Strategy', although the language surrounding such 'targets' tended to become more cautious as the years went by.

I showed that the argument, then quite popular, that tight monetary policy, by driving up the exchange rate and so reducing import prices, would reduce inflation, was fraught with dangers for exporters and those competing with imports. I emphasised the large error involved in estimating the Public Sector Borrowing Requirement; that ours was not particularly high by international standards; that reducing it would not necessarily reduce the growth of money supply; nor necessarily reduce interest rates significantly; and that any benefits to business of a reduction would quite likely be more than offset by the depressing effects on demand of a lower PSBR, which meant higher taxes, lower public spending, or both.

I argued that, in assessing the appropriate PSBR for, say, the year ahead, one should take account of the level of activity and its effect on public revenue and expenditure: if the economy were depressed, this would reduce tax receipts and increase spending on unemployment benefit and the like, so that one should plan for a larger PSBR than would otherwise be the case. Such a proposition was in fact advanced early in 1980 by Nigel Lawson while Financial Secretary to the Treasury, but when I mentioned this to Geoffrey Howe at a meeting shortly afterwards he was not impressed.

In my paper I was not arguing that 'money does not matter'. On the contrary, I believed strongly – and still do – that governments have to keep money supply, and public borrowing, under control for all sorts of reasons. But I wanted to show that the whole matter was far more complicated than some theories currently in vogue would suggest; that it could be dangerous to formulate policies largely by reference to precise targets for money supply and public borrowing; and that to rely on monetary policy alone to get inflation down could depress output, employment and profitability far more than intended.

The paper was not circulated outside Tothill Street – an indication of the sensitivity of the subject even when Labour was in power. (A Treasury friend begged me, in vain, to give him a copy.) But nearly all the arguments in the paper – including several I have not mentioned – were used in our representations to Conservative Ministers from the summer of 1979 onwards, many several times over.

About this time I started having trouble with my eyesight. The last straw was when, in the autumn of 1979 in Ireland, Margaret – whom I had after all taught to fish – started catching far more than I did, because I could not see the line and fly at all clearly. My eye doctor had said it was a cataract, that I would come back in six months and say it was worse, but that there would be nothing he could do, because it was a long way off surgery. Margaret said this was just not good enough. Fortunately we had met in Ireland another fishing couple where the husband was having the same trouble and recommended a brilliant eye surgeon, Eric Arnott, whom I went to see in London. He said he could remove the cataract and hopefully put a permanent lens implant inside my eye, starting with the worse one and then, after an interval if the first operation proved successful and I so wished, do the other. I agreed.

This was early in 1980. I told John Methven and we agreed that, so that there should be a reasonable number of senior CBI staff to mind the shop, I would postpone the operation until he returned from a month-long tour he had planned of the Antipodes, culminating in two speeches to an Employers' Convention in New Zealand. The preparation of these, and the tour itself, interrupted John's work with a few of the staff on the economic prospects, about which he was rightly concerned. He initiated this work in a highly confidential memorandum sent to just four of us on the Friday immediately before the National Conference in November 1979 at which he made his 'Last Chance Saloon' speech.

The short-term prospects could hardly have been gloomier and the medium term outlook was disquieting. I prepared a paper, including unpublished predictions up to 1983 by the London Business School, which assumed policies similar to those contemplated by the Govern-ment. They showed inflation falling to around 5%, but output, after falling markedly, barely regaining the level of mid-1979 – the time of the last Election – with unemployment rising to two million. (The first two predictions proved close to the mark but unemployment rose to over three million. Few could then have conceived of a government being returned to power with this number out of work; but equally, few could have foretold the Falklands war and its consequences, quite apart from the growing disarray in the Labour Party.) I warned that, unless different policies were pursued, the Government could finish up by increasing rather than reducing the overall burden of taxation (completely at variance with one of its major objectives) and by reducing to a dangerous extent our industrial base.

John was back in the office on Monday 10 March, 1980 and I went into hospital on Tuesday. The operation was wonderfully successful and, although my 'new' eye was not in full working order for some time, I caught as many trout as Margaret in Scotland that June. The operation on the other eye was equally successful, and I shall be eternally grateful to Eric Arnott and to all those who developed the techniques which obviated the previous need to wait until a cataract 'ripened' and also made 'implants' possible.

When I got back to the CBI after my first operation I learned that John Methven was himself going to have one – to remove a cartilage from his knee. He had been having trouble with it, particularly when sailing, and thought this would make him nippier about the boat. I had had a similar operation when a schoolboy and it seemed nothing to worry about. John went into hospital on Thursday 17 April but, after leaving his things and registering, insisted on coming out again to take part in a television programme and did not get back until quite late that night, before the operation on Friday. On Sunday, Margaret and I left flowers for him with the receptionist but, when asked if we would like to see him, declined as we thought it would be wrong to tire him with conversation so soon after his operation (although we later learned that he had hardly come out of the anaesthetic before beginning to dictate memoranda).

Monday and Tuesday were normal working days, except for John's not taking the chair at our weekly Directors' meeting; but we heard he was getting on famously, walking up and down the corridor in his dressing gown. On Wednesday the first engagement in my diary was to see the President – John Greenborough – to discuss our latest Trends Survey. But when I got to the CBI I was told that instead there was to be a special meeting of senior staff in his room on an undisclosed subject. At this we were told, to our horror, that John was dead. He was only fifty-four. It was a tragic loss of a man who had contributed so much and shown he had so much more to contribute.

During the interregnum before we got a new DG we moved from Tothill Street to Centre Point, a skyscraper at the top of Charing Cross Road which had achieved notoriety because its main owner, Harry Hyams, had kept it unoccupied for many years for complex financial reasons. I was sad to leave Tothill Street, even though it was getting a bit tatty; and Centre Point was less convenient if one wanted to go to Whitehall or the Reform Club, a visit to the latter having the added attraction when we were in Tothill Street – if one had the time – of a walk across St James's Park. Our new office was also much further from my home in Pimlico. But I was convinced by those who had studied the matter that the move was the right thing to do.

I was delighted when I learned that Terry Beckett was to be our next Director-General. He was a great catch for the CBI. As Chairman and Chief Executive of Fords he was by far the most senior businessman whom the CBI had attracted to the post. I had enjoyed talking to him on the relatively few occasions when we had met. These were mostly connected with the CBI, but I also remembered chairing a large international Congress, with participants from over twenty-five countries, organised by the (British) Society for Long Range Planning (now the Strategic Planning Society) of which I was President, at which Terry gave a fascinating talk on 'Success and Failure in Company Planning'. This included a description of the planning and development, for which he was responsible, of the Cortina and other Ford vehicles – an achievement he was justly proud of and mentions in *Who's Who*. He also recalled the first instance of lack of foresight in the company's history: 'When Henry Ford built his first car, the Quadricycle, in a brick shed in Detroit in 1896, he forgot one thing: the door of the shed wasn't wide enough to get the car out. So the dawn of a new era began, as Nietzsche recommended, with a sledgehammer.'

The theme of the Congress was 'The Management of Strategic Surprise'; so perhaps I should not have been so impressed as I was that Terry turned up at all, because only the day before a national strike at Fords had been made official. Not surprisingly, hordes of journalists came too – there is a photograph, in the printed proceedings of the Congress, of us shaking hands on the platform with the caption: 'Sir Terence Beckett, about to run the Press gauntlet, says goodbye to Sir Donald MacDougall' – and the media were much more interested in the strike than in the Cortina.

Terry had read economics at the LSE and retained a great interest in the subject. While on sick leave in 1981 he asked me for literature on the German hyper-inflation of the 1920s; but as he was particularly interested in the type of assets held by the more fortunate survivors of that experience he was, as he freely admitted, not simply keen to brush up his economic history, but thought there might be personal lessons for those living in today's uncertain world. Once settled into the job his life pattern was not one of such frenetic activity as Methven's had been. This meant, not less work, but less social life, opera-going and the like than John had indulged in; although Terry, like John, was a music-lover and he made annual pilgrimages to the Edinburgh Festival. Also, his other main recreation was ornithology, and I imagine that watching birds near his home in rural Essex was less exhausting than John's sailing weekends.

During the five-and-a-half weeks between joining us on 1 October 1980 and the National Conference early in November he certainly did not spare himself. Despite the need to spend a lot of time in London – for half-a-dozen regular, pre-arranged, meetings of members, plus one with the Chancellor, two of the NEDC, a press conference on our latest (very gloomy) Trends Survey, to say nothing of briefing meetings with his staff – he insisted on getting out and around the country; and somehow, I cannot imagine how, managed to visit no less than seven of the worst hit regions. And what he saw and heard there he did not like at all.

This influenced drafts of the closing speech he was to give at the Conference, in which he argued that the economy was being so rapidly deflated that 'if we are not careful, a lot of industry will not be around when the revival comes'. The short-term needs were therefore clear: a lower pound, lower interest rates and a reduction in the National Insurance Surcharge (NIS). In the medium term, numerous institutional changes were required. (These were elaborated in *The Will to Win*, mentioned later.)

In Brighton, on the Sunday before the Conference proper began, Terry asked for my comments on a semi-final draft of his speech. He told me that, as he did not want to make many more changes, he was showing it to no one else except our Information Director, then Mrs Dorothy Drake. (She was succeeded in 1981 by Keith McDowall, a very old hand at the game, having been a journalist for twenty years and then in the Government Information Service, working in innumerable Departments beginning with the DEA, which was a bond between us.)

I suggested some changes to Terry's draft, all of which he accepted save one – the omission of a passage on the possible need to increase taxes on 'booze and fags', because this could lose us members producing these articles; at least one did resign, but rejoined later. Terry had not yet lived through – at least as a staff member – one of our regular annual marathons, preparing our Budget Representations, when it sometimes seemed that nearly as much time was spent agreeing a few weasel words on excise duties, particularly on whether they should be raised in line with inflation, as was devoted to the rest of the exercise.

But during Monday, Terry, unknown to me, decided to strengthen his speech because he sensed that the membership wanted this. While a motion at the Birmingham Conference a year earlier, expressing concern at the damage being done by very high interest rates and an 'over-strong' pound, had been defeated by a large majority, a similar motion – the first to be debated on Monday in Brighton – was carried overwhelmingly. This reflected both the worsening situation and a greater readiness to criticise a Conservative Government. Also, as the Conference progressed, speaker after speaker elaborated on this theme; and James Cleminson and others called specifically for a cut of 4% in MLR (Minimum Lending Rate) – the successor of Bank Rate – both to reduce the burden of interest charges on business costs and to encourage a fall in the pound. Then on the Monday evening, when Terry did the round of parties given by CBI Regional Councils, he got the message that many members wanted him to make a really tough speech.

On Tuesday morning, immediately before the Conference reopened, I was sitting on the platform in the second row a yard or so away from Terry, and saw him exchanging pieces of paper with Dorothy Drake; and later he left the platform for some time before coming back holding the folder containing his speech. It was fairly obvious that some important changes had been made. In fact a passage had been added which included the following: 'We have got to take the gloves off. We are in a bare-knuckle fight in some of the things we have got to do'. It was a stirring speech, delivered with great conviction, and he got a prolonged standing ovation in which I happily joined. Immediately after the Conference, at a press briefing, he emphasised that his 'bare-knuckle fight' was not with the

Government but with anyone in the country or any other pressure group which was getting its way at business's expense. But it was widely regarded as an attack on the Government, as were other parts of the speech. A few member companies resigned in protest, but some only temporarily.

As soon as I got to Centre Point the next morning (Wednesday) I was summoned to see Terry Beckett and Ray Pennock who, as President, had chaired the Conference; told they had an appointment in an hour's time with Mrs Thatcher; and agreed to produce in a quarter of an hour, on one page, half-a-dozen reasons why a 4% cut in MLR was necessary and need not increase money supply or exacerbate inflation. This I did and off they drove to Downing Street.

The TV later showed them coming out of No 10 looking rather sheepish and saying 'she was magnificent'. One member told me they looked like naughty schoolboys who had just come out of the headmistress's study. Some thought they must have completely caved in and let the side down after the tough words so widely acclaimed in Brighton. But that was not the case. Before the end of quite an amicable discussion, in which, admittedly, Terry and Ray got rather few words in edgeways, Terry handed a copy of my paper to the PM and persuaded her to let him read it aloud while she also read it – a favourite technique of his. Apparently quite a lot of it came as news to her, and we are pretty convinced that this was an important reason why, twelve days later, MLR was cut from 16% to 14%; and possibly one reason why it was cut further to 12% on Tuesday 10 March 1981. But this latter cut was almost the only redeeming feature of the Budget measures announced that day, to which I have already referred.

This Budget was a real shocker. We regarded it as much too restrictive in general; and in detail it ran contrary to our Representations in almost every respect. Apart from hitting individuals hard, by failing to make any increase in income tax allowances to take account of inflation, and raising excise duties by much more than the rate of inflation, it also hit industry and commerce hard (in spite of a few minor concessions) instead of helping to reduce business costs as we had asked.

Terry Beckett issued a statement immediately after the Speech which began 'This is a disappointing Budget'. The next day Ray Pennock went a good deal further. Speaking in Manchester he said 'We have at best what might be described as a brush-off, and at worst a kick in the teeth'. Some Tory back-benchers were more scathing. Peter Tapsell put out a statement describing the Budget as 'economically illiterate', 'maladroit', 'muddle-headed', 'inept', and called on the Prime Minister to get another Chancellor.

(Interestingly, Tapsell received a Knighthood in 1985. Also, despite Ray Pennock's comments, and although at the CBI's annual dinner a few months later he described how Mrs Thatcher, the guest of honour, had been rejected by an ICI recruitment panel – and she turned the tables on him by saying that, had she not been, she might now be President of the CBI – he got his Life Peerage in the 1982 New Year Honours.)

The next day, Thursday 12 March, the Queen came to Centre Point to open our new headquarters. (During the reception she discussed with me whether, when the Chancellor raised taxes on alcoholic beverages, he wanted us to consume less – and she remembered this when I met her a couple of years later after she had opened the British Academy's new headquarters near Regent's Park.) Most of the leading CBI figures were at Centre Point to meet the Queen, so an emergency meeting was held immediately after she left, which mandated Ray and Terry to take a tough line and tell the PM of the CBI's serious concern about the Budget. This they did on the following day, but got precious little change out of her.

Then, would you believe it, only five days later, at a meeting of Council (which had, after all, endorsed our Budget Representations in January), quite a lot of speakers cut up rough about the CBI criticising the Government – an example of the tiresome way in which members can blow hot and cold when the Tories are in power. There was, however, agreement on the need to cut Government plans for current spending (not capital spending, which everyone felt strongly had been cut too much).

So a Working Party on this was set up, chaired by Malcolm McAlpine, of the civil engineering and contracting firm, Sir Robert McAlpine and Sons. It consisted mainly of CBI members but also included Leo Pliatzky who, as mentioned earlier, found himself in fundamental disagreement with the rest of the group, and did in fact resign. It proved possible to produce by September what I think was rather a good document. It naturally came to be called 'The McAlpine Report', although Malcolm disliked this, not because he disagreed with its contents but because he is a self-effacing, and charming, character. The Report analysed the scope for reducing the cost of the services the Government was planning to provide, and made practical proposals to that end. It did *not* discuss whether the planned level of services was appropriate.

The idea was not to depress total demand still further. That would have been absurd when the CBI was arguing that Government policies were too restrictive. The object was rather to increase efficiency in an important part of the economy. This would both increase overall national efficiency and, through its effects on the Government's finances, make possible more capital expenditure on the infrastructure, a reduction in business costs by cutting NIS and local authority rates, and other measures to encourage enterprise. Taken together with other elements in the CBI's package of policies, including a less tight fiscal stance, there should then be more jobs created in the market economy than were lost in the Government sector.

Demands for cuts in Government spending plans (though not necessarily in existing levels) had for long been a hardy annual in our Budget Representations and an important feature in other policy documents; and they had always included reduction in 'waste and inefficiency' as one way in which this could be achieved, but without giving very much supporting evidence.

The latest statement was in *The Will to Win*, published a few days before the 1981 Budget. This was a brain-child of Terry Beckett, on which we had been working hard over the previous few months. It was our first comprehensive policy document since *Britain Means Business 1978*. To emphasise that it was a discussion paper it had a green cover and was deliberately not bound but had the pages held together by a Treasury tag. It was taken to the grass roots at over sixty meetings of members throughout the country. Many of the presentations were by Terry himself. It included numerous 'action points' required by Government, management and unions (shades of the 'check-list of action required' in George Brown's National Plan – plus ça change . . .); and one of these was that 'public service sector administrative economies must be made to achieve savings of at least £3 billion p.a. by 1984/85'.

It was the formidable task of the McAlpine group to demonstrate in far greater depth than we had attempted before how this might be achieved. I was agreeably surprised by the amount of detailed, quantitative, information it was possible to unearth on, for example, the striking differences in the efficiency of different local authorities and of the National Health Service in different regions; the large savings already made by some authorities by 'contracting-out' services to the private sector; the relative numbers of 'front-line' workers and support staff in various fields, and how the numbers in administration had in many cases been increasing much faster than those at the sharp end. Much credit is due, not only to members of the Working Party but to the CBI staff involved, particularly two economists, Peter Lobban and Joanne Waldern, who toiled long and hard collecting and assessing this information. They, and a few of the rest of us, with our spouses, were rewarded by a delightful dinner given by Mr and Mrs McAlpine on my sixty-ninth birthday in Claridges. This must have increased *private* sector expenditure considerably.

Treasury Ministers told us the report helped them in their battles with colleagues, although some officials, in the Treasury and the main spending departments, were less complimentary – not surprisingly, perhaps, since the report could be regarded as criticising their efforts. Though I believed we had proved our case rather well, I had some sympathy with them. I knew from wartime how difficult it is to get cuts in the tail rather than the teeth of any organisation. Once, when manpower was being allocated – as it was in those days when people could be directed to particular forms of work – departments were asked to describe the consequences of, I think, a 10% cut in their manpower. The Admiralty said the Navy would be largely confined to port – because someone had worked out that at any one time not much more than one in ten of those they employed were at sea.

As in several previous incarnations I was concerned at the CBI with exchange rate policy. During my first three years the pound fell almost continuously till the autumn of 1976 when it was some 40% below its 1971 level against a basket of currencies. I regarded the fall during much of 1976, due in considerable part to withdrawals of funds by overseas holders of sterling, as excessive and unfortunate; it was one cause of the reacceleration of prices during Year 2 of Labour's pay policy which made Year 3 so difficult; and former Treasury colleagues told me later that the balance of payments crisis in 1976 was at least as traumatic as that in 1968, described in Chapter 8. CBI was right during this period to advocate strict domestic policies to prevent the pound falling through the floor. Towards the end of 1976 the pound pulled out of its nose dive and recovered to what I regarded as a reasonable level, given the need both to keep down inflation and to remain internationally competitive. The authorities then rightly 'capped' the rate during much of 1977 to prevent it rising further. This, together with the growing realisation that North Sea oil would strengthen our balance of payments, led to a large reflux of funds, and a strong recovery in our reserves, but also to a big rise in money supply which increasingly worried the Treasury. So in the autumn of 1977 they 'uncapped' the rate, which then rose markedly. On the day they did this John Methven and I went across to the Treasury to express our concern – privately – to my old friend Sir Douglas Wass, then Permanent Secretary, that this would worsen British industry's competitiveness.

Shortly afterwards, I had a visit from Arthur Knight, then Chairman of Courtaulds. I had known him for a long time, first through his friendship with Peter Vinter, a Civil Servant who had worked in Prof's branch during the war. Arthur too, and his company, were getting worried about the rising pound and he suggested an independent inquiry into how it was affecting other businesses. So the CBI invited Peter Oppenheimer, the Economics Don at Christ Church, to chair a group of five other economists to do this (four of them former pupils or colleagues of mine). They visited, in pairs, twenty-five companies and other organisations, in both manufacturing and other sectors, early in 1978. About half thought a lower pound would be beneficial; but the rest were mostly indifferent.

Partly for this reason, the CBI was for some time rather muted in its representations to Government on the exchange rate, though it warned against the dangers of a further rise and pressed for relaxation of exchange control, both for its own sake and to help hold the pound down by encouraging investment abroad. In the autumn of 1979 we carried out another survey, by post, of a much larger sample of manufacturing firms only, which are in general more exposed to international competition than the average business. This showed only a rather larger proportion – 55% – preferring a lower pound, although our competitiveness had worsened considerably in the meantime.

But by the time of the National Conference in November 1980, when the pound had risen to absurd heights, members showed in debate and by their voting their overwhelming concern about the damage being done. After that we really went to town and in our Budget Representations of January 1981, followed by *The Will to Win* in March, told the Government in no uncertain terms that it was essential to get the pound down, and how they might set about doing this. (We had had working parties discussing technicalities for some time.)

The pound fell quite a bit during 1981, as did the level of pay settlements, so that our competitiveness improved significantly. But we went on arguing that a further depreciation was necessary (in addition to a slower increase in our unit labour costs relative to our competitors', plus the abolition of NIS) to restore our competitiveness sufficiently. I argued this in public when giving evidence to the House of Commons Treasury and Civil Service Committee in July 1982; and in August Terry Beckett, in his presentation on 'Competitiveness' to the NEDC, gave an illustrative package (invented by me) which included an average 4% per annum fall in the exchange rate over the following three years, making 12% in all.

After the Conference vote in November 1982, described earlier, we were more circumspect in what we said; and in any event, during the period between Terry's presentation and the time I left the CBI in March 1984, sterling had already fallen by 12% and the abolition of NIS had been announced, although we had not done so well as assumed in reducing our relative unit labour costs in terms of national currencies.

We had a long, hard struggle to get the Conservatives to abolish NIS, although they had criticised it in opposition. I feared, when Healey introduced it, that this might be so because, with my Treasury experience, I knew what a terribly simple way of collecting revenue it was, and therefore a tax which any Chancellor would be loth to give up. Geoffrey Howe did not even begin to reduce it until his 1982 Budget, nearly three years after the Tories returned to power, and it was not until March 1984 that his successor Nigel Lawson announced its final demise on 1 October – six months after I left the CBI. Terry Beckett wrote a letter at the time to thank Nigel, in which he reckoned that the tax, over its lifetime, had drained British business of more than £17 billion and destroyed 300,000 jobs. He sent me a copy, with a nice personal note thanking me for the part I had played in the battle to get rid of what we called 'the jobs tax'.

When I came to the CBI in 1973, at 61, I expected to stay for four years, the normal retiring age being 65. In fact I stayed for over ten, and felt like the character who gave the title to the play *The Man Who Came to Dinner*. Well before I was 65, Methven asked if I would stay on longer. I said I would love to but would like a little more leisure. He said 'Why not a 4-day instead of a 5-day week – at the same pay?' I said 'Thank you very much, but may I take the extra leisure in the form of longer holidays?' He agreed. I reckon I did the equivalent of 4½ days a week.

Then in 1982, Dermot Glynn, who had been with the CBI during much of the time since he left Oxford, and Director of Economics for nearly ten years, decided that, at 42, it would be sensible to seek pastures new. I was reluctant to see him go, for he had done a tremendous job; but who was I, who had had half-a-dozen jobs by the time I was his age, to dissuade him? So he looked around and found another excellent post.

Terry and I agreed that his successor must be experienced; for I did not wish to stay on much longer and there was no intention of replacing me with an economist of similar seniority above him. We persuaded John Caff to take the job. A few years older than Dermot, he had read maths at Wadham and got a First. Then, after learning some economics at Harvard, he was elected to a Nuffield Studentship. I was his supervisor and also one of the examiners when he got a B Phil (now called M Phil) in Economics. (Doug McWilliams, whom I praised earlier for his chairmanship of a committee in Brussels, took the same degree over ten years after John. He joined the CBI soon after I did, and was still there when I left. He had a first class, versatile, imaginative mind and was an excellent expositor. He gave me tremendous support and played a large part, along with Dermot and others, in building up the high reputation of the CBI's Economic Directorate.)

After John Caff left Oxford he entered the Foreign Service; but I got
him seconded for a spell to Neddy in its early days, and later to the
Treasury in 1969. He never went back to the Foreign Office, and
transferred to the Government Economic Service a few years later, and
later still to the Administrative Service. While at the Treasury I sent him
to our Embassy in Washington for a couple of years, where he was one of a
long succession of economists – many of whom subsequently had distinguished careers – who have had a spell there reporting back to the Treasury
on the US economic scene. After all this, it is hardly surprising that, when
he told his wife Pat in 1982 that he was having lunch with me, she was
rather suspicious and said: 'What does Donald want you to do this time?'
He started at the CBI on 1 January 1983, and when it was clear that he
was settling in well, I agreed with Terry that from 1 April I would go on to
a 2-day week (it inevitably turned out to be more) and retire completely a
year later, at the end of March 1984.

My last Council meeting was on 22 February 1984 – there was none in
March – and I was asked to talk about the economic situation. There
being, unusually, no questions or discussion, the President then said
some nice things about me, including a reference to the memoirs I was
starting to write. I asked permission for a thirty seconds reply to say that, in
these, I would give as one reason for the effectiveness of Council the
convention of very short speeches from the floor, so I would just say thank
you and sit down. But the funny thing was that, in the debate on the next
item, an acrimonious one on the earth-shattering question of the stage at
which VAT should be charged on imports, there were several speeches
which I thought would never end.

During the following month or so Margaret and I were given a
tremendous send-off. First, there was a dinner given by the senior CBI
economists, at which we received gift vouchers for use at a chain of garden
centres, one of which – happily – is very near an Elizabethan cottage in
Constable country we had recently bought jointly with Margaret's daughter Anthea Hall, a journalist on the *Sunday Telegraph*, and her husband
Max Wilkinson, of the *Financial Times*.

Then there was a huge reception, for a couple of hundred, and a lunch
later for a couple of dozen, mainly selected from those who could not
come to the main party, at which Harold Watkinson sang my praises.
Although the invitations to these parties were from the President and
Director-General, I had the privilege of deciding who should be asked
and was overwhelmed by the response. We had eight of the ten surviving
Presidents of the CBI, past, present and elect – the last being James
Cleminson who, as Deputy President, was shortly to become President at

the AGM. (The only non-surviving President was my dear friend Sir John Partridge.) We had both surviving Directors-General, Terry Beckett and Campbell Adamson; John Methven and John Davies (the first DG) were, alas, no longer with us. There were lots of other staff, past and present; numerous CBI members who had become my friends; and many others from the Civil Service, Bank of England, TUC, Neddy, academics who had helped the CBI, the media. In my speech I reassured this last group that, although they knew I was related by marriage to the press, I read their papers avidly.

The invitation to the big party said 5.30 to 8.00 pm; but when Margaret and I got there at 5.20, four former Presidents had already arrived, presumably for the drink; and we cannot have got away before nine o'clock. The evening was full of surprises. While Campbell Fraser, the President, and I were receiving guests from outside as they came to the top of the stairs and onto the Concourse in Centre Point, several said what a splendid picture of me they had just seen downstairs. I was completely puzzled and only later discovered that Keith McDowall had got Glan Williams, who drew cartoons of MPs for their *House Magazine*, to do one of me; and this was displayed at the bottom of the stairs surrounded by a generous margin in which guests arriving could inscribe their signatures.

Then, after Campbell had done his stuff, with a characteristically witty, but grossly over-complimentary, eulogy of me, he pointed to a large object wrapped in tartan paper which he said was a 'symbolic chair'. The most important content was a cheque from the staff to buy a chair suitable for sitting on while writing memoirs. Then, before I had time to embark on my own speech, I was astonished to hear the skirl of the pipes. I turned and saw a piper marching slowly, in full highland dress, towards me, and he was playing 'For He's a Jolly Good Fellow' – which I had never before heard on the bagpipes. Following him was a waiter pushing a trolley, draped in tartan, on which was a cake; and behind him a charming girl, wearing a kilt and bearing a tray on which were what looked like two very generous drams. The thought of these must have hastened on my speech – which even so was far too long. When I had finished and could risk a decent drink, the piper and I toasted each other – in gaelic of course – and this gave me strength to cut the cake, which I did right across the middle before realising it was in the shape of a pound sterling (£); had I known, I would have cut it quite differently because I certainly did not want a fall of 50% in the exchange rate. The piper was a member of a pipe band of six, of whom five were English and one Welsh.

So I left the CBI in great style. But this was not the end. I stayed on the Economic Situation Committee as an "observer"; I kept popping into

Centre Point – for example, to get help with these memoirs; and Margaret and I were invited as guests to the National Conference in November 1984 in Eastbourne.

But these memoirs must come to an end, and when better than in Orwell's 1984? However concerned we may feel about so many things, it was certainly much less awful than he portrayed. For this we may be thankful. I am also thankful for having had such an interesting and varied life which I have greatly enjoyed, and hope I have conveyed this enjoyment to my readers.

INDEX